Other works by Max Haines

The Collected Works of Max Haines Vol. 4 (2000)

Canadian Crimes (1998)

Murders Strange But True (1997)

Celebrity Murders (1996)

The Collected Works of Max Haines Vol. 3 (1996)

Multiple Murderers II (1995)

Multiple Murderers (1994)

Doctors Who Kill (1993)

True Crime Stories Book V (1992)

The Collected Works of Max Haines Vol. 2 (1991)

True Crime Stories Book IV (1990)

True Crime Stories Book III (1989)

True Crime Stories Book II (1988)

True Crime Stories (1987)

That's Life (1986)

The Collected Works of Max Haines Vol. 1 (1985)

Murder & Mayhem (1984)

The Murderous Kind (1983)

Crime Flashback #3 (1982)

Crime Flashback #2 (1981)

Crime Flashback #1 (1980)

Calendar of Criminal Capers (1977)

Bothersome Bodies (1977)

UNNATURAL CAUSES

MAX HAINES

PENGUIN
CANADA

PENGUIN CANADA

Published by the Penguin Group

Penguin Books, a division of Pearson Canada, 10 Alcorn Avenue, Toronto,
Ontario, Canada M4V 3B2

Penguin Books Ltd, 80 Strand, London WC2R 0RL, England

Penguin Putnam Inc., 375 Hudson Street, New York, New York 10014, U.S.A.

Penguin Books Australia Ltd, 250 Camberwell Road, Camberwell,
Victoria 3124, Australia

Penguin Books India (P) Ltd, 11, Community Centre, Panchsheel Park,
New Delhi – 110 017, India

Penguin Books (NZ) Ltd, cnr Rosedale and Airborne Roads, Albany,
Auckland 1310, New Zealand

Penguin Books (South Africa) (Pty) Ltd, 24 Sturdee Avenue,
Rosebank 2196, South Africa

Penguin Books Ltd, Registered Offices: 80 Strand, London WC2R 0RL, England

First published 2002

1 3 5 7 9 10 8 6 4 2

Printed and bound in Canada on acid free paper ⊚

NATIONAL LIBRARY OF CANADA CATALOGUING IN PUBLICATION DATA

Haines, Max
Unnatural causes / Max Haines.

ISBN 0-14-301344-0

1. Murder. I. Title.

HV6515.H37 2002   364.15'23   C2002-903263-6

Visit Penguin Books' website at **www.penguin.ca**

To Jake Star

Acknowledgements

Many individuals and organizations contributed greatly to the writing of this book. I am particularly indebted to the Ontario Provincial Police, Quebec Provincial Police, Scotland Yard and the Federal Bureau of Investigation for their co-operation. I am also grateful to the wardens and other officials of several prisons who gave of their time and insight.

My thanks to the following people, whose contributions to this effort are incalculable: Susan Dugas, Clarissa Feliprada, Jillian Goddard, Julie Hornby, Bob Johnson, Julie Kirsh, Selena Ladd, Glenna Tapscott, Joyce Wagler and Kathy Webb Nelson.

This book would not have been possible without the dedication of co-editors Glenn Garnett and Liba Berry.

The title of the book is attributed solely to Roy McIntyre.

Contents

Contents   ix

Kiran Ahluwalia

(ENGLAND)

THE YOUNG GIRL WAS JUSTLY PROUD the day she received her bachelor of arts degree. It hadn't been easy. Kiran was the youngest of 10 children. Her father died when she was 3 months old, her mother when she was 16. Now she was leaving the Indian Punjab to join a married sister in Toronto. She planned to study law in Canada.

Kiran's family was pleased with her accomplishments, but they felt there were more important things in life. They coaxed her to find a suitable husband. If she had any difficulty in her quest, her brothers would supply a mate for their younger sister.

By 1979, Kiran was settled nicely in Toronto, pursuing her studies toward a law degree, when her well-meaning brothers informed her they had found her a potential husband. The candidate was a handsome engineer named Deepak Ahluwalia, who lived in Crawley, England. A meeting was quickly arranged. Deepak flew to Toronto. The 23-year-old Kiran had only a week to become acquainted with her future husband. She was pleasantly surprised. Deepak was charming, had a sense of humour and was so very handsome.

At the end of the week, the couple was married in a Toronto civil ceremony. Five days later they flew to England and were married in a Sikh temple in London. They moved into a modest but comfortable home in Crawley.

Two days later Kiran was shocked when, for no reason whatever, Deepak smashed the wedding presents his new bride had brought from Canada. That was the beginning. There would be more, much more. Within a week of becoming husband and wife, Deepak struck Kiran on the face with his fist and pulled her across the room by her hair. Kiran was in fear for her life. She attempted to run out of the house. Deepak blocked her way. Yelling and screaming, he made it perfectly clear that if she sought help or went to the police, he would hunt her down and kill her.

The days turned into months and the months into years. The abuse escalated. Deepak would strike out without warning. He hit his wife with anything within reach. Kitchen utensils, a telephone and a belt buckle were only a few of the items that came crashing down on Kiran's five-foot-two-inch frame. Several times she was severely burned after her husband threw hot tea in her face. Over the years Kiran suffered a broken hand, a broken nose and broken teeth. Nothing pleased her husband.

Three years of marriage took its toll. Kiran's hair turned grey. She grew despondent. Kiran pleaded with Deepak's family, who lived nearby in Crawley, but they showed her no sympathy. A woman's place was with her man and that was that. Besides, everyone agreed it was time for Kiran to have children. In 1984, a baby, Sanjay, was born into the dysfunctional family. Ravi followed two years later.

The birth of the children did nothing to interfere with the abuse heaped on Kiran. Twice, members of Deepak's family had to restrain him from choking her to death. On these occasions Kiran was rendered unconscious. Deepak's idea of marital sex was to rape his wife. Finally, Kiran mustered up enough courage to contact police. Deepak had held a knife to his wife's neck and had threatened to slit her throat. Injunctions restraining Deepak from assaulting his wife were issued. They had no effect. Kiran attempted suicide by overdosing on pills. She was rushed to hospital, where she recovered. After she was discharged, Deepak beat her unmercifully.

To add to Kiran's degradation, Deepak took a mistress. He bought his lady friend a car and was forever purchasing gifts for her. Kiran had difficulty running the house on the paltry amount of money doled out to her. She became a nervous wreck and lost a great deal of weight. Depression was a way of life. Kiran would burst into tears without provocation. Her body was scarred, her face swollen.

On May 8, 1989, after 10 years of hell, Kiran was a woman with no will of her own. She managed to gather enough strength to attempt to reason with her husband. She had tried in vain before, but all that day she resolved to try once more. After dinner she asked, "Can we talk about our future?" In response, Deepak said, "There is nothing more to say." He then attacked his wife. He twisted her legs until she thought they would break. Deepak grew tired of his sport and commenced to iron some clothing. Without warning, he threw his wife to the floor and placed the hot iron near her face, threatening to burn her if she didn't stop annoying him. At last, Kiran's demented husband released her and went to bed.

Kiran stayed up and thought about her plight. There was no escape, no way out. Deepak showed her no mercy. He should be made to suffer, to experience pain as she had for 10 long years. Well after midnight, Kiran took a stiff slug of whisky to calm her nerves. She then methodically made her way to a utility room off the kitchen, where she knew her husband kept a can of gasoline. Kiran poured some of the gasoline into a bucket. She put on oven gloves to protect her hands, lit a candle and picked up a small stick from the utility room floor. Thus armed, she made her way to Deepak's room. Her husband was sleeping soundly under a duvet.

Kiran poured gasoline over the duvet. When she proceeded to pour more of the liquid over Deepak's feet, he awoke with a start and jumped out of bed. As a matador faces a bull at the moment of truth, Kiran knew that the time had come. If she did nothing, she would suffer a severe beating, maybe one from which she would never recover. In a split second she took a few steps toward the bedroom door, dipped the piece of wood into the gasoline and lit it with a candle. It burst into flames. With one motion, Kiran threw the flaming stick toward the bed.

The gas vapours in the room burst into flame, engulfing Deepak. He fled screaming from the room. "I'll kill you, I'll kill you," he shouted as his pyjamas disintegrated. Deepak ran to the bathroom in search of water, but the water failed to extinguish the fire. He flung himself outside and rolled around in the garden. A neighbour saw the horrible sight of a man being consumed alive. Strips of skin were hanging from his body. Other neighbours came to his aid and attempted to extinguish the flames. One of them looked up and saw Kiran looking down at the scene from an upstairs window. She had burned her hands and arms.

The fire spread. Kiran grabbed her two children and evacuated the premises. Someone called the fire department. Soon firemen and an ambulance were at the scene. Unbelievably, despite his terribly burned body, Deepak managed to rise and make it to a phone. He told his mother of the hateful wife who had set him on fire.

Kiran was arrested on the spot and hustled off to jail, where she was charged with attempted murder. For six days Deepak lay in hospital, struggling to stay alive. When questioned, he told authorities about the wicked woman he had married. On the sixth day, he lost the struggle. The charge against Kiran was changed from attempted murder to murder.

In December 1989, Kiran stood trial for the murder of her husband. Her lawyer pleaded that his client was provoked to the point where she wanted to inflict pain on her husband, but not to kill him. The prosecution pointed out the singleness of purpose exhibited by Kiran as she went about gathering the implements of murder. They also stated that three hours had passed from the time Kiran had been abused by her husband to the time she had ignited the fire. They insinuated that she had calmly waited until her husband was sleeping.

The English jury found Kiran guilty of murder. She was sentenced to life imprisonment.

In prison, Kiran stated that she was leading a far better life than she had ever led under the same roof as her abusive husband. She blossomed while incarcerated, taking English lessons and studying fashion. In time, there was a great outpouring of sympathy from the public in general and the Asian community in particular concerning the plight of the charming, fragile woman behind bars. Various women's groups rallied, demanding that Kiran's case be appealed. Their efforts bore fruit. In July 1992, Kiran's appeal was heard. Unlike at her trial, her 10 years of intensive abuse was revealed in detail. Even her late husband's family testified on her behalf.

Kiran's murder conviction was quashed and a retrial was ordered. On September 25, 1992, at London's famed Old Bailey, the prosecution accepted Kiran's plea of guilty to manslaughter. She was sentenced to three years' and four months' imprisonment, the exact amount of time she had already served. Kiran Ahluwalia was released from custody and rejoined her two sons. Her release was considered a victory for abused women throughout England.

Amy Archer

(UNITED STATES)

IT ISN'T OFTEN YOU MEET A NYMPHOMANIAC who is a mass murderer. Folks, meet Amy Archer. In 1907, Amy arrived in Windsor, Connecticut, with her hubby, whom everyone called Big Jim. Amy wasn't a beautiful woman, but she wasn't plain either.

Amy and Big Jim purchased a House of Usher–type mansion, which soon opened for business as the Archer Home for Elderly People and Chronic Invalids. Amy passed herself off as a nurse. She also did all the cleaning and cooking for the five elderly gentlemen and four women who lived there. Big Jim fixed things, fetched things and cleaned out the bedpans.

Business boomed. You see, Amy's rates were dirt cheap, the cheapest in all of New England. There was one condition, though. To take advantage of the low rates, patients had to make Amy the beneficiary of their wills. In exchange, she would take care of their every need for the rest of their lives.

Unfortunately for the residents of the Archer Home, the patient death rate was unusually high. These deaths, tragic though they were, had a silver lining for Amy. She collected the recently departed's worldly goods and, at the same time, made room for a new resident. As you may have guessed, Amy was directly responsible for the rash of deaths: she was placing arsenic in her elderly wards' food. To break up the pattern a bit, she smothered several of the extremely frail.

Circumstances changed around the home on the day Michael Gilligan, a 30-something charmer, showed up. Michael was going door to door looking for work. Amy gave him a hot meal and assured him there was a lot that needed fixing around her establishment. Before you could say triangle, Michael moved in as a permanent member of the staff. Naturally, this did not sit well with Big Jim, who watched Michael's every move. He soon found out that Michael was a secret drinker. In fact, he was pretty well sloshed all the time.

When Michael had been firmly ensconced in Amy's home for only a few months, it was obvious to Big Jim that the new boy on the block was playing around with his wife. A rather talkative man by nature, Big Jim blabbered a lot around town. He told his friends that he was at his wits' end. His Amy loved her sex. Not just your average occasional romp in the hay. No, according to Big Jim, it would have taken a superhero to satisfy Amy. She wanted it all the time and Big Jim simply couldn't keep up, if you know what I mean.

At the same time as Big Jim was complaining to the locals, Amy was spreading the word that Big Jim was suffering from severe stomach cramps, possibly caused by overindulgence in the devil rum.

Amy's rumour-spreading proved to be timely. Big Jim suffered from stomach pains so severely that he was called to that great rest home in the sky.

His death caused little concern among the locals, who had become rather accustomed to the undertaker calling at Amy's home on a regular basis. Amy herself was heartbroken. At the wake she sobbed uncontrollably while serving cucumber sandwiches.

A few months after Big Jim's demise, Amy's attitude abruptly changed. She announced that Michael Gilligan had proposed marriage and that she had accepted. The marriage went off without a hitch, although a day before the blessed event, another of the elderly in the home went to his great reward. Never mind. The wedding was a joyous affair.

Now, folks, I have to tell you that Michael, like his predecessor, began to complain about Amy's sexual demands soon after they were legally hitched. He claimed that strong drink was the only thing that kept him going. Evidently, even this dubious remedy had its limitations. You see, to his chagrin, Michael found that he had become impotent. Amy learned quickly enough that her stud could no longer perform. A dash of white powder solved the problem. Amy whipped up a mess of cucumber sandwiches, sang a few hymns and dispatched Michael to the hereafter.

The home had been in operation for six years when Amy took to her bosom Mr. Runyon, a spry elderly gentleman who had, like all the residents, made out his will in Amy's favour. It was Mr. Runyon's misfortune to arrive at the home at the same time as a Mr. Andrews. Both men were on intimate terms with Amy. The situation became unmanageable and annoying. Never fear, Amy had a solution. She poisoned Runyon and smothered Andrews.

It is quite a feat to get away with murder year after year after year, but Amy did it. So confident had she become that she murdered two of her patients within hours of each other.

Eventually, she married Charles Smith, a resident of her home. Like all the others, he had made a will naming Amy as sole beneficiary. It took only a few months before Charles was gone and Amy collected.

Amy's reign of terror was finally causing tongues to wag. Soon the press and the police were receiving reports claiming that an inordinate number of people were dying at the Archer Home for Elderly People and Chronic Invalids. One reporter, Mike Toughy, decided to probe into the home's affairs. He discovered that of all the deaths over the previous 10 years, at least 40 were extremely suspicious.

Mike bribed a couple of gravediggers to exhume Mr. Andrews's body and ship it off to a Boston laboratory for testing. He was disappointed when the lab could find no trace of poison in the body, but he didn't give up. He had two more bodies exhumed, but again was disappointed. No trace of poison was detected. Of course, you and I know that Amy sometimes smothered her aged victims. It was her good luck that the bodies brought to the surface had not been poisoned.

Meanwhile, our girl kept murdering without missing a beat. Unbeknownst to her, Mike Toughy kept looking into her affairs. He hired an artist to produce a good likeness of Amy, which was shown to drugstore staff throughout the area. Sure enough, one pharmacist remembered Amy as the woman who had purchased a large quantity of arsenic. Mike felt he now had enough evidence to take to the state's attorney.

More bodies were exhumed. Amy's luck had run out. These bodies were laced with arsenic. Amy was immediately arrested.

On June 17, 1917, after 10 years of profitable murders, she was tried for her crimes in Hartford. There she stood, Bible in hand, maintaining that she was innocent of all wrongdoing. The evidence against this most unlikely killer was overwhelming. She was found guilty and sentenced to hang. Her lawyer was able to obtain a second trial on a technicality. Amy was again found guilty, but this time she was sentenced to life imprisonment.

Incarcerated in Weatherfield Prison, our Amy began to act irrationally. When she attempted to poison the warden and several guards, she was transferred to a lunatic asylum. Amy Archer's home for the rest of her life was a padded cell. She died in the asylum in 1928, at age 59.

Herbert Armstrong

(ENGLAND)

NEW YEAR'S EVE OF 1921 was not the happiest of occasions for lawyer Herbert Rowse Armstrong, but that's getting ahead of our story. Herb was a small, polite man who weighed no more than a hundred pounds. In 1906, at age 37, he moved to the small town of Hay, located just inside the Welsh-English border. When his partner died, he took over an established legal practice, which was one of only two in the town.

Herb met and married Katharine Mary Friend, a rather plain woman who usually wore a scowl. Let's face it, Katharine was as cranky as all get-out, especially when it came to hubby Herb. The Armstrongs lived in a large house, called Mayfield, about a mile outside Hay. They had three children, who were brought up in the strictest manner possible by their mother.

Herb led two lives. At home he was henpecked. His wife ridiculed him in front of the children. Nothing Herb did satisfied Katharine. She ordered him about without the least concern for his feelings. Alcohol and tobacco were not allowed in their home. Outside Mayfield, however, Herb was treated quite differently. Widely respected, he was active in social clubs and church affairs.

Herb's life was interrupted by the First World War. He served in various parts of England, achieving the rank of major. When he returned to Hay, he was forever after referred to as Major Armstrong. Herb loved it. But Katharine was as cranky as ever. She called him Herbert.

Professionally, the Major had his finger in many legal pies. When his only competitor, the elderly Mr. Griffiths, took in a partner, Oswald Norman Martin, Herb's practice declined appreciably. The fact that he could look out his window and observe Martin in his office directly across the street did nothing to diminish the growing envy Herb felt for the new boy on the block.

Martin's personality was quite unlike the popular Major's. He was straitlaced, aloof and not at all well liked, although everyone recognized him as an astute lawyer. A short time after setting up in Hay, Mr. Martin married Constance Davies, the pharmacist's daughter. Let's leave the Martins for a moment and get back to cantankerous Katharine.

In July 1920, Katharine, who was always complaining about some ailment or other, was once again under the weather. Solicitous Herb called in the family physician, Dr. Tom Hincks, who was quite accustomed to making house calls at Mayfield. He found Katharine suffering from depression. On August 22, Dr. Tom had her confined to the Barnwood Private Asylum in Gloucester, where she would remain for five months.

The Major, although heartbroken that Katharine was in such bad shape, enjoyed the relaxation of rules which her confinement afforded. It was pleasant to light up a Havana and pour a glass of Sandeman port without being harassed and insulted in what the Major considered to be his castle. Alas, all good things come to an end. Katharine, fit as a fiddle, returned home.

Folks, it pains me to report that back in the friendly confines of Mayfield, Katharine's health once again deteriorated. Actually, that's an understatement. On February 22, 1921, she died. The death, while tragic in the extreme, did allow the Major a certain degree of freedom. Out came the Sandeman and those big Havanas. Locals were invited to pleasant dinners at Mayfield. Over and above the civilized functions the Major held for fun, he also partook of other delights. Yes, Herb enjoyed the pleasures of the flesh. We know that for a fact because he contracted venereal disease around this time and was totally embarrassed to receive shots in the derrière from Dr. Tom to treat his delicate condition.

It was a busy time for the Major. He had no sooner planted Katharine than the annoying Oswald Martin began badgering him to close the sale of some property. Herb was acting for the vendor and Martin was acting for the purchaser. Martin's client had turned over a deposit to Herb, but Herb's client didn't have clear title to the property. He couldn't close the deal. When Martin demanded the return of the deposit, Herb couldn't come up with the cash because his client had spent it.

Martin was persistent. Herb invited him over to Mayfield for tea in order to discuss the matter. Nothing of a business nature was accomplished, but a rather pleasant interlude was concluded with Martin enjoying the Major's hospitality by accepting a buttered scone to accompany his Earl Grey. Martin had hardly reached his own home before he was laid low by a bout of vomiting and diarrhea. Dr. Tom Hincks was called immediately. He attributed Martin's discomfort to a bilious attack, and prescribed the appropriate medicine.

John Davies, the town pharmacist, who was also Martin's father-in-law, spoke to Dr. Tom, suggesting that Martin was being poisoned by Herbert Armstrong. Dr. Tom was aghast. Certainly Mr. Davies was in error. How could he make such a frivolous accusation against one of the leading citizens of the town? Davies related that on various occasions he had sold arsenic to Herb, who had signed his poisons book and asked what quantities would be required to get rid of persistent dandelions in his garden. Davies even mentioned that he wouldn't be a bit surprised if Herb had had something to do with Mrs. Armstrong's recent demise.

That got Dr. Tom thinking. He thought so much that he dashed off a note to Barnwood outlining his suspicions. The doctors at the

asylum agreed that it was quite possible they had mistakenly diagnosed Katharine's illness. All her symptoms were compatible with
arsenic poisoning. They recalled, as did Dr. Tom, that Katharine's
condition had improved dramatically in the asylum, only to take a
turn for the worse when she went back to Mayfield.

Dr. Tom informed police of his suspicions. They contacted
Martin, who was frightened out of his wits to learn that he was the
target of a man whom police now suspected of murder. Martin told
police he had once received a box of chocolates anonymously in the
mail, but as he and his wife didn't fancy chocolates, they had served
them to an acquaintance after dinner. The poor woman had taken ill
right there at their dining room table. Police examined what was left
of the chocolates and found that they were laced with arsenic. On
the last day of 1921, Herb was arrested and lodged in jail, which is an
extremely unpleasant way to spend New Year's Eve.

New Year's Day didn't prove to be much better for the Major.
Bright and early, authorities exhumed Katharine's body. It was found
to be chock-full of arsenic. It never rains but it pours. The Major was
charged with his wife's murder.

On April 3, 1922, Herb stood trial for murder, with his life in the
balance. The Crown revealed that when Herb was arrested, police
found a packet of arsenic on his person. Most people don't usually
carry around arsenic. The only reason Herb could give for having
the poison was that he'd been waging a war against dandelions. His
lawyer proposed to the court that Katharine could have died by her
own hand. The jury felt otherwise and found Herb guilty of murder.

On May 31, 1922, after all appeals failed, Herbert Rowse
Armstrong was hanged in Gloucester, England.

Charles Barafaud

(FRANCE)

WHEN WE THINK OF LIMOGES, FRANCE, we conjure up images of fine porcelain, but alas, the famous French city is not devoid of murder most foul.

In 1928, Charles Barafaud lived and loved with a vengeance. The son of a wealthy porcelain factory owner, he was an admirer of French wine of quality and wild French women in quantity. Charles was a playboy through and through. He spent money like a drunken sailor until, one day, his frustrated father laid down the law. Enough was enough. Charles would have to become accustomed to living within a strict budget.

Charles was stunned at this revolting state of affairs. He attempted to live within his budget for a few weeks, but gave up the idea as ridiculous and definitely not for him. Our boy came up with a diabolical scheme to raise cash. He would turn to murder.

He contacted a friend in the real estate business named Roux. He told Roux that he knew an elderly eccentric who owned timberland worth more than a million francs. He had an option to purchase the land for 600,000 francs. If they could sell it for the option price, they would each make commissions of 30,000 francs. Besides, whoever bought the property would be getting a real bargain.

It was one of those deals where everyone concerned would come
out smelling like roses. There was one small catch. The eccentric old
man had no use for cheques or banks. He insisted on being paid in
cash. Roux said, "No problem. I know just the man for the deal, the
lumber merchant Lascaux."

True to his word, Roux approached Lascaux, who agreed to
purchase the timberland at the bargain price. So far so good.
Basically, Charles planned to murder both men, grab the cash and
have their murders blamed on another party altogether, taxi driver
Etienne Faure.

Charles put his scheme into action. He made arrangements for
Roux and Lascaux to rendezvous with him for the several hours'
drive outside Limoges to meet the old man, who, between you and
me, didn't exist. He would pick the two men up at midnight on
January 12.

Early on January 11, Charles called an acquaintance, taxi driver
Etienne Faure, advising him that he was having car trouble outside
the city and required assistance. Following Charles's directions,
Etienne made his way down a dark road over the river Vincou. He
spotted Charles and asked if he could look under the hood. That's
when Charles hit him over the head with a hatchet, killing the unsuspecting taxi driver instantly.

Charles placed Etienne's body in his own car and hid the dead
man's taxi in nearby woods. Cunning Charles filled Etienne's pockets
with stones and threw him into the river. He then drove to where he
had hidden the taxi and changed cars. He drove the taxi to a garage
at his father's factory and parked it there.

Next day, at midnight, Charles picked up Roux and Lascaux for
the trip to the eccentric's home to purchase the timberland. The
scheme couldn't fail. He would kill the two men in Etienne's taxi and
the missing Etienne would be blamed. Meanwhile, he would relieve
Lascaux of those 600,000 francs.

Initially, all went well. As they approached the place where
Charles had left his car the night before, he told his companions that

he'd had car trouble; that's why he had borrowed the taxi. If they would excuse him a minute, he wanted to get something out of his stalled vehicle.

Minutes passed. Finally, out of the darkness, Charles was seen approaching, carrying a hatchet. Wild-eyed, he walked to the car. Lascaux had brought along a revolver to protect his money. He extracted the weapon from his pocket and pointed it at Charles. The two men stared at each other. It was Charles who broke the tension. "I played a joke on you," he said. "There was no timber deal."

The two men didn't take the news well. The drive back to town was tense. No one spoke. The men were furious. As they got out of the car, they made disparaging remarks about Charles's mental capabilities and his heritage.

No one was more disappointed than Charles that his scheme had gone awry. He had killed a man, received no money and had a taxi to get rid of. First things first. He drove the taxi to a ledge beside the river and managed, with a slight shove, to push it into the water. He watched as the car disappeared. Then Charles retrieved his own car and drove back to Limoges.

For three days nothing happened. Charles spent his time downing cognac with an old friend, Bertrand Peynet as if he didn't have a care in the world. On day three, Etienne's body washed ashore. A day later, children spotted the dead man's taxi just under the water.

The hunt was on for the popular taxi driver's killer. It didn't take an Inspector Maigret to locate the two men who had been seen driving around in Etienne's taxi. When they were questioned, they told of Charles's involvement.

Charles was picked up and interrogated. He told police that he was their man. He even promised to confess if he would be allowed to return home one last time to tell his father how very sorry he was that things had turned out in such a disagreeable way. Investigating officers, being suspicious by nature, suggested that he confess first. Charles agreed and related all the details of his strange scheme.

Under close guard, he was escorted to his father's home. Once there, it was learned that Charles's father was not in. Charles was greeted by his best friend, Bertrand Peynet. Charles asked permission to retire to an upstairs den with his friend to await his father's return. His guards thought this a reasonable request. The house was completely surrounded. There was no fear of escape.

Charles knew there were loaded hunting rifles in the den. He quickly grabbed a rifle and, for reasons known only to him, shot Bertrand Peynet in the chest. His friend was dead before he hit the floor. Downstairs, police heard the loud report. They dashed upstairs and found Charles with the smoking gun. "You killed him," the detective shouted.

"No, he killed himself." Charles went on to explain that he and his friend had quickly formulated a suicide pact. Peynet had shot himself and he had attempted to commit suicide himself, but the gun misfired.

Sixteen months later, Charles stood trial for the murder of Etienne Faure. The entire country followed the trial. Charles's father spent a fortune attempting to save his son from death by the guillotine. He succeeded.

Charles Barafaud was found guilty of murder and was sentenced to life imprisonment. Citizens of Limoges were so incensed at the lenient punishment that armed mounted soldiers had to be employed to disperse the mob of several thousand who milled about the courthouse as Barafaud was transferred to prison.

Marie Becker

(BELGIUM)

YOU MIGHT CALL MARIE BECKER a late bloomer, but once she got the hang of killing people, she took to the vile practice with a vengeance.

Marie hailed from Liège, Belgium. Her husband, Charles, couldn't ask for a better wife. For years Marie devoted herself to Charles and to Charles only. The quiet cabinetmaker looked forward to spending his twilight years in the arms of his ever-loving wife. But things didn't work out for Charles. You see, Marie, the hussy, took a shine to 46-year-old Lambert Beyer, and so hubby had to go.

There was Marie, a well-preserved 53 years of age, a touch of grey in her once jet-black hair, a tiny wrinkle here and there on an otherwise pleasant visage. As for Lambert, he was tall, rather handsome, with well-chiseled features, which sometimes appeal to women.

In the fall of 1932, Charles suddenly took ill and left this cruel world for a far, far better place beyond. Marie, the typical grieving widow, shed tears in abundance at graveside. Later, she served those attending the funeral selected dainty sandwiches and petits fours.

The widow didn't grieve for long. Charles was hardly cold in his final resting place before Marie was keeping company with men, not years, but decades her junior. She wasn't above downing quantities of rich red wine at local clubs and dance halls. Her neighbours' collective tongues wagged.

Now then, Marie was not left a fortune by her dear departed husband. A small insurance policy on his life helped a bit, but not enough. She became a dressmaker, though not because she had any ambition with needle and thread. No, she was looking for a way to gain entry to the moneyed homes of Liège.

Soon, Marie was not only dressmaker to the elderly aristocracy of the city, she was also their confidante and, in some cases, nurse. In this way, our Marie became a good friend of Madame Douphène. The two women grew so close that when Marie suggested that Madame Douphène move in with her, the older lady jumped at the chance.

Madame was so grateful that she made out a will leaving everything she possessed to Marie. It didn't take long. Two months after she entered Marie's home and loving care, Madame Douphène expired.

Her death wasn't that unexpected. She had often complained about an unreliable digestive tract. Her doctor duly signed the death certificate, attributing that malady to be the cause of death.

In the summer of 1932, Marie shifted gears. With her bank account once again reinforced, she lived the life of wine, men and song. She met Monsieur Hoby, who was younger than Marie, which was just fine with the merry widow. Her old beau, Lambert Beyer, had to go. But Beyer wasn't having any. He had the unmitigated gall to tell Marie that he loved her. Marie was annoyed.

You can just guess what happened. In November 1934, his death was attributed to epigastric trouble that failed to respond to his doctor's treatment. Everything he owned he left to Marie.

There is some evidence that Marie was actually fond of Monsieur Hoby. Perhaps that was the reason she allowed him to remain alive.

To keep herself in petty cash, the widow went on a poisoning spree. The year 1935 was particularly bountiful. She killed six women and profited from each murder. They were Julia Bossy, the widow Perot, Aline Louis-Damont, Madame Castadot, the widow Lambert and the widow Grulle.

While not as lucrative as 1935, the year 1936 was also hectic. Marie claimed three more victims: Anne Stewart, the widow Bultay and the widow Lange.

If you are keeping score, Marie poisoned 10 women, all of whom left her their worldly goods, as well as a husband and a lover. That's an even dozen victims for a woman who had been a kind, gentle lady until something snapped in her fifty-third year.

Our Marie could quite possibly have continued killing for profit indefinitely if she hadn't been so flippant. One fine day, a lady with homicide in mind inquired whether Marie had any good ideas as to how she could dispose of her husband. Instead of coyly feigning ignorance of such a dastardly deed, Marie volunteered, "If you want to poison your husband, I can give you a powder to leave no trace. Death appears to be natural."

The woman didn't take Marie's advice, but later, when she suffered from abdominal pains, she thought Marie might be responsible. She reported her suspicions to police. This act alone might not have ended Marie's killing spree, but it coincided with an anonymous letter to police in which the writer charged Marie with being responsible for Madame Castadot's death.

Once detectives got on the trail, they discovered the array of corpses left in Marie's wake. When she was arrested, her purse yielded a vial containing digitalis. All the victims had displayed symptoms compatible with digitalis poisoning. Marie claimed that the digitalis was for her own heart condition. Unfortunately, her doctor swore that Marie's heart was fine and that he had never prescribed that medication for her.

Marie's trial, held in the Palace of Justice in Liège, caused a sensation. She displayed no emotion throughout her ordeal. Taking the witness stand in her own defence, Marie changed her story about how she'd come to have poison in her possession. She now claimed she had purchased digitalis and had sold it regularly at a profit to a friend. Marie refused to divulge her friend's name.

The defendant gave colourful testimony. When asked how the widow Lambert had died, she replied, "Like an angel choked by sauerkraut." Marie was also asked if she had had an affair with Monsieur Castadot after she had killed his wife. She wouldn't admit to killing anyone, but she did confess that Monsieur Castadot became her lover after the untimely demise of his wife.

All of this was titillating testimony, especially since Monsieur Castadot was a police officer. Marie added that after she dropped him, he had acted extremely spiteful. It was he who had sent the anonymous letter to police.

The sensational trial lasted three weeks, but the decision of the jury was a foregone conclusion. Marie Becker was found guilty of multiple murder and sentenced to life imprisonment.

Leo Bertrand

(CANADA)

IT'S HARD TO SAY just when Leo Bertrand made the transition from a rosy-cheeked farm boy to a scheming, murderous rascal. We do know that at 21 years of age, the rather handsome Leo married Rose Asseline. The newlyweds settled in Ottawa, where Leo gained employment as a cab driver. In 1934, that occupation provided the Bertrands with little more than a meagre living. Leo wanted more from life. He cherished expensive clothing and trips to distant lands, all of which were well beyond his means.

Then our boy discovered that great source of illicit fast bucks—insurance. He learned he could insure Rose's life for $5,000 with a double-indemnity clause, which meant if Rose departed due to an accident, the payoff would double to $10,000, a veritable fortune in those days. Leo purchased a policy. It didn't matter a hoot to him that his wife was heavy laden with child.

The day after taking delivery of the insurance policy, Leo and his wife drove out to his parents' farm. The elderly couple was delighted with the unexpected winter visit. Although not wealthy, the elder Bertrands were generous, forever giving their son and daughter-in-law gifts from the farm. As Leo and Rose prepared to leave, they were presented with a crate of eggs, which they placed between them on the front seat of their vehicle.

Leo was next seen running through a stop sign where the St. Polycarpe road intersects the main road to Ottawa. He continued down the road, which was strange since it ended a short distance away at a pier on Lac St. Francis. Mon Dieu, what was Leo Bertrand doing with his pregnant wife on a pier in the middle of a cold winter night?

A short time later, Leo awakened Alcide Melthot, who lived some distance away from the pier. Hysterically, he blurted out that his car had gone over the end of the pier with his pregnant Rose and a crate of Grade-A eggs inside.

The two men rushed to the nearby White House Hotel, where they found several men in the beverage room. All rushed down to the end of the pier to attempt to extract the car, Rose and the eggs from the icy depths of Lac St. Francis. Leo frantically explained that when he had attempted to turn the vehicle, the front end had gone over the pier. It had balanced there. He had been able to get out, and had tried to yank the car off its precarious perch. His efforts didn't work and the car plunged into the water. The men worked all through the night before locating the car some 15 metres from the end of the pier.

Police smelled a rat. When the car was examined, there was Rose beside the crate of eggs. The driver's door was open, but the crate of eggs blocked her way out. The passenger door was locked and the door handle was missing. It was found in the trunk of the car.

In addition, police noted tire tracks in the snow, indicating that the car had accelerated greatly before plunging into the lake. This would explain why the vehicle was found so far from the end of the dock. The hand throttle of the car was found wide open. Investigators were certain that Leo had trapped his wife in the car and had jumped clear as it sped into the lake. Discovery of the insurance policy was frosting on the cake.

Leo was arrested and charged with his wife's murder. On December 2, 1935, he stood trial. Despite the overwhelming circumstantial case against him, Leo Bertrand was found not guilty.

A few days later, Leo collected the 10,000 big ones from the insurance company. That same day, he purchased a new wardrobe. The shiny new threads were closely followed by a shiny new car. Leo displayed an absolute talent for spending money. Within a few months he was hard up for cash.

Never one to let grass grow under his feet, Leo devised another get-rich-quick scheme. It was simple. He would rob a bank. Together with buddy Anatole Letreille, Leo made his way to the small town of Russell, Ontario. They planned on making an unauthorized withdrawal from the Bank of Nova Scotia.

Things didn't go well. Anatole approached the tellers and shouted in Humphrey Bogart fashion, "This is a hold-up. Stick 'em up." Manager Charlie Stewart heard the shout and took his bank-issued revolver out of his desk drawer. Leo, waving a weapon of his own, picked that very instant to walk into the manager's office. Leo fired. He missed. Charlie fired. He missed. The gunplay took all the fight out of Leo and Anatole. They raced to their car and got away with their lives, but no cash. Both men were traced and taken into custody within weeks of the aborted robbery.

On October 19, 1936, Leo and Anatole were tried in L'Orignal, Ontario. They were found guilty of attempted robbery and sentenced to 15 years' imprisonment. The ominous gates of Kingston Penitentiary closed behind Leo Bertrand. A few years before, he had been a young man working on his father's farm. In short order he had become a husband, a killer, a widower, a robber and now a convict.

Leo did well in prison. Three years after entering Kingston, he was transferred to Prince Albert, Saskatchewan, where he distinguished himself as an acolyte in the institution's Roman Catholic chapel. After serving more than 11 years of his sentence, on March 9, 1948, Leo was released. He made his way back to Ottawa, where he gained employment with the dry-cleaning firm Lyle Blackwell. Two years later, he was plant manager.

One day, quite by chance, Leo noticed an advertisement on the back of a matchbook. He applied for a correspondence course at a diploma mill. Magically, he was transformed into Leo Bertrand, Doctor of Divinity, Psychology, Philosophy and what have you.

Dr. Bertrand soon met cute and proper schoolteacher Ruth Bouchard. Ruthie was smitten. Leo was a busy boy. He opened an office, where he did a lot of counselling, kept his manager's position down at the dry-cleaning plant and wooed Ruthie on the side.

Still, he wasn't content. The 36-year-old Leo took a fancy to 53-year-old Marie Charette, a seamstress at the dry-cleaning plant. More precisely, he took a fancy to the two rooming houses Marie had inherited. Leo added Marie to his ever-expanding list of activities. On September 3, 1951, he married the widow Charette, but didn't give up his romance with Ruthie.

The newlyweds drew up wills leaving everything they owned to each other. Two months after the marriage, Leo rented an isolated cabin on the shores of Lac Ste. Marie, Quebec. He also purchased two five-gallon cans of Varsol.

One winter's night, several men driving along a country road came across Leo and his ditched Cadillac. It had snowed heavily and the men stopped to lend a hand. Leo told the men that his wife and he had been in a cabin nearby when a lamp had exploded, burning her hand. When he had gone to obtain bandages from his car, the cabin had burst into flames.

In the darkness the men assumed that the injured woman was in the back seat of the Cadillac. They offered to go to the cabin to see if anything was salvageable. Leo assured them that the cabin had burned to the ground.

The men instructed him to follow them into town and to be careful on the treacherous road. After they had travelled a short distance, they were stopped by a truck, which had skidded across the road, blocking their way. Leo got out to inquire about the delay. Only then did he reveal that his wife wasn't in the car. She was back in the cabin, burned to a crisp. The men were flabbergasted at Leo's lack of concern for his wife, who had apparently died such a horrible death.

Leo duly reported the accident to police. As they approached the burned-out rubble, Quebec Provincial Police found a wad of paper in the snow that smelled of Varsol. They also found a Coleman lamp beside Marie's incinerated body. The lamp was charred black but was intact. This was the lamp Leo claimed had exploded. Most incriminating of all were two empty five-gallon cans found near the lamp.

On May 12, 1952, Leo was tried for the murder of his second wife. When it was proven that the Varsol came from Leo's dry-cleaning plant, his fate was sealed. He was found guilty of murder.

On June 11, 1953, Leo Bertrand was hanged at Montreal's Bordeaux Jail.

Jane Callaway & Leon Hawkins

(UNITED STATES)

THERE IS SOMETHING about some of the affluent citizens of Texas that seems to compel them to go around shooting each other. That's what happened on September 2, 1987, to Judy Saragusa, the attractive 37-year-old wife of a multimillionaire wine and liquor distributor. Judy was active in Houston social circles and deeply involved in charitable causes.

Judy and Michael Saragusa lived in the exclusive section of Houston known as Pine Shade. Late in the afternoon in question, security guard Craig Nimer, employed to protect the mansions along Green Tree Street, heard the sound of a shot emanating from the Saragusa home. As he ran to investigate, he saw a maroon Cadillac leave the Saragusa driveway, and got a good look at the driver before he sped away.

Nimer entered the house and scanned the first floor before proceeding upstairs. Once there, he came across the fully clothed body of Judy Saragusa in the hall. Judy had been shot in the head. Nimer immediately notified Houston police.

Detectives examining the crime scene found a single spent .22-calibre shell, apparently fired from the murder weapon. As befits a multimillionaire's wife, Judy was bedecked with expensive jewellery, none of which was touched by her killer, nor had she been sexually interfered with in any way. The palatial home had not been disturbed. Nothing was missing from the residence. An examination of all doors and windows indicated there had been no forced entry.

Michael Saragusa was notified of the tragedy and was, understandably, devastated by his wife's death. He informed police that they had just moved out of their previous home a month before and were in the process of making extensive renovations to the home on Green Tree.

Michael furnished the police with an important lead. Two months earlier, he told authorities, Judy and his private secretary at Quality Beverages, 35-year-old Jane Callaway, had lunched together. Jane gave Judy a lift home. When the two women entered the house, they encountered an elderly man with a handgun. Without hesitation, Jane pulled a weapon of her own out of her purse and fired at the intruder. She missed, but scared the daylights out of the stranger, who turned tail and ran away.

Jane Callaway's name popped up in the murder investigation from another avenue. Security guard Nimer, who had seen the Cadillac speed away from the Saragusa residence, had been astute enough to memorize the car's licence plate number. A check of the plate revealed the owner to be none other than Jane Callaway.

Jane was questioned by police. She told them she had loaned her Cadillac to a relative from Lubbock, Texas. Detectives placed a call to Jane's relative then and there. The woman had no idea what the police were talking about. She insisted that she had never borrowed Jane's vehicle. Jane stuck to her story. In fact, she stuck to it for a full day before abruptly altering her yarn in every way. Jane now told detectives that an acquaintance, Michael Richardson, a 24-year-old former college basketball star, had borrowed her car on the afternoon of the murder. She claimed that's all she knew.

Richardson was picked up and taken into custody for questioning. He told police he had returned to the Houston area after graduating from college. He had met Jane through other members of his family.

She often contacted him to do odd jobs around her home and had, on occasion, loaned him money.

One fine day, he reported, Jane let him know she would pay well to have her boss's wife put out of the way. She kept after Richardson until he decided to milk her for whatever he could. Jane, who had the authority to transfer Quality Beverages' funds, was soon making cold hard cash available to Richardson. He received an initial payment of $20,000, but claimed he had had no intention of killing anyone. Jane kept phoning him, insisting that he complete his part of the bargain. One day when she called, he was with his stepbrother, 21-year-old Leon Hawkins. Jane heard Leon laughing in the background. She suggested he might be an excellent candidate for the unique task she had in mind. Leon said that for $50,000 and a shiny new Nissan 300ZX, he was just the man for the job.

On the day before the murder, Richardson, Hawkins and Jane met at Jane's house. She presented two pistols to Hawkins on a tray. He chose a .22-calibre handgun. Next day, the two men drove to Quality Beverages, where Jane gave Leon the keys to her Cadillac.

According to Richardson, on the day of the murder Hawkins called him and said, "Man, I've done something and I'm scared." Richardson's story was checked and found to be authentic in every detail.

Jane was charged with the murder of Judy Saragusa. While police were searching for Leon Hawkins, he walked into a police station, where he too was charged with murder. Richardson was held on murder charges as well.

On May 16, 1988, Jane Callaway stood trial for the murder of Judy Saragusa. As is the case in every murder trial, the accused's history came under microscopic scrutiny. It was learned that Jane was a regular churchgoer and sang in the church choir. She had been twice married and twice divorced. Her second husband, Charles Beaschler, was an 80-year-old church-choir director. It was this elderly gentleman who had purchased the murder weapon and was the intruder who had accosted the two women months earlier. Jane had staged the scene so that suspicion would later fall on the "intruder."

During Jane's trial, it was discovered that she was a millionaire in her own right. Her family was big in the grocery business in central Texas and had left her more than a million dollars' worth of stock in the family business. All of this leads one to wonder why Jane, a good-looking woman with an executive position and money to burn, would swindle her own firm and plot the murder of her boss's wife.

Are you sitting down?

It was revealed by Michael Saragusa that he and Jane had had a short-lived affair, which he had terminated about three months before his wife's death. Jane was madly in love with him and insanely jealous of his wife and her social standing in the community. She decided to have Judy murdered, and financed her wild scheme by embezzling a total of $138,000 from her employer's bank accounts, most of which went to pay middleman Richardson and trigger man Hawkins.

Jane Callaway and Leon Hawkins were both found guilty of murder and sentenced to life imprisonment. Michael Richardson was allowed to plead guilty to conspiracy to commit murder in exchange for his testimony. He received a 10-year prison sentence, which on appeal was reduced to probation for 10 years.

Bernard Cazes

(FRANCE)

CIRCUMSTANCES SURROUNDING SUICIDES and attempted suicides are sometimes deceiving. To illustrate the point, let's take a look at the life and apparent suicide attempt of Myriam Fraysses.

The 19-year-old Myriam met and fell in love with Bernard Cazes in March 1982 while she was employed as a waitress in the French town of Naucelle. She brought Bernard home to meet her *mère* and *père* on the farm. Not one to miss an opportunity to freeload, the unemployed Bernard moved in with Myriam's parents for six months. During that time he ate well, drank red wine and didn't once seek gainful employment.

On the other hand, Myriam was successful in upgrading her status when she obtained a position in a nearby textile mill. Eventually the young couple moved into a tiny home in the small village of La Capelle-Balaguer. The upkeep of the house was derived solely from Myriam's income. Bernard spent most nights, belly up to the bar, at watering holes in surrounding towns and cities. Funds supporting his extravagant habits came from what he could cajole out of Myriam and a monthly government unemployment cheque.

Life progressed in this relatively peaceful manner until the wee hours of July 30, 1984, when neighbours of the couple were startled out of their sleep by the loud report of a gunshot. Minutes later, Bernard was at a neighbour's door. He bellowed, "Help me! Call a doctor! Myriam has shot herself." The neighbour called for an ambulance and ran next door. There lay Myriam in the middle of the bed in her nightgown, the right side of her head blown away. Her arms were folded across her chest. There was surprisingly little blood on the floor and walls. A 12-gauge single-barrelled shotgun was on the floor beside the bed. When the neighbour felt for a pulse, she was surprised that Myriam was still breathing.

The horribly wounded woman was rushed to Toulouse, the closest city with facilities to treat her injury. Myriam surprised the ambulance staff by surviving the trip. The prognosis, however, wasn't good. Doctors held little hope for her recovery. They stated that if by some miracle she were to survive, she would remain in a deep coma because of the extensive brain damage she'd suffered.

Meanwhile, gendarmes investigating the incident were hampered by Myriam's parents, René and Marie Fraysses, who insisted that their vivacious, fun-loving daughter would never take her own life. Investigators examined the bedroom and the shotgun. The weapon was sent to a police lab where fingerprints were lifted from the stock and trigger guard. These were compared with Myriam's prints, obtained in the hospital from the unconscious girl. They matched. The lack of a large quantity of blood was a puzzle, but there seemed little doubt that Myriam had attempted to commit suicide. Weeks passed. Doctors confirmed that Myriam would survive, but she would be totally paralyzed and incapable of speech. Her distraught parents eventually took her home, where they and her brothers and sisters fed, washed and cared for the helpless girl.

As the months turned into years, Myriam's parents never wavered from their belief that someone had attempted to murder their daughter. They continued on a weekly basis to stay in contact with police, urging them to reopen the investigation. Gradually, Myriam's condition improved to the point where she could move two fingers. She managed to write, "I love you. I love you." Her parents, as well as the police, begged her to try to write more, but she never did. She only wrote, over and over, "I love you."

Three years after the shooting, police finally gave in to the urging of the Fraysses family, and agreed to conduct an extensive investigation into the shooting. They immediately established that it would have been possible for Myriam to have shot herself in the right side of the head with the single-action shotgun. However, they now felt it would have been impossible for her clear fingerprints to have been found on the stock and trigger guard. The weapon had a tremendous kick and the recoil would have smeared the prints.

Since Bernard and Myriam's house had not been sold or rented due to the superstition of the local populace, police were able to conduct tests at the scene. They found that the recoil of the gun discharging would have sent it flying far from the bed. You may have noted that the shotgun was lying beside the bed, on the floor, when neighbours first arrived at the scene.

Experts were asked to study the bedroom and address the fact that a woman had been shot at close range with a shotgun, leaving no appreciable blood spatters on the floor and walls. They concluded that for her to have discharged the weapon was altogether impossible.

Even though three years had passed, technicians were able to scrape traces of blood from the ceiling, walls and floor of the kitchen. The blood proved to be the same type as Myriam's. Investigators concluded that Myriam had been shot in the kitchen before being placed on the bed. Doctors agreed that it was within the realm of possibility for a person to shoot themselves in bed and be left with arms folded neatly across their chest, but it was highly unlikely.

Bernard was taken into custody. He was no sooner behind bars than a drinking companion contacted police to inform them that Bernard had confessed to killing Myriam after a bitter argument. She had put her foot down and declared he had to quit his carousing and drinking. Bernard had seen red and had blasted half her head off with a shotgun. Another buddy contacted police. He told them that

Bernard had often bragged about committing the perfect crime. Both these witnesses had not come forward sooner as they had feared for their lives. With Bernard in custody, they felt safe to contact police.

In May 1988, Bernard stood trial on a charge of attempted murder. He was found guilty and sentenced to 20 years in prison.

Today, in a small town in France, a 31-year-old woman is still being cared for by her family. When given a paper and pencil, she scrawls, "I love you. I love you." No one but Myriam knows to whom she is directing her message.

Steven Cheshire

(UNITED STATES)

IT ISN'T OFTEN that the love of a father for his children leads to bloody murder, but it does happen.

At 28 years of age, Darrel Durbin was convinced that his life had finally taken a turn for the better. After years of searching for his biological father, he had finally located him. What's more, the man who had not laid eyes on Darrel for 28 years was pleased and receptive to the anticipated meeting with his son. The pair arranged to get together within a week of their first telephone contact.

Darrel, who had a good position with a metal extruding company in St. Augustine, Florida, had another bit of good fortune. His girlfriend, 30-year-old Mary Cheshire, had consented to marry him. Mary and her two sons, ages 12 and 6, by a previous marriage, had moved into Darrel's trailer home in nearby Palatka.

Darrel had spent a fatherless, tumultuous youth. Maybe that's why he enjoyed being with Mary's two boys. Within a few months in the fall of 1988 he had become engaged, was in the process of acquiring two sons and had found a long-lost father. No wonder he told everyone he knew that his life had turned around. The future looked bright.

At around 2:30 a.m. on October 30, Darrel's neighbour awoke with a start. He thought he had heard a car backfire and looked across the street. When he saw nothing unusual, he figured he had been dreaming and went back to sleep. Next morning, his wife said she thought she had heard gunshots. His curiosity aroused, Darrel's neighbour went across the street to investigate. He immediately noticed something peculiar. All four tires on both cars in the driveway had been slashed. The neighbour took no chances. He called police.

The first officer at the scene found the trailer unlocked. Inside he discovered Darrel's nude body lying on a bed. Mary's body was in a sitting position on a sofa in the living room. A sheet had been tossed over her lap.

Homicide detectives soon arrived at the crime scene. Just outside the trailer they noticed what appeared to be a fresh footprint. A plaster cast was made of the print.

It was discovered that both victims had been shot directly in the chest with a shotgun. An autopsy revealed that Darrel had been shot with the barrel of the gun placed not more than a few inches from his chest. Mary had been shot from a distance of five or six feet. The shells recovered from the scene indicated that the weapon was a 12-gauge shotgun.

The medical examiner estimated that death had occurred between 7:30 Saturday night, when both victims had been seen alive, and 1:00 p.m. on Sunday, when their bodies were discovered. After interviewing Darrel's neighbour, investigators felt that he and his wife had heard the fatal shots, putting the exact time of death at 2:30 Sunday morning. They also confirmed that Mary's two sons were away that weekend visiting relatives in St. Augustine.

Mary's estranged husband, Steven Cheshire, had not taken his separation from Mary well. She had sued for divorce, citing physical cruelty as the grounds for the action. A rider on the petition requested that Steven not be told where she was living.

In the meantime, Steven had acquired a girlfriend of his own. Coincidentally, she lived only a short distance from Darrel's mobile home. In addition, a local patrol officer told investigating detectives that he had seen Steven drive down the road close to Darrel's mobile home at about 2:00 a.m. on the Sunday of the murder. He was certain it was Steven because he knew him personally, and besides, Steven was driving a distinctive Department of Transportation yellow pickup truck.

Detectives realized that Steven could have been in the murder area visiting his girlfriend. When they questioned her, she confirmed he had arrived at her home after midnight Sunday morning. He often dropped in at odd hours, so she didn't find the visit unusual. She did add that Steven appeared upset about something.

Police contacted Mary's relative in St. Augustine, where her two sons were staying for the weekend. They learned that Steven had visited the boys that Saturday. The reunion didn't go well. For the first time he found out that Mary was living with another man. His eldest son told him, "Mummy wants me to call the other man Daddy." Coming from his son, this information was devastating. Steven was beside himself. He insisted that they give him their mother's address.

Detectives attempted to pick Steven up at his home, but he wasn't there. They obtained a search warrant to enter the house. Inside they recovered two 20-gauge shotguns, but the 12-gauge shotgun they knew Steven owned was nowhere to be found.

Investigators realized their bird had flown. They had no difficulty locating him at the home of a relative in Newport, North Carolina. The first thing Steven said to his interrogators was: "I believe I would like to invoke the right to counsel." He did, however, consent to turn over his shoes to detectives. Experts agreed that one of the shoes could have made the print lifted from outside Darrel's trailer.

A search of the Department of Transportation truck unearthed a bloodstained T-shirt and a pair of jeans. Both of these items had been mentioned by Steven's girlfriend as the clothing he was wearing when he visited her in the wee hours of Sunday morning. That was enough. Steven was charged with two counts of first-degree murder. He waived extradition and was returned to Florida to stand trial.

A short time later, a Grand Jury indicted Steven on two counts of first-degree murder, burglary of a dwelling while armed, shooting into an occupied dwelling and criminal mischief. The burglary charge stemmed from a few items missing from Darrel's mobile home. The criminal mischief charge covered the slashing of the occupants' tires.

At a pretrial hearing, the chief prosecutor informed Judge Robert Perry that the defendant had refused a plea bargain arrangement. The State had proposed dropping the two charges of first-degree murder if Steven would plead guilty to two counts of second-degree murder and the other charges against him. Steven would have none of it. He insisted he was innocent and demanded a speedy trial.

On May 22, 1989, Steven stood trial. After deliberating eight hours, the Florida jury found him guilty of all five charges. They recommended life sentences on each of the murder charges. Two months later, Judge Perry dismissed the jury's recommendation and sentenced Steven to death in Florida's electric chair. He also handed down an additional 16 years' imprisonment on the three remaining charges.

Over a year later, the Florida Supreme Court ruled that the judge had erred in not considering the jury's recommendation when he'd imposed the death penalty. The death sentences were reduced to two sentences of life imprisonment to run consecutively.

Steven Cheshire was 38 years old at the time of sentencing and will not be eligible for parole for 50 years, at which time he will be 88.

Donald Lewis Clark

(UNITED STATES)

THERE IS SOMETHING TITILLATING about a man of the cloth straying from the straight and narrow. It doesn't happen often, but when it does it tends to erode one's faith.

Donald Lewis Clark was born down Alabama way to a God-fearing religious couple who taught their son the Golden Rule and other good and pure values. When Donald was in his twenties, he joined the U.S. Navy, not to further his religious education, but rather to see the world.

After his discharge, Donald married Norma, a winsome Southern belle, whom he found downright annoying within three months of tying the knot. Donald joined the civilian labour force as an advertising salesman, an occupation which many feel bears a certain relationship to religion. When he wasn't selling, he served the Almighty as a lay minister.

At age 45, Donald gave up the thrills and spills of the advertising game to become an ordained minister. He caught on as spiritual head of the Lurgan United Brethren Church just outside Shipensberg, Pennsylvania. While thus employed in the service of the Lord, he distinguished himself by leading many heathen to the light and being an all-round darn good preacher.

Such exemplary work did not go unnoticed. Soon Donald was in demand. When his contract was up, he became a free agent. Just like a ballplayer who seeks real grass rather than Astroturf, Donald too sought greener pastures. He moved to Greencastle, Pennsylvania, where he ministered to the faithful of the Macedonia United Brethren Church.

It came as a terrific shock to all concerned when Norma simply vanished off the face of the earth. Just imagine, the new minister's wife might have been kidnapped or could have met with a terrible accident. Why, the congregation had hardly gotten to know poor Norma. The flock spent a lot of time praying for her safe return. They prayed and they prayed until they kind of forgot about what's-her-name—oh yes, Norma.

Donald mourned the loss of his first wife until he met Phyllis, whom destiny had decreed would become Donald's second wife. Phyllis was attractive and wasn't annoying at all. She was also healthy and robust. That's why everyone was so surprised when word spread throughout the congregation in October 1981 that Phyllis was suffering from stomach cramps. We are not talking about a mere tummy ache. We are talking about excruciating, body-racking pain. Plans were afoot to have the reverend's wife admitted to hospital, when she fell down the parsonage stairs. Phyllis was rushed to hospital, where she expired seven days later.

Reverend Clark was understandably devastated. He cried, became depressed and did all those things that caring, sensitive spouses do when they lose their loved one. Everyone thought it proper and fitting when the reverend requested that the doctors not perform an autopsy. He couldn't stand the thought of lovely Phyllis's body being desecrated. Donald spoke of suicide, which is definitely not reverend-like.

The elders of the church were concerned when month after month they observed Donald's behaviour going from bad to worse. They had no way of knowing that their minister had secretly married Ronaele "Candy" Rotz. Now, Candy, despite her nickname, was a religious woman. She was a member of the Lutheran Church Women and the altar guide. Of a Sunday, she could be heard belting out inspirational tunes as a member of the First Evangelical Lutheran Church choir. In her spare time, Candy taught Sunday school.

The reverend was hoodwinking everyone, but not for long. The elders, still ignorant of wife number three, smelled a rat. They dismissed Donald for erratic behaviour and gave him notice to vacate the parsonage within a month. Candy didn't know her husband was a minister. He told her he was an undercover drug squad agent with the government. That's why he lived in Greencastle and Candy lived in Chambersburg, some 10 miles away.

You can imagine the shock and outrage experienced by Candy's fellow church members when, on April 7, 1983, she was found stark naked and dead in her bathtub. There was an electric fan heater in the tub with Candy.

It was soon learned that Reverend Clark was the husband of the deceased. This time around, Donald's wife's death was investigated. Police discovered that he had put down police officer as his occupation on his marriage certificate. They knew this was a barefaced falsehood. Everyone was well aware the reverend was a reverend.

Investigators also learned that Donald had collected $50,000 on Phyllis's death, the proceeds of an insurance policy he had taken out only six months before her demise. That Donald was a creature of habit. Eight days after his marriage to Candy he had taken out a similar policy on her life valued at $50,000, with a $200,000 payoff if she departed as the result of an accident. So sure of himself was our Donald that he put in an offer on a $90,000 home even though he knew he had lost his ministerial position and had absolutely no income.

While investigating Candy's death, detectives looked into the lives and deaths of all three of Donald's wives. The mystery of Norma's disappearance has never been solved. Phyllis's body was exhumed. Pathologists found she had been fed small doses of arsenic over a period of time. In excruciating pain, she had fallen down the stairs. Candy had been struck on the back of the head, rendering her unconscious. She had been placed in the tub, after which Donald had tossed in a connected electric heater fan, electrocuting her.

Donald was a scalawag through and through. Nosy detectives learned that he had an able and willing teenager on the side, so to speak. This innocent had no idea that Donald was married. He had proposed marriage to her in anticipation of Candy's accident.

After concluding their investigation, police swooped down on the parsonage. They were too late. Reverend Donald Lewis Clark lay naked and dead on his bathroom floor. He had taken a lethal dose of poison. Beside his body lay several suicide notes explaining how sorry he was for any pain and sorrow he had caused. He also mentioned that the flesh is weak, which we all know is true enough.

Joyce Cohen
(UNITED STATES)

JOYCE AND STAN COHEN HAD IT ALL. I mean, the whole enchilada.

The Cohens lived in what can only be described as palatial digs at 1665 South Bayshore Drive in the exclusive Coconut Grove section of Miami, Florida. A shiny Porsche was parked beside the Mercedes in the driveway. The swimming pool glistened under the hot Florida sun.

In addition to their Coconut Grove home, the Cohens owned a 650-acre spread named Wolf Run Ranch in Steamboat Springs, Colorado. They dashed from one home to another in their own private jet. Stan's very successful construction company financed the couple's extravagant lifestyle. To the casual observer, all was definitely right in the Cohens' world.

Both Joyce and Stan had brought children from previous marriages to their union. Stan had a son, Gary, and a daughter, Gerri, who were self-sufficient adults when our tale takes place. Gerri was a well-known TV news reporter on a local channel, while Gary was a lawyer with a practice in Miami. Joyce's son, Shawn, by a previous marriage, attended a private school in Tennessee. By 1986, the Cohens had been married for 12 years. Stan was a big, blustery 54-year-old tycoon. Joyce, a svelte 35, was usually dressed in designer outfits.

The good life changed abruptly at around 3:00 a.m. on the morning of March 7, 1986. That's when someone fired two shots into Stan's head while he slept in bed.

Joyce related what had happened to Patrol Officer Catherine Carter, the first officer on the scene. She claimed the only occupants of the house that night were Stan, herself and Buddy, a Dobermann pinscher. Stan was asleep in the upstairs master bedroom, while Joyce was sorting clothes for a garage sale in a downstairs bedroom, which had formerly been occupied by her son, Shawn.

A loud noise from the kitchen frightened Joyce, but she ran toward the racket to see what had caused it. Someone had thrown a rock through the window in the kitchen door. She realized the burglar alarm had not been engaged. Her first reaction was to turn it on, knowing full well that the police would automatically be dispatched.

Joyce claimed that while all this was happening she heard footsteps running down the stairs. She looked up to see two dark male forms dash out the front door. She ran upstairs and found Stan lying in bed, a large quantity of blood around his head. Joyce attempted to wash his wounds with a towel and waited for the police to arrive. Stan was very dead.

Officer Carter and the grieving woman talked for a few minutes until the house filled with other police and medics. Carter answered several phone calls and thought it a bit peculiar to be fielding calls from Colorado at that hour of the morning.

Following the principle that if two people are occupying a house and one is murdered, the other occupant is immediately suspect, police asked Joyce down to headquarters for a friendly chat. Detectives didn't take kindly to her story. Although her version of events remained basically the same, she did elaborate. According to Joyce, at about 11:30 p.m. she went downstairs for a glass of warm milk to help her sleep. She heard a strange noise, went back upstairs and told Stan, who had been watching the late news on TV. Stan took his gun—standard equipment in most Florida homes—with him to investigate. They found the front gate open, but nothing else suspicious. The alarm system was off because Joyce had felt she might accidentally set if off while wandering around the house.

Joyce added that when she left her son's room after sorting clothing, she received a phone call from a friend, Kimberly Carroll, from Steamboat Springs, Colorado. She hung up when she heard a noise from the kitchen. After finding the rock that had been thrown through the kitchen window, she activated the burglar alarm system, saw the dark figures dash out the front door and ran upstairs to her husband's room.

While the police were questioning her, Joyce suddenly had a change of heart. She refused to discuss the case further and ordered investigating officers to leave her home. The police were stunned. Never before had a wife or husband halted an investigation in progress when their spouse was the victim of a crime. The officers were required to obtain a search warrant, which took nine hours. As a result of the delay, doctors had some difficulty establishing the time of death. More importantly, Joyce was instrumental in casting suspicion on herself.

Homicide investigators did receive one break when police found a .38 Smith & Wesson revolver in some bushes beside the Cohen residence. It proved to be the murder weapon; it was also Stan's own gun. It had been wiped clean of fingerprints. Joyce was quick to point out that when her husband had investigated the noise downstairs, he had taken his gun with him. When he returned to the bedroom, he left it on his night table.

Detectives believed that Joyce Cohen was in some way involved in her husband's death. So did his children, Gary and Gerri Cohen. To protect her interests, Joyce retained a lawyer. There were a lot of bucks at stake. Stan's estate was valued at US$13 million. Liabilities would bring the net figure down to four or five million, still a substantial amount and more than enough to constitute a motive for murder.

When Joyce's lifestyle was laid bare under the relentless scrutiny of a murder investigation, officers learned that she was a cocaine user who loved to party into the wee hours. In recent years, Stan had slowed down, preferring a somewhat quieter existence. It was possible that Joyce had tired of her husband, but wouldn't think of divorcing him. She might very well have wanted all of their substantial wealth. Despite the suspicions, there was no concrete proof that Joyce had had anything to do with her husband's murder.

One phone call changed the entire complexion of the case. Frank Zuccarello, a 21-year-old member of a gang of hoodlums who specialized in home invasions, contacted police from the Broward County jail. He told them that for certain considerations he would identify the killers of Stan Cohen. Frank got the officers' attention when he told them that Joyce Cohen had hired him to do the hit. He requested and received total immunity from prosecution in any crime connected with the murder.

Under questioning, Frank told all. Anthony Caracciolo, Tommy Lamberti and he were all members of a home-invasion gang who had been hired by Joyce to knock off her old man. Each was offered $10,000 for the job. The trio received the plans of the Cohen residence from Joyce. They knew in advance that Joyce would have the burglar alarm system deactivated and that Buddy, the Dobermann pinscher, would be locked in a room. The plan was to kill Stan with his own gun.

Sometime after 2:00 a.m., Frank drove up to the Cohen residence. Joyce met the men at the door. Tommy Lamberti showed her how to fake a break-in. Frank stood guard at the front door to make sure that they wouldn't be interrupted. Anthony Caracciolo went upstairs. Joyce had told him where to find the gun. It was Anthony who shot Stan while he slept. The three men fled the premises. Anthony had dropped the Smith & Wesson in the bushes in his haste to get away.

During the gang's negotiations with Joyce, she told them she had two reasons for wanting her husband out of the way. She no longer loved him and she wanted the money that would allow her to lead the life to which she had become accustomed. The authorities verified

Frank's story in every possible way. Indeed, Frank knew details that only the intruder could know.

Joyce was arrested and charged with murder in the first degree, conspiracy to commit murder and display of a firearm in the commission of a felony. She was found guilty of all three charges. Upon hearing the verdict, Joyce fainted. She was sentenced to life imprisonment with no possibility of parole for 25 years for the murder of her husband. For conspiracy to commit murder, she received an additional 15-year sentence to be served consecutively to the life sentence. In addition, for the display of a firearm during the commission of a felony, she was sentenced to 15 years to run concurrently with the other prison terms.

To avoid Florida's electric chair, Anthony Caracciolo and Tommy Lamberti pleaded no contest to reduced charges of second-degree murder. Caracciolo received a sentence of 41 years, while his buddy Lamberti was sentenced to 39 years.

Joyce Cohen received not one cent of her husband's estate. Gone are the cars, houses, ranch and airplane. She is now incarcerated in the Broward Correctional Institution, a maximum-security facility for women in Florida.

Tony Craven
(ENGLAND)

ON RARE OCCASIONS when a murder is committed, someone on the perimeter of the case takes an unusual interest in the investigation. On even rarer occasions, that person is the murderer.

Who can forget the interest Richard Loeb displayed in the death of little Bobby Franks? When the smoke cleared, he and his confederate, Nathan Leopold, confessed to the murder. Far less known but every bit as horrific was the murder of seven-year-old Angela Flaherty.

On Saturday, August 10, 1991, Angie went out to play with her new bicycle in the peaceful Huddersfield suburb of Rawthorpe, England. When she didn't return home, her frantic parents called police.

All that night and next morning the hunt for the missing child continued. At midday, not more than 500 metres from her home, Angie's body was found in a thicket by a mounted police officer. She had been subjected to a vicious sexual assault and had been killed by several blows to the head with a rock. Bruising along her throat indicated she had also been choked.

Local officers soon learned that children in the neighbourhood often frequented the thicket, mostly to play house. The area was secluded, with bushes forming a circle that provided some privacy.

Investigators theorized that if Angie was abducted or lured to the thicket, her assailant must be a local man who knew the area.

When officers studying the crime scene discovered Angie's bicycle tracks leading into the thicket, they surmised that the little girl was acquainted with her killer and had gone there willingly. Her bicycle was found nearby, undamaged.

The murder of little Angie Flaherty made headlines throughout Europe. News-gathering agencies reported every scrap of information about the victim and her family. Reporters became so aggressive that the Flaherty family attempted to distance themselves from the media. They looked for a friend or relative to act as their representative. The family settled on 17-year-old Tony Craven, a pleasant lad who had been friends with Angie and her three older sisters.

Although saddened at the brutal rape and murder of his friend, Tony relished the importance of his unaccustomed role. He held informal press conferences, dispensed little-known details and behaved in an all-round conscientious manner.

Youthful Tony was a great help to the Flaherty family in their hour of need. Everyone, except the investigating officers, felt Tony was doing an outstanding job.

One detective believed something wasn't strictly kosher. He noticed that when the police were in the neighbourhood Tony made a point of asking detectives how the investigation was proceeding. In addition, they observed that he seemed to hang around with boys and girls years younger than himself.

A few days into the investigation, Tony sought out the lead investigator and told him he believed he had seen the killer. He claimed the man had been near the thicket on the afternoon of Angie's disappearance. Tony said he didn't know the man but was able to describe him as middle-aged and bald. At the same time, he had seen Angie on her bicycle in the general area.

The officers listening to Tony's dissertation doubted the lad was telling the truth. They decided to conduct an investigation into Tony's background. In his neighbourhood, Tony was regarded as a bit immature and naive. Otherwise, everyone had a good word to say about the boy.

At his place of employment, Tony's reputation was quite different. Fellow employees teased him incessantly about his aversion to members of the opposite sex. Police learned he had never had sex and had never dated a girl his own age. His colleagues told police they taunted the boy unmercifully, often showing him pornographic material, which infuriated Tony. Sometimes he lost his temper and screamed at his tormentors. On occasion he told them he hated all women.

Was it possible that the razzing at his place of employment had driven Tony to seek a sexual experience? Certainly he didn't have the courage to make the acquaintance of someone his own age. Perhaps he had gravitated to the most vulnerable female he knew, little Angie Flaherty? Despite their grave suspicions, detectives could come up with nothing of a concrete nature to connect Tony to the rape and murder.

The investigation continued. Authorities decided to test all 9,000 males between the ages of 10 and 26 in the area. Tony, as usual, displayed great interest in the procedure. Detectives told him they would draw blood from all the males in the area and compare it with evidence left by the killer at the crime scene. They were quick to stress that the foolproof procedure would be voluntary. Tony immediately volunteered to take the test. Detectives were disappointed. They felt that if he had committed the crime, he would make some excuse not to be included.

Tony was among the first group tested. His DNA matched semen taken from the victim's body. While still at large that Christmas, Tony sent a card to Angie's family. Soon after, he was arrested and charged with Angie's murder. In custody, he was extremely helpful and continued to exhibit great interest in all police activities. He confessed that he had raped and killed Angie Flaherty. He told police that he had grown tired of the constant taunting at work over his virginity and decided to do something about it.

After luring Angie to the thicket, he had played a game of daring her to take off her clothing. When she became reluctant, he forced her to undress. Then he raped her. Angie started to cry and he couldn't get her to stop. She said she was going to tell her mother what he had done. He begged her not to but she wouldn't listen to him. He had to make sure she wouldn't tell. Tony said he tried to strangle her, but found that he couldn't do it. That's when he picked up a rock and hit her several times on the head until she was dead.

Detectives asked the one question that still puzzled them. Why had Tony submitted to the blood test when he knew he was guilty? Unsophisticated Tony told them that he thought his blood had to match blood found at the scene. Since he had not left any blood at the location of the crime, he thought he was home free.

Tony Craven attempted to kill himself three times while in jail awaiting trial. Three times he failed. In May 1992, he pleaded guilty to the murder of Angie Flaherty and was sentenced to life imprisonment with no possibility of parole for 17 years.

Alain de Bernardi

(France)

THE MARQUIS Alain Jules Antoine Romain Gaspard de Bernardi de Sigoyer wasn't a marquis at all. He was really Alain de Bernardi, a scheming con artist who dabbled in murder.

In 1944, Paris was occupied by the German army. Times were tough for the civilian population, but our boy Alain was an exception. With years of nefarious business dealings behind him, the neatly turned-out con man with the trim beard had no difficulty gaining favour with the German occupation forces. And no wonder: Alain was in the wine business. From his Paris office he wheeled and dealed, sometimes legally, more often illegally, but deal he did until he became a wealthy man.

No one carrying on business with the cunning Alain knew that the wine agent had been in and out of jails and asylums most of his adult life. It was wartime. No one checked up on business acquaintances.

On March 28, 1944, a distraught mother showed up at a Paris police station to report that her daughter, Jeanne, had failed to return home. Jeanne's mother didn't make a good impression. She claimed her daughter was the beautiful 23-year-old Marquise Jeanne who had left her home to visit her estranged husband, the Marquis

Alain de Bernardi. She had never stayed out all night without check-ing in on her children. According to her mother, Jeanne had gone to see her husband about child support.

Detectives promised to investigate. They called on Alain, who readily admitted his wife had paid a visit to him to dicker about the amount of alimony he was forwarding to her each month. They had quarrelled, apparently not an unusual occurrence. Jeanne was in the process of obtaining a divorce, which apparently was just fine with the marquis. He assured detectives his wife had left in a huff and he had not seen her since that evening of March 28.

When it became obvious that the tides of war were turning, Alain attempted to change his allegiances. As the Allies advanced toward Paris, he tried to ingratiate himself with resistance forces, but it was too late. He was well known as a friend and provider of wines to the German army. Alain was arrested as a collaborator shortly after Paris was liberated.

There was Alain, firmly ensconced in prison with the equivalent of hundreds of thousands of dollars on deposit in various Paris banks. From time to time he wrote letters to friends, beseeching them to help. All were read by his jailers. One such letter, mailed eight months after his incarceration, caught their attention. It was addressed to Mademoiselle Irene Lebeau, who had been his wife's maid. He requested that Irene dispose of several dresses belonging to Jeanne. What made the authorities take notice was the cryptic phrase "Be fearful of the red armchair." The police decided to call on Irene to get an explanation.

Upon seeing detectives at her door, Irene was frightened out of her wits. She informed police that the answer to many of their questions could be found in old vaults under the marquis's home. Gendarmes immediately scampered over to Alain's residence. Initially, they found nothing but broken casks in the wine vaults, but when police started digging, they uncovered clothing that Jeanne's mother identified as having been worn by her daughter when she'd disappeared almost a year earlier. Digging still deeper under the damp earth, they uncovered the decomposed body of Jeanne de Bernardi.

Irene had more to tell. She confessed that she had been the marquis's mistress for years, predating his marriage to Jeanne. He had treated Irene badly, often abusing her physically. After his marriage, she often observed him treating his wife in the same manner. Finally Jeanne had left her husband and had moved with her two children to her mother's home.

Irene had been present the night Jeanne showed up at her former residence demanding funds to support her two children. At one point, while Jeanne was sitting in the red armchair, Alain positioned himself behind the chair and commenced to strangle her with a length of cord. Irene claimed she attempted to intercede, but the marquis said he would kill her if she interfered. She went on to explain that if Jeanne divorced Alain, she would have stood to receive one-half of his estate. In Irene's opinion, Alain had killed his wife to prevent her from getting half his fortune.

Once again, detectives questioned Alain in jail. They asked him what he had been referring to when he wrote about the red armchair. Jokingly, Alain replied, "So Irene would know what to expect if she talked." The statement wasn't a confession of murder, but it was good enough. Alain was charged with Jeanne's murder.

When Alain's charges were made public, a hue and cry ensued. The populace wanted to know how a Nazi collaborator, who had spent time in asylums and prisons, could have amassed a fortune under the collective noses of the authorities. Irene didn't fare well either. Investigators felt that she might have been an accomplice, rather than an unwilling witness to murder.

In December 1946, the marquis and the former maid stood trial for murder. Irene Lebeau took the witness stand and reviewed her life from the time of her first meeting with Alain. All the while she was giving evidence, she couldn't help but glance at the ominous red armchair displayed beside her in court. Irene related that she had been seduced by Alain in 1940 when she was 17 years old.

After his marriage to Jeanne, she was hired to look after the couple's only child. In 1943, there was an unwelcome addition to the family. It was Irene who had given birth to Alain's second child. That's when Jeanne packed up, returned to Mama and instituted divorce proceedings. Irene professed that Alain had murdered Jeanne on the red armchair exactly as she had already related to police.

Alain took the witness stand in his own defence. He swore he had nothing to do with his wife's death. Moreover, the marquis said that after he and Jeanne had agreed to divorce, they had reconciled. The reconciliation hadn't succeeded because Irene constantly argued with his wife. Modest to a fault, Alain told the court that the two women continually argued over him. In the heat of one such argument, Irene shot Jeanne in the head. The strangulation, he maintained, had been a figment of Irene's imagination.

Alain's testimony was scintillating courtroom drama but its effect was a surprise. The presiding judge ordered Jeanne's body exhumed and the head X-rayed. No semblance of a wound or a bullet was found. As they say in the poultry business, Alain's goose was cooked. The stupid lie he'd told from the witness stand sealed his fate.

On December 22, 1946, the French jury took only half an hour to find Alain de Bernardi guilty of murder. Irene Lebeau was found not guilty. A month later, in Paris's Santé Prison, the bogus marquis had his head removed from his body by means of the guillotine.

Roy Donell

(UNITED STATES)

TODAY WE ARE GOING TO DELVE into the lives of the very rich. I mean loaded.

William Keck made his first big dollars in oil leases. In time he amalgamated his holdings into Superior Oil with assets in the billions. In 1964, William died, leaving his fortune to his three children, William Jr., Howard and Willametta. In 1983, William died. Willametta passed away a year later.

On the surface, it would appear that Howard stood to inherit the whole kit and caboodle, but there was a catch. William had set up a trust back in 1964, stating that his entire fortune was to pass along to his grandchildren upon the death of his last surviving offspring, who turned out to be Howard.

At this juncture, I would be remiss if I failed to elaborate on the Keck family's wealth. Superior was sold to Mobil Oil for $5.7 billion. Howard and his wife, Libby, lived in an 11,000-square-foot home in Stone Canyon, located in California's posh Bel Air neighbourhood. The house was custom built for Libby, who modelled it after a pavilion in Versailles, France. The estate cost $42 million and was called La Lanterne.

At 65 years of age, Libby, an attractive woman, was director of the

Los Angeles County Museum of Art, the Museum of Contemporary Art, the Huntington Museum and the Los Angeles Music Center. For fun, Libby dabbled in horse racing. The jewel in the crown of her stable was a thoroughbred named Ferdinand. With jockey Willie Shoemaker in the irons, Ferdinand won the 1986 Kentucky Derby. Howard and Libby once endowed the California Institute of Technology with $70 million. You get the idea. The Keck family was one of the wealthiest clans in the entire United States.

As mentioned above, Howard and Libby had three children of their own, as well as a daughter from Libby's previous marriage. Evidently, Howard Jr. became anxious in the service. He launched a lawsuit to clarify his rights to the Keck family fortune in the event of his father's demise.

Father didn't like this move one little bit. He put forward the proposition that Howard Jr. wasn't really his son at all, but had been sired by another. He also threatened to adopt children, thereby diluting Howard Jr.'s inheritance.

No doubt about it, the Kecks were a troubled family. Around this time, Libby and Howard decided to divorce, although both continued to live in separate quarters in La Lanterne while their case ground through the courts. The very rich do things like that.

The Kecks' domestic difficulties had a spillover effect on other people. Their butler and all-around man, Roy Donell, had been with the Kecks for 11 years. He was a conscientious employee who acted more as a manager than a butler. Roy purchased all the food brought into La Lanterne, which amounted to well over $5,000 monthly. Roy, 61, and his wife, Christina, who was employed as a cook at the estate, could see their secure, well-paying jobs evaporating as the Kecks' marriage deteriorated.

Now I'll let you in on a little secret. Roy desperately needed every cent he earned, because he was leading a double life. Yes, Roy had a sweet morsel, Ester Ariza, stashed away in an apartment on Santa Monica Boulevard. While Christina was a frail 67, Ester, a warm-blooded Colombian, had seen only 45 summers come and go.

There were complications. Ester, who had expensive tastes, had been led to believe that Roy had divorced his wife, but felt honour-bound to support her. As if that weren't enough, in a moment of weakness, he had promised to pay her 20-year-old son Andy's way through college.

The Kecks had priceless antiques and works of art sprinkled throughout their home. Some were so well known, such as a Gainsborough, that they were impossible to sell. But there were other paintings. In fact, the Kecks had so many that they kept several in storage in their original crates. In September 1986, Roy took one of the crated paintings, entitled *Fête Gallante,* a miniature by French artist Le Clerk des Gobelins, out of La Lanterne and kept it in his apartment until it was time for him to take his vacation.

Despite having worked in the United States for years, Roy had never given up his Swedish citizenship. He travelled to Sweden with the painting, paid a few hundred dollars to customs to get it into the country and called on Beijars Auktioner, one of the country's largest art dealers. An expert examined the painting and declared it to be genuine. Beijars were delighted to auction off the painting for their new client, Roy Donell. Within a week it was sold and Roy collected the proceeds, some $5,000 after the auctioneer's commission was deducted. Roy had passed Art Theft 101 with flying colours.

At the end of his vacation, the cunning butler and his wife returned to their duties at La Lanterne $5,000 richer. Roy knew that he couldn't retire on selling such paintings, nor could he peddle Gainsboroughs. He looked around the estate for something in between. To his way of thinking, the most saleable work of art in the collection was an 1888 canvas by Sweden's Anders Leonhard Zorn, which Libby had purchased in 1982 for $88,000. The painting, entitled *I Fria Luften (In Free Air),* depicted a nude dressing her son near a pond.

Roy stayed on at the Kecks' turbulent household for a few months before giving his notice. He explained that he and Christina had decided to retire to Sweden. Roy took a photo of the Zorn, had a slide produced and brought it to Rossi Photographic Custom Lab where he asked for an enlargement the exact size of the original. When the enlargement was produced, Roy was not happy with the quality of the reproduction. He was told by the manager of the lab that they couldn't do any better from a slide. They required the original. A few days later, Roy appeared with the painting and stayed with it while a large negative was produced. A week later he picked up an exact replica of *I Fria Luften*. Roy put the photograph into the original frame. No one looked very much at the valuable paintings anyway. After all, there was a proliferation of well-known works around the house.

The butler left for Sweden, not with his wife but with his mistress, Ester. He dropped off the valuable painting at Beijars and collected a down payment of $85,000 while he toured Europe. The painting brought $550,000 at auction. After the auctioneer's commission, Roy pocketed an additional $355,000, for a total of $440,000 on the deal. Mission completed, the couple returned to Los Angeles.

Roy had pulled off a successful caper, right up until the day four months later when Libby stared at *I Fria Luften*. Son of a gun, it was smooth as silk! The authentic painting, an oil, had a rough surface. Libby's first reaction was to scream. Her second was to call the police.

Detectives confirmed that to make such a photograph, the original had to be removed from the frame. As there had been no breach of the extensive security system that protected the estate, authorities decided that the theft was an inside job. Only two employees had recently left the Keck household, namely Roy and Christina Donell.

It didn't take long to trace Roy to an apartment in Los Angeles. He was taken into custody without incident. A search of his apartment uncovered a brochure from Beijars Auktioner, as well as transfer receipts from Beijars to the Security Pacific Bank in L.A. In all, $85,000 had been transferred to the bank. Police also found a price list from Rossi Photographic Custom Lab.

Roy was lodged in jail while the airtight case against him was developed by police. Ester and Christina, the two women in Roy's life, claimed they had no knowledge of Roy's thieving ways. They were never charged with any crime.

Roy went to trial facing two counts of grand theft. From the witness stand he admitted that he had stolen both paintings. But hold on a minute. Roy claimed that he had done it all under instructions from Libby Keck. What's more, he had given her all the money. According to Roy, he had helped Libby because she had wanted to accumulate cash in her own name due to her impending divorce.

To counteract this rather startling evidence, Libby took the stand and stated she didn't need to raise what she called a pittance. She provided the court with figures that revealed the quality of her lifestyle. Pending her divorce, she was receiving a $5,000 a month grocery allowance, $25,000 for clothing, $1,200 for lunches, $3,300 for dinners and $10,000 for dinner parties. She also had $11 million in accounts she controlled. Would she enter a scheme with her butler to steal $440,000? As Libby said from the witness stand, "I could have written a cheque for the whole amount."

The jury was faced with the problem of who to believe. Strangely enough, they chose to believe Roy Donell and returned a verdict of not guilty. That elusive $440,000 never did show up.

Michael Dowdall

(ENGLAND)

BY THE TIME HE WAS EIGHT YEARS OLD, Michael Dowdall had lost both his parents. His father was killed in 1942 while in active service in the British army. Six years later his mother passed away of natural causes. The little boy, along with his brother and sister, was brought up by an aunt in the Welsh mining village of Llanhilleth.

Michael was a handful and quickly gained a reputation for being a problem youngster. He periodically stole useless items, tortured cats just for fun and once broke into a school where he vandalized several classrooms. Michael left school at age 15 and enlisted as a drummer boy with the Welsh Guards. He knew of his father's history during the war and wanted to follow his career.

Michael was a heavy drinker. I'm not talking social drinking here. No, when Michael hit the booze he kept right on going until he passed out. He displayed a hair-trigger temper when intoxicated and was so belligerent that his colleagues in the service left him to his own devices. Often they would have to carry him back to barracks.

Sometimes Michael didn't make it back to camp at all. On one of these occasions, he was confined to cells, where he attempted to hang himself with a kimono cord. To add to his woes, Michael, small in stature, was often teased about it by his mates. Moreover, although he was not a homosexual, he was the subject of taunts because he was never seen with a member of the opposite sex.

This then was the picture of the extremely disturbed drummer boy. At 18 years of age, Michael had been in and out of trouble all his life. And there was more trouble just around the corner.

Veronica Murray was a 30-year-old prostitute who plied her trade in London's West End. On December 19, 1958, Veronica's girlfriend tried to get in touch with her. When she couldn't reach her, she asked Veronica's landlord to look into her room. The landlord took one look and called police.

Veronica's nude body lay on her bed. She had been battered about the head with a dumb-bell, which she had been in the habit of using as an exercising device. Strangely, there were tiny circular abrasions over various parts of her body. The little circles were arranged to form the letter V. Pathologists stated that the abrasions had been inflicted after death. Apparently, some deranged person had lingered over the dead body applying the small circles. A professor at London University, who was an expert on voodoo rituals, assured police that the circles had nothing to do with these practices.

Veronica's room was in total disarray; the killer, obviously in a rage, had tossed furniture and clothing all over the place. As a result, police were able to obtain several fingerprints. They believed some of them were the killer's. From the time of Veronica's death, fingerprints from all robberies and murder scenes were compared to those lifted from her room.

The first clue that the killer was still operating came to the attention of authorities when the suite of actor George Sanders at London's Westbury Hotel was burglarized. The thief left his fingerprints on a bottle of whisky after consuming most of the contents. In the ensuing weeks, no less than 15 burglaries yielded prints that matched those taken from Veronica's room. In each case the thief had helped himself to copious quantities of liquor. He also chain-smoked while he drank.

Ten months after Veronica's death, Mrs. Mabel Hill was attacked by a young man who had made her acquaintance on a train. The young man, obviously suffering from a hangover, insisted on accompanying Mrs. Hill to her home on Ismalia Road, Fulham. She asked him in for a cup of coffee. Next thing Mrs. Hill knew she was regaining consciousness in a hospital. Her 13-year-old son had found her unconscious in the kitchen. Nylon stockings had been tied so tightly around her neck that a religious medal had been imbedded in her throat. On her face, neck and chest, her attacker had made tiny circles, one inch in diameter, which were arranged so that they formed a larger circle.

Although it had been almost a year since the murder of Veronica Murray, police connected the two crimes. Fingerprints found in Mrs. Hill's kitchen matched prints lifted from Veronica's room.

The break-ins continued. When the thief burglarized the home of Mr. and Mrs. William Sloane in November 1959, one of the items he took was a distinctive cigarette lighter. A photo of a similar lighter was given wide publicity by the press. This avenue of the investigation gave authorities their first break in the case.

An officer at the Welsh Guards camp at Pirbright, Surrey, saw one of his men using the lighter.

Detectives sped to the camp and took Michael Dowdall into custody. He was shown several items that had been confiscated from his quarters. Michael looked at a tube of toothpaste and said, "I like the taste of that. It belonged to the actor George Sanders." He was immediately made aware that the police were concerned with a far more serious incident than burglary.

Michael gave police a comprehensive statement: "It is when I get drinking I do these things. It has been worrying me for a long time and I have wanted to go to a doctor. I'm glad it's over." He went on, "I picked up a prostitute in Trafalgar Square. She called a taxi. At her house I had sex with her and went to sleep. When she woke up we had a row over something and she called me a filthy little Welshman. I pulled her onto the bed. I hit her on the head. I took a bottle of whisky and then I left the place. I went back to the Union Jack Club and went to sleep. When I woke up I found blood on my hands and on my shirt and suit. I tried to wash the shirt, but could not get rid of the blood, so I chucked it away in a dustbin at the camp. I sent the suit to the cleaners. A day or two afterward I read in the newspapers that a prostitute had been found murdered at Kilburn and I knew that I had killed the woman."

Michael blamed all his problems on his drinking: "When I was very drunk I would try anything."

In January 1960, Michael pleaded not guilty to the murder of Veronica Murray. His legal counsel based his defence on diminished responsibility. It was felt that although Michael talked at length about every aspect of the case, he claimed to have had no knowledge as to why, in two cases, he had made the strange circles on his victims' bodies; nor could he recall what instrument he had used to make the circles.

The British jury believed that Michael Dowdall did suffer from a degree of amnesia. He was found guilty of manslaughter and sentenced to the maximum term for such an offence—life imprisonment.

Lucien & Christine Duc

(France)

EVERYONE WHO KNEW EUGÈNE AND THÉRÈSE DUC in the farming area of La-Côte-Saint André, France, believed they had done a good job of bringing up their three sons.

Let's see now, there was the eldest son, Roger, 48, a well-respected construction worker. He was happily married and was the father of several children. Salt of the earth, that Roger. Marius, 40, drove a truck for a living. He too was a devoted family man. Both sons lived in Grenoble, about 30 miles east of their parents' farm. They often helped out their elderly parents financially.

Lucien, 29, was the apple of his father's eye. Being appreciably younger than his two brothers, he was doted upon by the entire family. In June 1982, Lucien married Christine Jacquin, a local girl who had been brought up by foster parents. At the age of 16, Christine charged foster parent Robert Rodet with sexually molesting her over a period of two years. The charges were eventually dropped, but the experience so traumatized Christine that, at age 18, she was institutionalized in a psychiatric clinic at Saint Eygreve.

In April 1982, Christine left the clinic to marry Lucien. The couple settled down in nearby Saint Marcellin, but times were tough. Lucien lost his job in a textile factory and worked as a farmhand. His brothers felt their baby brother would eventually find himself. Things would work out. In the meantime, they accepted Christine as a sister.

On September 8, 1982, Roger phoned his parents but failed to reach them. This was most unusual. They rarely wandered far from home except to visit with one of their three sons. The next day, Roger was concerned enough to call police and ask them to look in on the elderly couple.

Police entered the quiet farmhouse. The house appeared to be vacant. Officers made their way down to the cellar, where they found Eugène and Thérèse Duc lying dead on the cold cellar floor. Both were bound and gagged. A medical officer at the scene thought the two victims had been asphyxiated. They had been beaten about the head and gagged with scarves so tightly that they were unable to breathe. He estimated that the Ducs had been dead for approximately 48 hours, placing the time of death sometime on Saturday evening.

A search of the area around the farmhouse uncovered a clublike branch of a tree stained with dried blood. White hair was clinging to it.

Nothing had been disturbed in the house. Police could find no money. Although the Ducs were far from rich, they normally kept a few francs in the house. Detectives felt if robbery was the motive, the perpetrators knew where the money was located. They wondered if a family member or a friend could have been responsible for this horrendous crime against the elderly, defenceless pair.

Adding credence to the police theory were the unwashed dishes in the sink, indicating that four individuals had had dinner together on Saturday evening. However, it was possible that the dinner guests had left the Ducs alive and well after dinner and had nothing to do with the killings.

Detectives searching the house found an unsigned and undated note in Thérèse's bible. It read, "You fat sow. You'd better send us a cheque. If you don't you're going to catch it. A farm burns good. Your animals will make a fine barbecue."

Police suspected that the Ducs were being blackmailed. Although the couple had precious little money, they did have a small bank account in Grenoble. A meeting with bank officials revealed that a flurry of cheques signed by the Ducs had been received by the bank immediately after the couple's death. The cheques, which amounted to the equivalent of $4,000, had been cashed in hotels, stores and restaurants around Grenoble. All had been forged.

Whoever wrote the cheques realized they wouldn't be honoured by the bank, but they obviously didn't care. It appeared the killers were well acquainted with the Ducs and their habits. The killers weren't after cash, they wanted their victims' chequebook and knew where to find it.

Detectives questioned friends. None could throw any light on who had murdered the Ducs. Police contacted all the businesses where cheques had been cashed. The killers had picked large, busy establishments. As a result, the descriptions given to police were sketchy, but several remembered that a pretty woman had accompanied the bogus cheque passer.

Finally, with nowhere else to look, gendarmes had to consider the Ducs' three sons. Roger and his wife had been entertaining friends in their home in Grenoble on the night of the murders. He proved without a doubt that he had nothing to do with the deaths of his parents. Marius was driving a truck on the night in question and had been nowhere near his parents' home.

That left the youngest son, Lucien. Detectives learned that although he was a placid, rather lazy individual when sober, he could be argumentative and violent when intoxicated. Questioned by police, Lucien and Christine vehemently denied being involved in the crime. Their interrogators realized that Christine was the stronger of the two personalities. As a result, they decided to question Lucien separately. It didn't take long before he broke down and confessed to the murder of his own parents. Police were amazed as this man, who had been loved and catered to all his life, described what he had done as if he were talking about last week's soccer match.

"I rang Mum up and said we'd like to come for dinner on Saturday. Mum said it would be all right and if we wanted we could stay the night. On the way we picked up a good strong club in the woods and left it outside the house so they wouldn't see it. After dinner, Mum and Dad went up to get the room ready for us and we got the club and waited at the foot of the stairs. We didn't know which one would come down first, but it was Mum.

"I hit her over the head with the club and she fell on the floor, but she wasn't dead and she was groaning, so I hit her some more, but she still didn't die. Christine brought me a scarf from the hall rack and said to stuff it in her mouth so she'd be quiet. We tied her wrists then and dragged her into the laundry room. A few minutes later Dad came down and I hit him with the club. He fell on the floor and I started pounding his head on the tiles.

"I was kneeling on him and he said, 'I'm not old yet. I want to live. Don't kill me.' Christine brought me another scarf and I stuffed it in his mouth. Afterwards, we dragged both of them down to the cellar. They were still moving and trying to say something.

"We found only 300 francs in the house, but we got the cheque-book so it was all right. We never had any trouble cashing the cheques."

When Christine, who was four months pregnant, had the tape of Lucien's confession played to her, she agreed to all the details. Both were arrested. Five months later, Christine gave birth to her baby in prison.

At the Ducs' trial, Lucien rather gallantly insisted that he had been the instigator of the murders and that his wife had taken no physical part in the deaths of his parents.

On June 16, 1985, Christine Duc was found guilty of aiding and abetting a homicide. She was sentenced to 10 years' imprisonment. Lucien Duc was found guilty of murder and received the lenient sentence of 18 years imprisonment.

Lori Esker

(UNITED STATES)

THE TINY TOWN OF BIRNAMWOOD, WISCONSIN, is an unlikely locale for a brutal murder. The main topic of conversation in the community revolves around the price of milk. Deep in America's heartland, dairy farming is the prime industry. Murder is something that takes place in Minneapolis or Chicago, not Birnamwood.

Lori Esker was only 17 when she started dating Bill Buss. Here were two young people with deep-rooted rural backgrounds whose families had farmed in the area for well over a hundred years. Lori was following in her parents' footsteps. Already she had received recognition from Future Farmers of America and had won several 4-H awards. As a teenager she thought of little else but developing her own herd of dairy cattle and settling down to life on a prosperous farm. Bill definitely figured in Lori's plans for the future. She was madly in love with tall, handsome Bill, who seemed to care for Lori as much as she worshipped him.

Probably the happiest time in Lori and Bill's life was that summer after high school graduation when blond, blue-eyed Lori won the Dairy Princess of Marathon County contest at the county fair. There on the stage before hundreds of her friends and neighbours stood Lori, accepting the honours every young girl in the county coveted. Bill was understandably proud of his girlfriend. About the only cloud in the wholesome scenario was Lori's parents' feelings toward Bill. It wasn't that they had anything against the boy, it was just that they thought 25-year-old Bill was a bit old for their 18-year-old daughter. No doubt they breathed a sigh of relief when Lori left town to attend the University of Wisconsin in River Falls, a distance of some 175 miles. Lori phoned and wrote Bill almost every day. Each week, she came home to spend the weekend with her boyfriend.

Slowly, ever so slowly, Bill became disenchanted with Lori. Friends noted the change, but not Lori. That's why it was such a shock to her when Bill told her that it had been great fun but it was over. Lori was devastated. She had planned on marrying her Bill and had always considered that they were unofficially engaged. When she learned that Bill now had eyes for another local girl, Lisa Cihashi, she decided to fight for her man.

Lori's idea of fighting was to approach Lisa and berate her in front of friends. She even spoke to the Busses' farmhands and attempted to have them talk Bill into returning to her. Nothing seemed to work. She now openly referred to Lisa as "the bitch." Despondent, Lori continued to attend university. Soon word drifted to her of Lisa and Bill's engagement. None of her efforts had had the desired effect. There must be something she could do.

In desperation, Lori purchased the scantiest nightie she could find. She made her way to the Busses' farm in the middle of the night, climbed through a window in Bill's room and performed a seductive dance around his bed. Bill wasn't impressed. He ordered Lori out of the house. When Lori came back for a return engagement, which involved jumping on Bill, he physically escorted her out of the farmhouse.

While Lori was attempting to entice Bill to return to her, Lisa prepared for her forthcoming marriage and carried on with her regular routine. Each morning, she drove 35 miles to the Howard Johnson restaurant, where she was employed as sales and catering manager.

On September 20, 1989, Lisa drove to work at the restaurant. After putting in a full day, she failed to return home. Bill and her mother were apprehensive and drove a few miles down the road looking for Lisa's Oldsmobile. Standing everyone up wasn't typical of Lisa, but she had stayed over at girlfriends' homes before without notifying her parents. Next morning, Lisa Cihashi's body was found in her Olds in the Howard Johnson parking lot. She had been strangled to death.

At the University of Wisconsin, Lori Esker was shocked when she learned of her rival's murder. Many felt that Lori, with her well-known hatred of Lisa, may have been responsible, but of course this was impossible. Lori had been at university, 175 miles from the murder scene, at the time of the crime.

Detectives travelled to River Falls to question Lori. They confirmed that she had been on campus early on the morning after the murder. A week later, Lori consented to being fingerprinted and to taking a polygraph test. When she failed the test, police were sure they had identified the murderer. A sympathetic officer spoke to Lori, explaining that accidents happen and that the law, and even God, take such circumstances into consideration. Eventually he struck a responsive chord. For two hours Lori, the Dairy Princess of Marathon County, related how she had killed Lisa Cihashi.

Lori told detectives that on the night of the murder she had decided to have a heart-to-heart with Lisa. She rented a car, drove the 175 miles to Howard Johnson and waited in the parking lot until Lisa finished her shift. Lori beckoned to Lisa, who unhesitatingly invited her into her car. When Lori pleaded with her rival to give Bill up, Lisa interrupted, stating emphatically that she intended to marry Bill. She told Lori off, calling her a slut and a whore. According to Lori, at the height of the argument, Lisa clutched her by the throat. In desperation, Lori grabbed a leather belt from the back seat and wound it around Lisa's neck. As the two teenagers struggled and cursed at each other, Lisa's body went limp. She was dead.

Lori knew instinctively that no one would believe it had all been a terrible accident. She immediately thought of self-preservation. She raced back to River Falls, returned the rented car and went to sleep.

Lori was indicted, but three days later was released on $100,000 bail after her parents pledged their farm as security. A year later, she stood trial. Was it an accident that had occurred spontaneously in the heat of battle, as Lori's statement suggested, or was it a planned, cold-blooded murder?

Prosecuting attorneys paraded 50 witnesses before the court who had overheard or had been told by Lori that she hated Lisa. On several occasions, Lori had stated that she wished her rival were dead. Defence counsel pointed out that if Lori had planned to commit murder, she would never have rented a car in her own name, nor would she have faced Lisa unarmed.

The Wisconsin jury disagreed. They found Lori guilty of murder in the first degree. Three months later, Lori Esker was sentenced to life imprisonment in the Taycheedah Correction Institute. She will be eligible for parole in 2003.

Virgil Fox
(UNITED STATES)

DOWN KANSAS WAY, certain industrious individuals are in the habit of augmenting their regular income by growing marijuana. The plant grows like the devil and once in the ground requires very little care. Cunning growers have been known to plant their crop between rows of corn, making it practically impossible to spot the illegal weed from the air.

Tony Arthur, 22, and his best friend, Doug Ashby, 23, of Pittsburg, Kansas, took in a fine home-cooked meal at Tony's parents'. After dinner, the two young men attended a poker game with friends. During the game, Tony and Doug openly discussed how they could make some easy money by sneaking into a marijuana field and stealing a quantity of plants. No one could remember seeing either Tony or Doug after they left the poker game around midnight.

A few days later, on September 18, 1980, an abandoned car was spotted partially submerged in the water of an old strip mine. The vehicle, a 1978 Chevy, belonged to Tony Arthur.

Before the car was found, authorities assumed that the two local men had taken off on their own and would soon show up. Now their absence took on far more serious implications. Divers scoured the bottom of the mine, but came up empty handed. The area around the mine was searched for any clues that might lead to the missing men. None was uncovered.

Two days after the discovery of Tony's car, a man, walking along the railway tracks, was struck by a strong odour emanating from nearby bushes. On investigating the source of the foul smell, he found the bodies of the missing men. Both had been shot twice in the back of the head. In addition, each had sustained a severe beating about the head and body.

Because of the inference that marijuana was involved, the Federal Drug Enforcement Agency was brought in to assist the Kansas Bureau of Investigation. They theorized that the two men had attempted to rip off a marijuana field, had been caught and had been severely beaten before being murdered. The slain men's poker buddies were questioned again. This time they revealed more details. After all, the investigation had progressed from a search for two friends who were probably off on a spree, to apprehending the killer of two well-known local men. The victims' poker buddies told drug enforcement authorities that Tony and Doug had stumbled across a marijuana field near the town of Opolis, Missouri, just across the Kansas state line. They had left the poker game with the intention of ripping off the marijuana field.

It didn't take long for detectives to locate the big field with its lush illegal crop. Employing scores of agents, they completely surrounded the area. As soon as the lead agents advanced toward a farmhouse at the edge of the field, they were met by ferocious guard dogs. The officers used a loudspeaker to address the occupants of the house. They urged them to call off the dogs and come out with their hands raised. The alternative was a shootout. Two men emerged from the house with their hands held high over their heads.

Once outside and under arrest, the men were informed that they were now caught up in the middle of a murder investigation. One of the men broke down. He explained that he had been hired to take care of the marijuana crop, but murder was something else again. He had no intention of shielding anyone. He stated that he and his partner were to split 10 percent of the profits from the marijuana in return for guarding the crop. The previous Saturday night he had caught two young men when the guard dogs had cornered them against the barn. He had tied up the thieves and called his contact, Dick Adams, for advice. Adams was in charge of this particular field and three others, acting as foreman or overseer of the lucrative local marijuana crops. Adams in turn had called Virgil Fox, the owner of the crops.

Virgil was a well-known local businessman who was involved in several ventures, including the promotion of rock concerts. No light-weight, Virgil lived in a large, luxurious home and was considered to be worth several million dollars. Currently he was free on a $150,000 bond. Some weeks before the double murder, he had been indicted for attempting to sell 1,500 pounds of marijuana to Oklahoma City interests.

On the night of the attempted ripoff of the crop, Adams and Virgil had shown up at the scene. Virgil was furious. He had proceeded to punch and kick Tony and Doug, all the while warning them they would be killed if they went to the police. Finally, it was decided to drive the two bound men to an isolated area and turn them loose.

That was as much as the men could relate as eyewitnesses, but Adams later told authorities what had transpired during the rest of the early morning hours. Tony and Doug had been placed in the trunk of Tony's car. Virgil drove. Adams followed at some distance in his pickup truck. When he caught up, he saw that Virgil had pushed Tony's vehicle into the water-filled pit. It was his intention to have the vehicle and its human cargo disappear forever. Instead, the front wheels caught on some rocks, leaving the rear of the car exposed. Adams helped Virgil pull the two men from the trunk.

Adams reasoned with Virgil. Tony and Doug had undergone a terrible beating. After their experience in the water, they were terri-fied. If released, it was doubtful that they would cause any more trouble. Virgil agreed and the two men were untied and left to walk down the nearby tracks.

Virgil Fox couldn't get over the fact that two locals had attempted to steal his marijuana. As he and Adams drove along, he became more incensed. Finally, he turned around and headed back to the railway tracks. Tony and Doug, bleeding profusely, were stumbling slowly along the tracks. According to Adams, Virgil jumped out of the pickup and quickly caught up to the injured men. He unceremoniously shot both in the back of the head with his .357 Magnum. Adams admitted that he had helped Virgil drag the men into the nearby bushes.

Adams was taken into custody. He quickly confirmed the story as related by the two men guarding the marijuana field, but swore he had no idea that Virgil intended to commit double murder. Besides, as events unfolded, he was afraid that if he didn't do as Virgil commanded, he too might become a victim.

Virgil had confided in Adams that he and his wife planned to disappear, forfeiting his $150,000 bond before the pending marijuana case came up for trial. His scheme was already in motion.

Investigators soon found out that Virgil Fox and his wife had flown the coop. Virgil had been converting his assets into cash for weeks before the double murder. His fingerprints and mug shot were flashed across the country. Meanwhile, in exchange for his co-operation, Dick Adams was allowed to plead guilty to two counts of kidnapping. He was given two concurrent 10-year prison sentences.

It took a full year before Virgil Fox was located in Los Angeles living under the name of a dead relative. He was found guilty of marijuana trafficking and sentenced to eight years' imprisonment. On October 11, 1982, he made a deal with the State. It was agreed that the State would drop the two first-degree murder charges. In return, Virgil was permitted to plead guilty to two counts of aiding and abetting a murder. He was sentenced to two life terms in prison, which he is currently serving.

Danny Garrett & Karla Faye Tucker

(UNITED STATES)

BEAUTIFUL KARLA FAYE TUCKER had attended the school of hard knocks all her life. When she was only 8 years old, she smoked marijuana. By age 10 she was shooting heroin. In time, the wild teenager was deeply entrenched in the Houston, Texas, drug scene. Karla dropped out of school in Grade 7, about the time her parents separated. She married at 15, divorced at 21. Karla and her sister Kerri became streetwalkers, hustling their bodies to anyone who could pay the price.

In January 1983, Karla met 37-year-old Danny Garrett, a fellow drug user. She moved in with the part-time bartender and biker whose main ambition in life was to become a small-time thief. When Danny teamed up with Karla he was well on his way to fulfilling his ambition. The attractive 24-year-old hooker and the flamboyant biker were perpetually under the influence of booze and drugs. Theirs was a life of highs and lows. Mostly they managed to function in a fuzzy never-never land, totally dependent on drugs.

On occasion, difficulties arose in their lives. These were either deflected or neglected. Usually minor problems went away, but acquaintance Jerry Dean was no minor problem. When Jerry's ex-wife told Karla that she still had Jerry's bank card, the two women agreed to clean out his bank account. In short order, Jerry discovered that he had no money in the bank. Understandably, he was furious. He managed to get his hands on Karla's childhood picture album, her most cherished possession. Jerry slashed the album to ribbons.

Karla told Danny about the destruction of her personal property. He agreed to seek revenge. Danny came up with a great idea. They would give Jerry a beating and steal the expensive motorcycle parts he kept in his apartment. They could sell the parts, buy guns and go into the business of robbing stores for big money to feed their drug habits. Karla agreed that the idea was a good one. The unholy twosome enlisted a mutual friend, Jimmy Liebrandt, to accompany them on their mission.

When the appointed day rolled around, Danny and Karla drove to Jimmy's house to pick him up. Unreliable Jimmy was out cold on booze and drugs. No amount of pushing, shoving or shouting could wake him. The conspirators placed Jimmy in their vehicle, but realized he wouldn't be much help. When they arrived at their destination, Jimmy remained asleep in the car.

Danny and Karla had no trouble gaining entrance to Jerry's apartment. They made their way to the bedroom. Jerry woke up with a start. Danny hit him over the head with a hammer. The blow was a glancing one and didn't appear to do too much harm. This seemed to infuriate Danny. He swung again and again until Jerry was only semiconscious, making guttural sounds. Karla, who later claimed she acted to put an end to the strange sounds, spotted a pickaxe in a corner. She clutched the axe in her hand and swung it at Jerry's back. The annoying sounds didn't abate. She implored Danny to put a stop to the noises. Danny took the axe and plunged it several times into Jerry's back. The noises ceased.

With their work apparently concluded, Danny left the room. That's when Karla made her startling discovery. Trembling in terror, hidden under blankets with her head under a pillow, was a nude woman. Karla didn't hesitate. She grabbed the pickaxe and swung. Thirty-two-year-old Deborah Thornton knew she was in a struggle for her life. Karla swung the axe for the second time. Debbie feebly clutched at the handle but could do little else.

Just then, Jimmy Liebrandt, who had been asleep in the car, walked into the room. He looked in horror at the two women, wheeled and fled the scene. Karla left the room and told Danny about the woman in the bedroom. He returned to hear Debbie plead, "Oh, God, it hurts. If you're going to kill me, please hurry up." Danny struck Debbie another blow with the pickaxe. All was quiet.

Danny and Karla looted the apartment of motorcycle parts. Later that night, they met with Jimmy and watched the news on television. By that time the two bodies had been found. Karla was ecstatic at the carnage they had wrought. She enjoyed the entire scenario. Karla went on to tell her companions that when she struck Debbie with the pickaxe she had been sexually aroused. She boasted to her sister Kerri and to Kerri's husband, Doug, that she had had a hand in killing her former friend and his lover. Doug, who was Danny's brother, was stunned at the cold-hearted attitude of his sister-in-law.

Karla had another plan. She confided in her sister and brother-in-law that she needed help to commit another murder. Both she and Danny felt that Jimmy Liebrandt could not be trusted to keep his mouth shut. They planned to kill him.

For weeks Kerri and Doug were in fear for their own lives. They now had guilty knowledge of a double murder committed by two drug addicts. It didn't matter that Kerri was Karla's sister and Doug was Danny's brother. Karla would do anything to stay on drugs and out of jail. Finally, Kerri and Doug Garrett decided to call police. They told their story and in so doing provided the first clues to solving what had become known as Houston's Pickaxe Murders. Detectives decided they needed more evidence other than the word of the sister and brother of the two killers. They asked Doug if he would wear a wire to gain incriminating evidence against Karla and Danny. He agreed.

In due course, a meeting was set up. Doug had no trouble bringing up the subject of the murders and the plans to kill Jimmy

Liebrandt. Minutes after police heard the incriminating conversation, Danny and Karla were arrested and charged with double murder.

At Karla's murder trial, much was made of the horrendous childhood she had endured. Her lawyer reviewed her entire life in an attempt to point out the effects alcohol and drugs had had on the pretty brunette. Nothing helped. It took the Texas jury only a few hours to find Karla guilty of murder. She was sentenced to death. Danny Garrett was also found guilty and received the same sentence, but died in prison before he could be executed.

On February 3, 1998, Karla Faye Tucker was executed by the state of Texas.

Juan Gonzales
(UNITED STATES)

IT'S A FACT OF LIFE that many victims of violent crime happened to be in the wrong place at the wrong time. Some were doing nothing more than eating in a restaurant or simply walking in the street when fate or plain bad luck decreed that they would cross the path of a killer.

On July 7, 1986, Rose Cammarota, 71, left her Manhattan apartment to visit a sick friend on Staten Island. She had heard the weather forecast on the radio. It was going to be a scorcher. The weatherman said it could reach 100 degrees Fahrenheit. Rose decided to catch the Staten Island ferry at 8:35 a.m. in order to enjoy the early-morning breeze. It would also give her the opportunity to get a good look at the Statue of Liberty, which had undergone a major restoration and had been rededicated on the Fourth of July.

Rose's husband had died a year earlier. Since then, she had devoted herself to volunteer work and was deeply involved in several charitable causes. At 8:35 a.m. she boarded the *Samuel I. Newhouse* for the 25-minute trip to St. George on Staten Island. The ferry was crowded with over 400 passengers. They were a mixed bag. Many were regular commuters. Others were tourists intent on getting a look at the Statue of Liberty.

One of Rose's fellow passengers was 61-year-old Jordan Walker, a security guard at a TV station in Manhattan. Everyone who knew Jordan spoke highly of him. He had just completed the night shift and was on his way to his home on Staten Island. Jordan was well aware that it was going to be an extremely hot day and was looking forward to the cool trip across the harbour. Rose and Jordan never met, yet they were to be indelibly linked in death when they had the misfortune to meet a madman on the Staten Island ferry.

Juan Gonzales had fled Communist Cuba in 1977 in little more than a rowboat. He was picked up by U.S. Coast Guard authorities and was later granted refugee status. Within a year he was in trouble with the law. Juan was one of those hustlers who operated from a cardboard box, dealing three-card monte on the streets of New York in an attempt to relieve unwary tourists of their dollars. Those who knew Juan realized that he was deeply disturbed. He constantly told acquaintances that he heard voices which commanded him to do terrible things. Sometimes he claimed that he spoke directly to God. These voices, combined with his natural bad temper, made Juan a very dangerous young man. He was prone to violent outbursts, which often cost him his menial jobs.

On July 3, while the rest of New York was preparing to celebrate the holiday, Juan, who was then living in the Fort Washington Men's Shelter, attacked several occupants of the home. He was so violent that police were called. Juan ended up in Presbyterian Hospital, where he was evaluated for two days. On July 5, he told doctors that he was feeling better and was no longer being bothered by the voices. They suggested he check himself into Harlem Hospital. Juan assured them that he would do as he was told, but he lied. On July 6, Juan Gonzales was listening to his voices on the streets of New York. They commanded him to do one of those terrible things. This time he listened and obeyed.

Juan made his way to a store in Times Square that specialized in martial arts equipment. He purchased a two-foot-long ceremonial sword. That day he filed the blade until it was razor sharp. On

Monday, at 8:35 a.m., he caught the Staten Island ferry and made his way to the saloon deck. No one noticed anything amiss. Indeed, who would have paid attention to the scruffily attired man carrying the two-foot-long parcel wrapped in newspaper.

Juan sat down and slowly undid his cumbersome package. He removed the sword from its scabbard and shouted, "Freedom for all!" With that initial shout, he lunged at the closest passenger and viciously slashed the astonished man. As passengers screamed, Juan continued shouting in Spanish and swinging his sword. A deckhand attempted to intervene. He too was stabbed. People scurried to get out of the madman's path. Some were superficially wounded, while others were more seriously hurt. Rose Cammarota and Jordan Walker were killed on the deck of the ferry. Nine others received slashes to various parts of their bodies.

The death toll would certainly have been higher had it not been for the actions of one man, Edward Del Pino. Edward had been an officer with the New York Police Department for 24 years. In all those years he had never fired his gun. After retiring from the force five years previously, Edward was enjoying semi-retirement. To supplement his pension, he was employed as a night guard in Manhattan. On this fateful morning, he was returning to his Staten Island home.

There seemed to be a commotion not more than 20 feet from where Ed was sitting. He got up to get a better view. That's when he saw a man with a sword plunge the weapon into a woman's back. Ed shouted, "Drop it!" as he pulled out his .38-calibre Smith & Wesson. At a glance he knew he couldn't fire low without hitting passengers. Ed fired over the man's head. The roar of the report got the sword-swinging killer's attention. He dived under a row of benches.

Ed advanced to the cringing Juan. He directed him, "Drop the sword." Slowly, the defused madman pushed his weapon from under the seats. Ed had him lie on the benches, face down. He placed his .38 against Juan's head with the terse warning, "Don't move or you're dead."

Ferry personnel radioed ahead for assistance. The nine wounded passengers were rushed to nearby hospitals. It was too late for Rose Cammarota and Jordan Walker. A SWAT team took Juan into custody. It wasn't easy. He became violent and had to be placed in a body bag before he could be carried off the boat.

Ed Del Pino was the hero of the day. Had he not acted as he did, no doubt several more passengers would have been killed. He modestly pointed out that he had acted on reflex and was far from being a hero.

Juan Gonzales's record of instability was soon uncovered. He was confined to a mental institution for an indefinite period.

Manfred Graf

(GERMANY)

WEALTHY JEWELLER MANFRED GRAF had a problem. He had met a luscious Nordic beauty, Karin Best, who could perform better in bed than Cleopatra on one of the latter's good nights. But wouldn't you just know it, Manfred had a wife, 27-year-old Ursula and 2-year-old son, Marco. To make matters even stickier, Ursula was eight months pregnant.

Ursula's daddy, a prosperous jeweller, had retired and left his business to his daughter and son-in-law. Ursula owned half the business. A divorce was out of the question.

The Grafs lived in a luxury villa in the German village of Hoesbach. Their jewellery business was located in Goldbach, a few kilometres away.

On October 1, 1987, Manfred sneaked up behind his unsuspecting wife and clubbed her over the head with a piece of birch firewood. Ursula slumped to the floor of the villa, dead from the single crushing blow. All the while, Marco slept undisturbed in his room.

Manfred then hopped into his white hardtop Mercedes and drove along the autobahn until he came to a convenient turnoff with a gas station and large parking lot. He opened his trunk, returned the keys to the ignition and climbed into the trunk. Manfred pulled the trunk door down from the inside. It locked automatically. Then, exactly as he had planned it, he smashed out one of the rear lights, ripped off a piece of his jacket, set it on fire and stuffed it through the hole to attract attention.

It wasn't long before the smoke coming from the broken light attracted a garage customer to the Mercedes. He heard Manfred screaming for help and immediately ran into the gas station for assistance. The trunk didn't have to be forced. The keys were in the ignition. That Manfred had thought of everything.

Manfred told police that two men had forced their way into his villa. While one held Ursula hostage, the other had forced him to drive to his jewellery business in Goldbach to open the firm's safe. He was helpless to do anything but comply with the robber's wishes. The intruder then had him drive to the turnoff, where he locked him in the trunk of his own car.

Police rushed to the Graf villa. They employed extreme caution as there was grave suspicion that the robbers could still be inside gathering up more loot. The house was surrounded. After a few hours of waiting for the robbers to emerge, a SWAT team swarmed the villa. They found Marco peacefully asleep in his bed. Ursula was found dead on the floor. When Manfred was told of his wife's death, he went out of his head, crying uncontrollably and punching walls.

Homicide detectives studied the crime scene. With the assistance of medical and laboratory staff, they were able to ascertain that Ursula had not been raped or sexually interfered with in any way. The killer or killers had not left any clues. No doors or windows had been forced. Jewellery and other works of art lying about the house, valued at approximately $400,000, had not been touched.

Manfred was questioned in an attempt to obtain a description of the killers. The best he could do was to describe both men as being dark, of average height and weight. He said they spoke German with an Italian accent.

Investigators were in a quandary. Why wouldn't robbers steal the valuables there for the taking? Why kill Ursula and not Manfred?

After all, both had seen the intruders. Detectives were puzzled. Like good detectives everywhere, they turned inward, to the closest relative of the deceased—Manfred himself.

Initially, police couldn't find any reason why Manfred would want his wife out of the way. Their marriage appeared to be a happy one. However, they learned that Manfred often slipped away for golf weekends. They also learned that he was a lousy golfer. By trailing him on one of these weekends, they discovered that he took part in, arguably, far more enjoyable sporting activities than golf. Her name was Karin Best.

After much soul-searching, authorities decided that if they didn't arrest Manfred, he would succeed in getting away with murder. They agreed to make the arrest late on a Friday. Because the courts didn't open until Monday, it would be impossible for Manfred's lawyer to obtain a writ of habeas corpus until after the weekend. This would give police labs a couple of extra days to gather up the suspect's clothing and perform tests on them, as well as on his Mercedes.

At the time of the arrest, Manfred was fit to be tied. He ranted and raved, threatening lawsuits for harassment and false arrest. None of his protestations did any good. Manfred was made to cool his heels in the lockup for the weekend.

Lab technicians found wool fibres from Manfred's sweater adhering to the murder weapon. When the Grafs' housekeeper was questioned, she told police that she had carried the firewood into the house. In fact, the fireplace had not been used yet that season and there was no reason for Manfred to even touch the wood, unless, of course, he had used the hunk of firewood to club his wife to death.

In addition, a small amount of Ursula's blood was found on the inside of a knitted vest Manfred had worn the day after the murder. He had had the vest laundered and the spot was invisible to the naked eye. Technicians, however, were able to detect it and bring it out. Manfred had been cunning enough to destroy the clothing he had worn on the day of the murder, so it was a mystery how he had managed to get the tiny spot of blood on the inside of his vest.

Experts felt that although he had destroyed his clothing and washed himself on the day of the murder, he must have had a bit of his wife's blood in his hair. When he pulled the vest on over his head, the blood was transferred to the inside of the garment.

Despite vehemently protesting, Manfred was placed on trial for his wife's murder. Because of his wealth and the fragile nature of the scientific evidence against him, many thought he would be acquitted. Such was not to be the case. Manfred Graf was found guilty of manslaughter and sentenced to 14 years' imprisonment.

Karin Best proved that she had no guilty knowledge of the murder and hadn't even known that her lover was married. She was never charged with any crime.

Stan Graham

(NEW ZEALAND)

EVERY SMALL COMMUNITY HAS ONE—a deranged individual who makes threatening gestures to strangers and is known for a bad temper. Usually residents come to accept this person as just one of the characters around town. When tragedy strikes, they look back and lament, "Someone should have done something."

Stan Graham of Koiterangi, New Zealand, had a nasty temper. Almost everyone in the area left him to his own devices. He was simply one of those fellows who marched to his own drummer.

Stan, his wife and two children lived on a dairy farm. Although his cows were well cared for, Stan let his milking plant deteriorate to the point where the local dairy wouldn't accept his product. Maybe the final straw occurred in 1941 when health authorities condemned his barn.

From that time on, Stan firmly believed everyone was against him. The world was conspiring to ruin his life. On several occasions during the next year he threatened other farmers, business acquaintances and, above all, neighbours, who he claimed were poisoning his cows.

On October 8, 1941, a local farmer, Anker Madsen, was cycling past the Graham house. Stan ordered him to stop. When Madsen didn't comply, the enraged farmer picked up a rifle and took aim. Stan was ready to shoot, when a car pulled up between him and Madsen. The moment passed and nothing happened. So upset was Madsen that he reported the incident to the police. As the day wore on, Stan threatened several other people who passed his farm. Constable E. M. Best drove out to the farm and attempted to talk some sense into the man, who was by now threatening almost everyone with whom he came in contact. Stan wouldn't listen.

Constable Best returned to police headquarters and reported his lack of success with Graham. Authorities agreed that something had to be done before the situation got out of hand. Constable Best, Sergeant W. Cooper, Constables F. W. Jordan and P. C. Tulloch drove out to the farm. Cooper and Best chatted with Stan, who seemed to have quieted down. He named the farmers who he claimed were poisoning his cows. The officers left to question these farmers, who totally denied having ever been near Stan's cows. The police returned to the Graham farm.

This time Stan met Best and Cooper at the front door. He was told that he couldn't go around threatening people. They asked him to give up the several weapons they knew were in the house. Stan ran to the kitchen and reappeared in seconds carrying a rifle. Mrs. Graham attempted to intervene. Her husband pushed her aside. Cooper clutched the rifle barrel. Stan fired, shooting Cooper in the arm.

The two officers, Tulloch and Jordan, who had been lingering outside at the gate, now came running up to the house. Stan fired twice, hitting both men as they entered his home. They fell dead to the floor. Best implored the gunman to stop shooting. Ignoring his pleas, Stan shot, hitting the constable in the hand.

Not knowing if his comrades were alive, Best bent over the fallen men. Stan calmly shot Best in the back. Cooper attempted to escape the carnage. He ran out of the house and along a path leading to the road. Stan took careful aim and shot him as he ran. Cooper fell dead to the road. Stan went over to the motionless officer and fired another shot into his body.

Of the four police officers who had arrived at the farmhouse, only one was still alive. Constable Best, although seriously wounded and helpless, never lost consciousness. He pleaded with the gunman to call a doctor. Stan agreed, but only if Best would sign a statement confessing that the police were out to get him. He ordered his wife to fetch pencil and paper and had her write: "I, E. M. Best, intended to murder Stan Graham." Best signed the document.

Stan abruptly left the house, but lingered in the yard. Mrs. Graham ran from the house to find a doctor. Neighbours and passers-by were attracted by the noise of the shooting and the hysterical Mrs. Graham shouting for medical assistance. Most thought that some kind of accident had taken place.

A neighbour, Mr. Hornsby, recognized the sound of gunfire. He ran to the house, carrying a rifle. Stan sighted him and shouted, "Drop that rifle!" Hornsby did as he was told. He asked, "What the hell went on here?" and received no reply. Another neighbour, Mr. Ridley, rushed into the yard. Seeing bodies on the ground, he took in the situation and picked up a rifle. Stan barked, "Are you going to let it go?" Ridley replied, "No." With that, Stan fired. Ridley slumped to the ground, seriously wounded. Unhindered by the killer, Hornsby carried Ridley out to a car.

Stan gathered up food, weapons and ammunition and made his way to woods adjoining his farm. By now the word was out. A madman was killing police officers and anyone else who stood in his way. The Home Guard was called out. Together with police, they converged on the farm and surrounding woods. As night fell, several Home Guardsmen were posted in Stan's house in case the killer returned.

Sure enough, as soon as it grew dark, the deranged man appeared before two startled Guardsmen, Gregory Hutchison and Leo Hagar. Without hesitation, Stan opened fire. Hutchison was hit as Hagar dived for cover. The shooting was heard by Guardsman Max Coulson, who was posted outside the house. Coulson ran toward the farmhouse and through the front gate. Stan brought him down with a single shot. Coulson crawled a few metres, but then lay still. He was dead.

A horde of Guardsmen converged on the house, but Stan had retreated into the woods once more. Two days after the gun battle, Gregory Hutchison died of his wounds in Westland Hospital. In all, 30 police officers and 150 Guardsmen were employed in the search for Stan Graham. At one point, two airplanes were used in the hunt. The search party was given orders to shoot to kill if they sighted Stan. Isolated farmhouses were evacuated. Scores of farmers joined in the hunt.

For two weeks, Stan evaded capture. Then, on October 20, a farmer who had evacuated his home during the height of the killing rampage returned to find that someone had broken into the house and removed food and other supplies. Police were quickly summoned. They searched the area and spotted Stan, who was heavily armed. An officer took aim and shot. Stan fell to the ground. As he lay there in obvious pain, he shouted, "Don't shoot again! I'm done."

Stan was rushed to Westland Hospital, where he died during the night with his wife and a minister at his side. Tragically, Mr. Ridley died of his wounds some time later.

The madman of Koiterangi had taken eight lives during his senseless slaughter. So outraged were the citizens of the area that they had the Graham farmhouse burned to the ground.

Demetrius Gula & Steve Sacoda

(UNITED STATES)

THE FINE ART OF KIDNAPPING seems to have gone out of fashion. Sure, occasionally some scion of industry is plucked off the streets of a South American city and held for ransom. But where are those desperate types who indulged in kidnapping as a profession? Let's turn a page back to the Dirty Thirties, when kidnapping was at its pinnacle as a means of turning a dishonest dollar.

On December 5, 1937, Gertrude Fried was awakened by the ringing of her telephone. It was 4:00 a.m. when Mrs. Fried awoke with a start. Earlier the previous evening her husband, Arthur, had gone out to pick up his car in Brooklyn and had not returned. Now her worst fears were realized. A harsh voice on the phone said, "Your husband's in the Bronx. Don't worry."

This call was followed by several others. It was clear Arthur had been kidnapped.

The Frieds were not wealthy and it was a mystery why Arthur had been chosen as a kidnap victim. The abductors initially demanded $200,000, but after being told this amount was well beyond the Frieds' ability to deliver, settled for the sale price of $1,800.

Arthur's brother Hugo took over negotiations with the kidnappers, who led him by phone all over New York. Despite the FBI's guidance, the New York press inexplicably got hold of the story and featured the kidnapping in the newspapers. Once that happened, there was no further contact from the kidnappers and no further word of the fate of Arthur Fried.

Investigators learned that on the night of Arthur's disappearance, several teenagers driving home from a party had observed a Buick cutting off a coupe, forcing it to an abrupt stop. A man with a gun had dashed over to the coupe, pushed the driver aside and driven off. The Buick followed. The teenagers said the first two letters of the coupe's licence plate were BM, the same as Arthur's licence. They thought the Buick's licence started with 7N.

FBI agents believed that Arthur had been taken off of South View Avenue, near his mother's home, where he had picked up his car.

Christmas came and went. In March, a similar kidnapping took place. Benjamin Farber, a coal merchant, was picked up off the streets of Brooklyn. His brother Irving received several phone calls from the abductors. Like Hugo Fried, he was told to go to certain bars and phone booths throughout New York to receive instructions.

Finally, Irving was ordered to wrap $1,800 and throw the package off the Williamsburg Bridge so it fell on South Fifth Avenue in Brooklyn. Under police instructions, Irving did as he was told. True to their word, the captors pushed Benjamin Farber unharmed from a car in Manhattan.

Benjamin could tell police little of importance, other than four young men were involved. His eyes had been taped and cotton wool had been stuffed in his ears.

Four months passed before the gang struck again. Two young men in their late teens, Norman Miller and Sidney Lehrer, were on their way home from a movie and had stopped at a red light. It took only seconds for two armed men to hustle them into another vehicle. Their eyes were immediately taped. Both were terrified, but independently decided to keep their wits about them.

The car radio was on. They heard a vocalist warble, "A tisket, a tasket, a green and yellow basket," to the music of the Tommy Dorsey

Band. After they had driven some distance, the vehicle came to an abrupt stop. One of the bandits pushed Sidney out of the car and gruffly ordered, "Grab a taxi, buster, and tell Miller we'll get in touch with him." With that remark, he thrust a dollar into Sidney's hand. The car sped away with Norman Miller.

The haggling by phone with the Miller family commenced. This time around, the kidnappers held out for $13,000, probably because Norman's father was substantially better off than the families of their previous victims. In due course, the $13,000 was successfully transferred. Once again, true to their word, the kidnappers unceremoniously released the victim on the streets of New York.

Norman was able to tell the FBI that he had attempted to keep track of the time. He felt that 20 minutes had passed from the time Sidney was released until he was delivered to the gang's hideout. Norman said the driver had stayed within the speed limit and had stopped at all traffic lights. In addition, he estimated that he had travelled about 25 minutes from the gang's hideout until he was dropped from the gang's car between 11th and 12th Streets in Manhattan.

Agents contacted the Columbia Broadcasting Corp. and were able to pinpoint the exact time that "A Tisket, A Tasket," was on the air. The song had started out at precisely 46 minutes past midnight. Based on Norman's estimates and the time the song was on the air, the FBI was able to formulate a general idea of the location of the gang's hideout.

Norman, who had remained alert while in captivity, volunteered that he had heard a church bell ringing. Police figured the bell had rung at 10:00 a.m. Sunday. Norman had also heard clicking noises in the hideout, which he speculated might be from someone shooting pool. While being taken blindfolded into the hideout, he had bumped into something that he thought might be a stack of folding chairs. He revealed one further bit of information. When he was being released, one of the kidnappers said nonchalantly, "I fingered your old man at the Empire City track, kid."

Agents checked out the clues. They learned that the Frieds, Farbers and Millers had all frequented the races. It was logical to assume that the kidnappers were racetrack habitués as well. With $13,000 in their pockets, they no doubt had headed for the track. At that time, a big racing meet was being held in upstate New York in Saratoga.

The FBI canvassed Saratoga, looking for a Buick as described by the teenagers, with a licence number beginning with 7N. As luck would have it, they found a 1937 Buick of the correct description, but it had 1938 plates. The car's previous licence was checked. Sure enough, in December 1937 its licence was 7N–900. It was registered to Dennis Gula, who turned out to be a respected New York businessman. He told police that his son, Demetrius, drove the vehicle all the time.

Dennis Gula operated a pool room in the basement of the Ukranian Hall, located in the area believed to contain the gang's hideout. Nearby was a church with a carillon of bells. Church officials confirmed that the bells were activated at ten o'clock each Sunday morning. At the entrance to a hall off the pool room was a stack of folding chairs.

Demetrius Gula was taken into custody. It was learned that his best friend, Steve Sacoda, was already in custody for another crime. Demetrius sang like a bird. He revealed that the other two members of the gang were friends, John Virga and Willie Jacknis. Steve Sacoda was the brains behind the gang. It was he who had made the phone calls to the victims' families.

The burning question remained. Whatever had become of Arthur Fried?

Demetrius told detectives that the gang had panicked when they read of Fried's kidnapping in the newspapers. At that time, Arthur was being held in Sacoda's apartment. Steve walked in the room, took a gun out of his pocket and shot Arthur in the head, killing him instantly. Demetrius and Steve carried the body down to their car and transported it to the basement of the Ukranian Hall, where it was pushed into the furnace. Demetrius and Steve passed the time chatting beside the furnace for four hours. They added coal to the raging fire from time to time until the body was totally consumed.

A year after Demetrius confessed, all four kidnappers were placed on trial. John Virga and Willie Jacknis, who had not been present at the time of the murder, were found guilty of kidnapping and sentenced to life imprisonment. Demetrius Gula and Steve Sacoda were found guilty of Arthur Fried's murder. They were later executed at New York's Sing Sing prison.

Susan Harrison

(ENGLAND)

SUSAN HARRISON THOUGHT she was the luckiest girl in Sunderland, England. Trim, attractive Susan had fallen under the spell of one of the most eligible bachelors in town. Michael Meade swept Susan off her feet. He was kind, charming and spent money freely. Nothing was too good for his Susan.

Unfortunately for Susan, she knew nothing of Michael's background. As a teenager he had the drive and ability to make money. By the time he was 21, he had been in and out of several profitable ventures. In 1971, Michael drove his Jaguar to a gas station, where he met attractive 22-year-old Joan. The young couple married in December 1973. Within a week, Michael was flirting with every female he met. In addition, he beat Joan severely and bragged to her that he had bedded several women during their short marriage.

Joan immediately left her husband and moved in with her parents, but Michael didn't take the rejection well. He showed up at his in-laws' home and hurled bricks through every window in the house. Clutching Joan by the hair, he threatened to cut her throat and kill her parents if they interfered.

Joan returned to Michael, whom she now considered to be a monster disguised as a human being. She thought of killing him before he killed her but couldn't muster up the courage. Instead, she escaped to Spain, where she lived in fear that Michael would find her. It would be seven years before she felt safe enough to return to England.

Poor Susan Harrison. In 1979 she felt she was madly in love with this kind, gentle man who treated her so well. Susan moved in with Michael and became his common-law wife. Soon she was pregnant with their first daughter, Shelley. The pregnancy seemed to set off a switch in Michael's psyche. He became verbally abusive to Susan and took great delight in punching her in the stomach. Occasionally, he would take off his belt and whip her unmercifully.

Susan, who had been a cheerful young woman, had a wide circle of friends. Michael took special pleasure in demeaning her in front of her girlfriends. He would throw dishes at her and laugh when he made her clean up the mess. Friends looked on in amazement as Susan cowered in fear. It was commonplace to see her with ugly bruises on her arms and legs. When Shelley was born, Michael displayed no affection toward the child and went out of his way to ignore her. Any time Susan hinted at leaving her abusive common-law husband, he threatened to kill her.

When the subject of having another baby came up, Susan was aghast. She had no desire to bring an additional child into the living hell she was now enduring. Michael was adamant and ordered his wife off the Pill. In 1982, the couple's second daughter, Prophecy, was born. Her birth brought out the very worst in Michael. He commenced to abuse his two daughters, inflicting severe beatings to the children. Sometimes, for imagined poor behaviour, he would lock the two girls in their rooms without food for up to three days. Susan managed to push scraps of food under the bedroom door when her husband wasn't around.

When Prophecy was only two years of age, she fell out of an upstairs window. A neighbour found her on the ground with a broken leg. Michael had left the children alone in the empty house. When told of the accident, his reaction was to build a roof over Prophecy's crib.

Michael often had business acquaintances over to his house and invited them to fondle Susan, charging them for the privilege. He seemed to enjoy what he considered to be a profitable game.

The constant abuse took its toll on Susan. She lost weight and became extremely nervous. There didn't seem to be any way out of her predicament. The most obvious solution was to simply leave, but Susan knew in her heart that Michael would hunt her down and kill her and the two girls.

Susan came up with an alternate solution. She would have her husband killed. She contacted a close friend, Rhonda Stoker, to whom she had confided her abusive relationship. When Susan told her idea to Rhonda, her friend wouldn't hear of such a thing. It took a couple of months, but slowly Rhonda came around. She agreed to try to find someone to do the job. And that's exactly what she did. She put Susan in touch with Danny Boyes, the 21-year-old doorman at the Victoria Public House in Sunderland. Susan and Danny met several times, discussing the hit. She turned over a photograph of Michael to Danny.

Clifton Britton, 34, head doorman of the Victoria, was brought into the scheme. The price for the job was set at £5,000, but the initial price was later tripled by the conspirators. Susan agreed to the new price, although she knew she'd have to sell her flat to raise such an amount.

Meanwhile, the abuse escalated. Michael held a knife against Susan's throat and told her it wouldn't be long before he slit her throat and killed the girls as well. A couple of weeks later, Michael found a fingerprint on the lens of his camera. He was furious and accused nine-year-old Shelley of playing with his equipment. He beat the child severely with his belt. When Susan saw her daughter crying hysterically as bright red welts appeared on her arms and legs, she made up her mind—no more delays: Michael must die.

That same night, she and Michael were to eat out at the Shagorika Indian Restaurant. Michael let her know that outdoor sex would be perfect on such a warm summer night. Susan informed the hit men.

After dinner, Susan drove the family Volkswagen to a secluded spot beside the River Wear. The night was still. Michael spread a blanket on the grass. As they prepared to have sex, Danny Boyes slipped out of the shadows brandishing a shotgun. He ordered Michael into the back seat of the car and instructed Susan to drive to a field a few miles away near Hylton Bridge. Once there, Michael was ordered to lie face down. A wire was wrapped around his neck until he was dead.

The plan had been for Clifton Britton to follow the Volkswagen in his own car and transport the body, but Clifton didn't show up. Later he revealed that he had abandoned the scheme and pretended to get lost on back roads.

What to do? Susan and Danny stuffed Michael's body into the trunk of the Volkswagen. Susan drove home and parked the car in her driveway. There it stayed, with the body in the trunk, for a full day. Finally she and Danny drove the car to a prearranged location. Danny promised he would take care of disposing of the body. Unbeknownst to Susan, Danny lost his nerve and went on a three-day drinking spree. Days later, Susan checked to make sure that the car had been moved. She was amazed to see it right where she had left it. Susan was to later claim that she had paid two men 500 pounds each to dispose of the body. These two men have never been traced.

The two mystery men drove a short distance to Cold Hesledon. When they spotted a hole in the pitch-black earth, they threw Michael in and covered the body.

Two days later, Tom Veitch showed up at the old miners' digs, from which he had been extracting coke left over from a previously producing mine. Tom couldn't understand why someone had filled in his coke hole. When he started to shovel, he found out. There was a body in his one-man mine.

After the discovery of the body, Susan realized she would have to go to the police. Others came forward, advising investigators that Danny Boyes and Clifton Britton had told them of the murderous plot. No one had believed the two men would actually go through with the scheme. Now that the body had been discovered, they knew better.

All three conspirators were charged with murder. On May 8, 1990, Susan, Danny and Clifton pleaded not guilty. Susan admitted she had been sitting in the Volkswagen and had heard Michael gag as Danny twisted the wire around his neck. Danny gave a conflicting story. He swore that Susan had helped him twist the wire. Both stated that Michael's last words were, "Kill her as well."

Over and above the actual killing, the most sensational aspects of the trial were the details of the abuse handed out by Michael over a period of 10 years. Many witnesses were aware of the abuse. All testified for the defence.

The three defendants were found not guilty of murder. Clifton Britton was cleared of all charges and walked out of court a free man. Danny Boyes was found guilty of attempted murder and sentenced to 10 years' imprisonment. Susan Harrison was found guilty of manslaughter and received a seven-year prison term.

Dr. Patrick Henry

(UNITED STATES)

TO FRIENDS, acquaintances and professional colleagues, they were the perfect couple. Dr. Patrick Henry, a successful dermatologist, was a distinguished man. Tall, handsome, charming and pleasant were adjectives used by many to describe the prominent physician. His attractive spouse, Tina, was a loving wife and doting mother to Stevie, their only child.

By 1972, Dr. Henry was an integral member of the United States Public Health Service in Mobile, Alabama. In time, he would become the organization's director. There they were—the Henrys—established career and comfortable home. Only Tina knew she had married a real-life Dr. Jekyll/Mr. Hyde. From the very beginning, her Patrick was weird. He grew worse.

Soon after they married, Tina realized that the dashing med student was less than perfect. Patrick ignored her for days at a time. He looked through her, walked around her as if she didn't exist. Tina thought a baby might change her husband's disposition. Stevie's birth had no effect on his father. In fact, Patrick often ignored the child, as he did his wife.

When he did talk with Tina, the doctor would go into great detail about what he would do to people who crossed him in any way. He told her that he would cut out their stomachs, gouge out their eyes and stick pins up their fingernails. She often begged him to stop or would run out of the room.

One day, Tina rushed to her crying baby to find that one of the child's arms had turned blue. She suspected that Patrick had caused the strange incident. Little Stevie came around after Tina gently rubbed the arm for some time. On another occasion, Tina was swimming when, unknown to her, an alligator came dangerously close. Patrick warned her to quickly swim ashore, but seemed more interested in taking photos of the close call than in assisting his wife.

Photography was Patrick's hobby. When Tina was pregnant he took pleasure in snapping her picture when she had morning sickness. He also placed a thick glass in front of the camera lens, thereby horribly distorting Tina's face when he took her picture.

Tina worried about the safety of her child. She thought of exposing her husband's abusive behaviour, but didn't believe anyone would believe her. Dr. Henry was a pillar of the community. Her accusations would be attributed to the ravings of a hysterical wife.

The disturbing incidents continued. When Stevie developed diarrhea, Patrick gave his wife a capsule to administer to the child. Instead, Tina phoned a pharmacist, who admonished her not to even think of giving Stevie that particular capsule. It was a narcotic that could prove fatal. Tina put down the phone, her hands shaking. She now knew without a doubt that her husband had attempted to murder his own son.

In 1977, when Patrick was attending a convention in New York, Tina took advantage of the opportunity and left her husband. With Stevie, she returned to her parents' home in Tucson, Arizona. When Patrick learned that Tina had left him, he begged her to return. He promised he would turn over a new leaf, but Tina wouldn't be deceived. Despite the distance between them, Tina was forever fearful that her husband would seek revenge, as he had so often told her he would. In time, the Henrys were divorced. Patrick remarried. Months passed.

On December 6, 1977, a man wearing a wig and bulky oversized clothing was stopped at the Tucson airport. He was carrying a brief-case and insisted it be checked as luggage on the aircraft he was attempting to board heading for Dallas. When an airport-security employee became suspicious, the briefcase was X-rayed. Although the X-ray didn't reveal anything definite, it did indicate that the case contained several metal objects. The suspicious-looking man, a Mr. Donald Vester, was asked to open the briefcase but he claimed he had lost the key. Officials told him he could proceed, but the briefcase would not accompany the flight. They promised that if the articles inside were harmless, they would forward the briefcase to Dallas on the next flight.

Bomb specialists opened the briefcase. Inside they found a glass cutter, cord, pins, a Boy Scout hunting knife and an Ivor Johnson .32-calibre pistol with nine rounds of ammunition. Dallas was contacted and told to detain Mr. Vester for questioning. He turned over his wallet to his interrogators. They found a Visa credit card and a U.S. Public Services ID card, all in the name of Dr. Patrick Henry.

The impostor admitted he was not Donald Vester, but was in reality Dr. Patrick Henry. Security officials were stymied. What was this doctor doing, wearing a ridiculous wig, baggy clothing and trav-elling under an assumed name? The doctor, who claimed he was in Dallas for a dermatology convention, would not give the authorities any further information. Police checked with convention officials and learned that Syntex Laboratories of Palo Alto were sponsoring the convention and that Dr. Henry was indeed an invited guest.

But the good doctor had more surprises in store for the police. He complained that it was stifling hot and asked permission to remove his coat. Police stared as Dr. Henry stripped. Under his oversized clothing, he was wearing what amounted to a padded suit, which added 50 to 75 pounds to his appearance. From his airline ticket, detectives learned that Dr. Henry had flown from Dallas to Tucson. Among the pencilled notes was a Tucson address. Upon checking out the address, Tucson police located Tina Henry, who was the proprietor of a nursery school located next door to her parents' home.

Tina informed the police that she was divorced from Patrick, who had remarried and was presently living in Baltimore. Nervously she told the detectives that the day before, she had seen the strangely dressed man staring at her from across the street. He was totally disguised, but she was sure it was Patrick. Further questioning revealed that someone had broken into the nursery school and that the family dog had barked at about 3:30 a.m. on the morning of December 6. He had barked so loudly that Tina's father had arisen from bed and investigated with a flashlight. In doing so he had probably saved his daughter's life. Later that morning the dog had been dopey and had vomited. Eventually the vomit was analyzed and found to contain a tranquilizer. Studying Dr. Henry's written notes, detectives were able to decipher certain words and initials. Among them they found the address of Tina's parents' home, reference to the family dog and the initials MT, which they interpreted to mean "Murder Tina."

Dr. Henry's scheme was plain enough. He flew from the convention in Dallas to Tucson with the intention of killing his wife and returning to the convention. A dog barking had stopped him from murdering his wife and an alert airport security guard had uncovered a can of worms.

Dr. Patrick Henry was arrested and charged with attempted murder. Lead prosecutor Randy Stevens had a tricky point of law to overcome. Cunning Patrick admitted that he had left Dallas with the express intention of murdering his wife but had changed his mind. Thus, no crime had been committed. You can prepare to commit a crime but stop short of committing it. This defence argument is most commonly called abandonment.

On the other side of the coin, if the accused is forced to stop due to some external influence, he is guilty of the attempt. You can't give murder a whirl and be stopped by chance. That's still attempted murder.

The jury agreed with prosecutor Stevens. Dr. Henry was found guilty of attempted murder and sentenced to a term of from 5 to 15 years' imprisonment in the Arizona State Prison.

The grey walls of Arizona State Prison closed in on the once-prominent doctor, but the world hadn't heard the last of Dr. Patrick Henry. In 1982, prosecutor Randolph Stevens wrote a book on the case, entitled *Deadly Intentions*. The book was later made into a television movie.

In February 1986, after serving six and a half years, Dr. Henry was released from prison and reunited with Nancy, his second wife. Within two years, Nancy, who had never believed anything derogatory about her husband, contacted police. She had found a munitions box in her home containing manuals on explosives and fake identities, as well as a pistol. Evidence indicated Patrick was planning to construct a bomb to blow up prosecutor Randy Stevens in the U.S. Attorney's Office in Tucson. A quantity of marijuana was also seized in his home.

Patrick Henry was prosecuted on the weapons and marijuana charges. He was found guilty and sentenced to 15 years' imprisonment. In addition to those items already mentioned, police recovered three vials of blood serum containing the AIDS virus and a container filled with ricin, one of the deadliest poisons known to man.

Barbara Hoffman

(UNITED STATES)

BARBARA HOFFMAN DECIDED on an abrupt career change. She was a few credits shy of a degree in biochemistry at the University of Wisconsin when she took up the unscholarly profession of masseuse in a Madison, Wisconsin, sex shop. Barbara was beloved by all at Jan's Health Spa, where she invented a few tricks that were not included in the average sex shop employees' repertoire.

Barbara was different in many ways. She was a slim, attractive young woman with an IQ of 145 and had sailed through school. Her university entrance-examination scores placed her in the 98th percentile of those tested. She received a full scholarship to attend university, where she proceeded to get straight A's before dropping out to go into the sex-for-hire game.

Harry Berge was something different altogether. Harry was born on a marginal Wisconsin farm, where his parents eked out a living. By 1966 the farm was producing less than its cost of upkeep. The Berges moved to Stoughton, where Harry caught on as a forklift operator at the Uniroyal plant. Within a five-year span, both of Harry's parents died of natural causes.

Harry was totally alone. His most exciting social activity was attending a movie in Madison. His only other hobby was his model trains, which practically filled the basement of his house. At 46 years of age, Harry had never been on a date with a member of the opposite sex. That all changed early in 1977 when he strolled into Jan's Health Spa and was serviced by Barbara Hoffman.

A new world of sexual delights dawned for the strictly raised Lutheran farm boy. Harry became a regular at Jan's. Life had never been so exciting. A beautiful girl seemed to be taking a special interest in him. Sometimes they met for drinks outside the sex shop. As the months passed, Harry would do anything for his Barbara. The couple even talked marriage. Harry, totally under his lover's influence, altered his $34,500 life insurance policy, naming Barbara as sole beneficiary.

Life appeared to be sweet for Harry, but in reality cunning Barbara had another fish on the line. Gerald Davies was born into poverty and a broken home. After finishing high school in 1968, Jerry obtained a job at the University of Wisconsin as an assistant in the audiovisual department. Jerry's salary hovered around the $10,000 per year level. He had never been intimate with a woman until the day he gathered up his courage and entered Jan's Health Spa.

Once Jerry sampled Barbara's unique sexual favours, he was smitten. Barbara seemed to respond in kind. She dated Jerry outside the spa. Before you could say triangle, Jerry was in love. The odd couple became serious. There wasn't just talk of marriage, there were wedding plans. Finances were a bit of a problem. Jerry's salary at the university wouldn't go far. Still, they would get by. The couple considered themselves engaged.

Unbelievable as it sounds, Barbara talked her future husband into the necessity of having adequate insurance. Her idea of adequate was three million dollars. They tried to buy that amount of insurance, but understandably were turned down by several companies. Finally, by claiming Jerry had an undisclosed income from the ownership of health clubs, the couple was able to obtain $750,000 in term life insurance from Transport Life of Fort Worth, Texas. Barbara Hoffman was named as sole beneficiary on the policy. Jerry handed over a cheque for $6,618.30, the first semi-annual premium. Six months later, he and Barbara paid the second instalment. As the third payment was about to come due, the well had run dry.

What to do? Barbara implemented her plan. She invited Harry Berge to her apartment on the bitterly cold night of December 22, 1977. Poor Harry was clubbed to death, most probably with a frying pan. Next day, Jerry Davies was invited to Barbara's apartment. She informed him that the evening before, she had arrived home to find a unique object in the bathroom. The object was a dead man. Barbara swore to Jerry that she didn't know his identity. Maybe one of her well-heeled clients from the health club had planted the body in order to get her into trouble. The nude corpse now lay outside the back door in a snowbank. Barbara implored Jerry to assist her in disposing of the body.

Jerry suggested they call police. Barbara wouldn't hear of it. She insisted they get rid of the corpse. Finally Jerry agreed. He pulled his car around to the rear of the apartment building and, with Barbara's help, lifted Harry into the car. It was quite a job. The temperature was 22 degrees below zero. Harry was frozen solid. The desperate pair deposited the nude body in a snowbank in the country. When Jerry dropped off Barbara in front of her apartment, she told him to vacuum and clean the car. Barbara had thought of everything.

Jerry was upset. He had never done anything like that in his life. He drove to his mother's ramshackle house, but didn't sleep a wink. All in all, Jerry had a lousy Christmas.

On Christmas Day 1977, Jerry Davies drove to Madison police headquarters and told the desk sergeant, "Last night I helped bury a body in a snowbank." Jerry spilled his guts. Within hours, Harry's frozen body was recovered and later thawed. Barbara was charged with murder but released on bail.

Strangely, Jerry and Barbara grew closer after her release. She claimed to be totally innocent of taking anyone's life and felt that Jerry had done the right thing by notifying police. Together they would ride out this adversity and eventually marry.

Barbara had other problems. She had to forfeit the $13,236.60 invested in that $750,000 life insurance policy or kill Jerry. It is alleged that she opted for the latter alternative.

Jerry lived in an apartment on South Park Street. The tenant in the apartment above Jerry's complained to the building superintendent that the electric fan was making a terrible racket in Jerry's unit. When he couldn't contact Jerry, the superintendent entered the apartment. No wonder the noise hadn't bothered Jerry. He was lying nude and dead in the bathtub.

Police arrived in a matter of minutes. Jerry had no bruises or abrasions on his body, nor was there any sign of a struggle. For some time, despite their grave suspicions, police believed Jerry had committed suicide. Substantiating the suicide theory was a letter written in longhand by Jerry. He stated that he had become insanely jealous and had made up the story of Barbara's involvement in the disposal of a man's body. In the letter, he wrote that he must have been crazy to make up such a story. Barbara was not involved in any way. In death he wanted to set the record straight.

Police were stymied. Were they dealing with an accident, a suicide or a murder? No one had seen anyone enter Jerry's apartment. There was no evidence that any other living soul had been in the apartment. Several weeks after an autopsy had been performed and after extensive testing, it was ascertained that Jerry had eaten a chili dinner laced with cyanide. Detectives also discovered that Barbara had access to cyanide at the university, where she had recently enrolled as a part-time student. A quantity of the deadly substance was missing from one of the labs.

It was all too much. Barbara was arrested and charged with double murder. At her trial, the prosecution stated that Barbara had planned to kill Jerry for the large insurance payoff. She had killed Harry to finance the third payment due on Jerry's policy.

The defence pointed out the obvious. No one had seen Barbara kill anyone. Jerry Davies had refuted his earlier accusation that Barbara had elicited his help in disposing of Harry's body.

At the conclusion of one of Wisconsin's most infamous trials, Barbara was found not guilty of murdering Jerry Davies but guilty of murdering Harry Berge. She was sentenced to life imprisonment.

Barbara Hoffman entered prison on June 25, 1980. When she was incarcerated, Wisconsin law allowed inmates sentenced to life imprisonment to apply for parole after serving 11 years and 3 months. Barbara applied in 1991 and was denied parole. Subsequent paroles have also been denied. She has spent 21 years in prison and is presently incarcerated in the Taycheedah Correctional Institute for Women at Fond du Lac, Wisconsin.

Neta Hoyt

(UNITED STATES)

THE TINY HAMLET OF RICHFORD is located about 25 miles from Ithaca in upstate New York. Most of the inhabitants earn a meagre living from the soil. Many hold down part-time jobs in nearby towns.

Neta Nixon was born in Richford in 1946. During her formative years there was nothing to distinguish her from the other farmers' daughters in the area. She was pleasant-looking, quiet, an average student. Tim Hoyt, a slim six-footer, took a shine to Neta while both were in high school. In her senior year, 17-year-old Neta married Tim. A month later she was pregnant. On October 17, 1964, Neta went into labour and was taken to Tomkins County Hospital in Ithaca. Seven-pound Eric was born later that day. Nurses recorded that he was a healthy baby with no abnormalities.

Neta later told relatives that little Eric was susceptible to "spells." A couple of times she took him to hospital, but doctors could find nothing wrong with the baby. On January 26, 1965, at the age of 3 months and 10 days, Eric died. His death was attributed to SIDS (sudden infant death syndrome). No one thought it strange in any way.

Looking back, members of Tim's family recalled that Neta never displayed the usual maternal closeness to her baby. She never cuddled little Eric. The death was considered an unfortunate tragedy and the less said the better.

A short time later, Neta's second pregnancy ended in a miscarriage. About eight months after Eric's death, she was pregnant again. On May 31, 1966, Neta gave birth to Jimmy, another healthy son. Julie was born on July 19, 1968.

On September 5, 1968, Tim was at work at a construction site. Neta claimed she was feeding Julie rice cereal when the baby started choking and turning blue. She ran out of their trailer home shouting for help. A neighbour, Evelyn Bond, called an ambulance. Attendants tried to revive the baby but it was no use. Julie Hoyt was dead at age 1 month and 17 days. The child's death was attributed to an accident. There was no autopsy, no investigation.

Three weeks after Julie's death, tragedy struck again. According to Neta, Jimmy was outdoors playing. She heard him screaming and found him with blood coming from his nose and mouth. A neighbour called an ambulance. Attendant Henry Robson tried to revive Jimmy with mouth-to-mouth resuscitation. Only when a doctor arrived and told him to stop did Robson give up. Jimmy was dead.

Tim Hoyt requested an autopsy to determine the cause of death. The results were inconclusive. Jimmy's death caused some talk. Tim wondered if some genetic force was at play. Others were more suspicious, whispering that Neta was never what you would call a loving mother. What's more, she seemed to relish being the centre of attention. The loose talk came to nothing.

On March 18, 1970, Neta gave birth to Molly, her fourth healthy, normal child. On the baby's eighth day at home, Neta said that Molly, asleep in her crib, turned blue and was barely breathing. She improved when brought outside into the fresh air. That same day, Molly was taken to a doctor, who could find nothing wrong with her. A week later, the same thing happened. This time Neta called her physician and told him she was able to save her baby's life with mouth-to-mouth resuscitation. The doctor advised Neta to have the baby rushed to hospital by ambulance. Once there, the infant was fine.

Molly underwent several tests. All proved negative. Released from hospital, the baby suffered a third spell. This time her doctor suggested she be taken to Dr. Alfred Steinschneider of Upstate Medical Center. Dr. Steinschneider was involved in SIDS research. He was working on the connection between SIDS and sleep apnea, a condition which results in the interruption or cessation of breathing while asleep and the resumption of breathing without assistance. He accepted Molly into his research program. The doctor diagnosed the baby as suffering from apnea.

Molly had various tests, all of which indicated she was normal. She was sent home with an apnea monitor. A day later, when Tim was out, Neta called Dr. Steinschneider to report that Molly had stopped breathing. Fortunately, Neta had revived her. The doctor had the baby rushed back to hospital, where she was observed for 10 days before being returned home. Once again, Neta said she had to resuscitate her daughter, who was once again rushed to hospital. After being discharged, Molly had another mysterious attack. She died as ambulance attendants worked over her.

Nurses, who had grown attached to Molly during her hospital stays, commented it was strange all the child's attacks occurred when she was at home. She had never experienced any distress while in their care. An autopsy failed to establish the cause of death.

In May 1971, Neta gave birth to Noah. Because hospital personnel knew the Hoyts had lost four children, none of whom had lived beyond two years and four months, it was decided to keep the boy for further evaluation. Noah spent his first month of life in hospital wired to an apnea monitor. Finally he was sent home. The next day, he was rushed to hospital. Neta said that the baby had stopped breathing. She had saved her son's life by mouth-to-mouth resuscitation.

Tim was now convinced that he carried some kind of genetic defect which affected his offspring. That summer, he had a vasectomy.

Noah was released from hospital, but not for long. The very next day Neta was back reciting her all too familiar story. Miraculously, she had saved her son's life again. On July 27, Noah went home for the last time. The following day he turned blue and died. Neta claimed she had tried her hardest, but couldn't bring him back.

In all, Noah had been in hospital 78 days and had never had a medical emergency. He was at home for a total of three days and each time had to be rushed to hospital. Twenty-five-year-old Neta Hoyt fainted at the funeral of her fifth child.

In 1972, Dr. Steinschneider published a paper based on the Hoyt children in the prestigious medical journal *Pediatrics*. He identified them as the "H" family and connected apnea to cyanosis (bluish discoloration of the skin due to the presence of oxygen-deficient blood) sufficiently severe as to require resuscitation. The doctor wrote that two of the children had died the day after being released from hospital, indicating that apnea was responsible for SIDS. This first-time research project revolutionized SIDS research. Dr. Steinschneider's theory was widely accepted.

Meanwhile, the Hoyts had adopted a 9-month-old boy named Jay who grew up to be a healthy teenager.

Twenty years after Dr. Steinschneider wrote his paper on apnea, a new district attorney, Bill Fitzpatrick, took office in Onondaga County. He decided to look into a file of unsolved mysterious deaths. In this way, he discovered Dr. Steinschneider's article. The D.A. was able to identify the "H" family as the Hoyts. He decided that the case warranted further investigation.

Fitzpatrick obtained the decades-old medical records. Experts studied the reports. Slowly, a pattern of infanticide by asphyxiation emerged. When a forensic pathologist specializing in pediatric cases was told all the facts surrounding the Hoyt-baby deaths, a motive became evident. Neta Hoyt was suffering from Munchausen's syndrome by proxy.

The strange condition known as Munchausen's syndrome involves individuals who have an overwhelming urge to be the centre of attention. They gain this attention by faking medical difficulties. Many have been known to study medical books so they can present the correct symptoms to doctors and hospital emergency departments.

Munchausen's syndrome by proxy is a mental condition in which an individual seeks attention by inducing illness in a second party; for example, typically, a mother who suffers from this disorder will purposely make her child ill. The mother is often praised for her devotion and heroic measures in helping her child. Experts believed Neta Hoyt had killed all five of her children by asphyxiating them.

Neta was questioned by a female investigator. A murderous odyssey, dormant for more than 20 years, was about to come to light. After only 15 minutes of urging, Neta sobbed, "You're all going to hate me. Everyone's going to hate me." With those words, the floodgates opened. Neta continued: "I caused the deaths of all my five children." She described how she had smothered each child, recounting every detail of her vile actions. Her husband, Tim, never suspected his wife had murdered their children.

Neta Hoyt stood trial for the murder of her five children. She was found guilty of murder in the second degree in all five cases. The judge sentenced her to a minimum of 15 years to life for each murder, the sentences to run consecutively. In all, the sentence amounted to 75 years' imprisonment before Neta would be eligible for parole. Neta Hoyt will spend the rest of her life in prison.

Pernell Jefferson

(UNITED STATES)

THIS IS THE STORY OF PERNELL JEFFERSON. He was handsome, charming, talented and educated. He was also a stalker and a killer.

Pernell was raised in the small town of Benson, North Carolina. His father deserted the family when Pernell was three years old, leaving Joan Jefferson to bring up her two sons by herself. The boys grew up poor but proud. Pernell and his brother, Willie, did well in school, but it was not in the classroom that the brothers excelled. Both were outstanding athletes. Pernell, in particular, was a star football player at every level.

When Pernell entered South Johnston High School, he was already looked upon as one of the most talented athletes in the state. By the time he was a senior he was a state all star. Pernell was small for a football player, standing only five foot ten, but he was quick and versatile.

Toward the end of his senior year, Pernell was offered a football scholarship to Guilford College in Greensboro. Guilford wasn't Notre Dame, but it did prove that someone recognized his talent. Goodbye Benson, N.C. Pernell Jefferson was on his way.

Pernell starred on his college team from the very first day. Almost single-handedly, he lifted the squad from its perennial losing ways to a respectable record in its small college league. Naturally enough, Pernell was noticed by members of the opposite sex. Helen Ramon, a fellow student at Guilford, met Pernell when she was a sophomore and he was still a freshman. They became friends and dated frequently. Helen found Pernell the most charming boy she had ever dated. It didn't matter that she was white and he was black.

As Pernell gained prominence on the football field, Helen noticed a marked change in his personality. He became demanding and possessive. One day when she didn't agree with him, he struck her in the face. Pernell begged forgiveness, promising it would never happen again. But it did. Over and over. Helen attempted to break off their relationship, but Pernell would threaten her and she would always come back. She wore long-sleeved shirts to hide the bruises and made excuses for the visible black-and-blue marks on her legs and face. Helen was in a living hell and didn't know how to extricate herself.

In 1984, Helen graduated and accepted a position with a grocery brokerage company in Chapel Hill, North Carolina. Pernell was named a small college all-American. On a visit to Helen, he beat her so severely that it was necessary for him to rush her to hospital. Doctors called police, but Helen refused to press charges against her boyfriend. Pernell was arrested and released on his own recognizance. When he was fined $200, Helen paid it. It was as if he held her in some kind of thrall.

Then it happened. The big break every youngster dreams about. The Cleveland Browns offered Pernell a signing bonus of $1,500 to attend a five-day training camp. Later he would be invited to the Browns' regular camp. If he made the team, he would receive a salary of $55,000 for his rookie year. After that, the sky would be the limit.

Pernell attended the camp and collected his signing bonus. He also attended the Browns regular camp. This was different. He was no longer the star. Everyone seemed to be bigger, stronger, faster. He grew depressed with his performance. The steroids he took regularly helped some, but he was lonesome for back home. Here there was no adulation, only hard work. Frustrated, Pernell walked out of camp. To all intents and purposes, his football career was over.

When Pernell returned to North Carolina, he again physically abused Helen. After enduring one of Pernell's brutal beatings, Helen moved to Miami, where she enrolled in St. Thomas University to pursue a master's degree in sports administration. From time to time Pernell visited her there and beat her unmercifully.

Pernell took up weightlifting. With the assistance of steroids he won local competitions. It was while working out one evening in a gym that Pernell was introduced to Jeannie Butkowski. Jeannie was smitten. Soon the pair were dating on a regular basis.

Right from the beginning, Jeannie's friends didn't like the way Pernell was so possessive about their friend. He seemed to have a vice-like control over someone who, a few short months earlier, had been a fun-loving extrovert. In addition, they felt he had been spying on her. He always knew where she had been and what she had been doing. It was sort of weird.

In 1988, an unusual event took place in Jeannie's life. Out of the blue, her ex-husband, Tony, showed up. Tony's second marriage had just crashed and he wanted to see if he and Jeannie might be able to patch up past differences. Although Jeannie was pleased to hear from her former husband, she had to be careful. Pernell was always lurking about, phoning and showing up without warning. Jeannie told Pernell that their relationship had come to an end. Outwardly, Pernell took the news well. Inside, he was fuming.

Pernell didn't go away. He phoned Jeannie frequently, threatening her and her family with violence. Meanwhile, she and Tony had rekindled the old flame. They planned to remarry. Jeannie visited Tony's family in Pennsylvania. When she returned, Pernell was waiting for her in her apartment. All that evening and night, he alternately beat and raped her. When he left he warned Jeannie that he could have her killed by someone else without lifting a finger.

After the attack, Jeannie moved in with a longtime female friend. One day, her friend came home to find that Jeannie was missing. Her answering machine was flashing. When she pressed play, the friend heard the disturbing details of a terrible fight that had culminated with Pernell dragging Jeannie out of the apartment. The police and Jeannie's parents were notified of the apparent kidnapping. During the first few hours of the investigation into Jeannie's disappearance, she drove up to her apartment. She had been beaten and raped. Despite everything Pernell had done to her, Jeannie was reluctant to press charges.

In the days following this most recent attack, Jeannie sank into a deep depression. When Tony broke off their engagement, it was as if Pernell had won. He had, in effect, ruined any chance she had for happiness. Then Jeannie simply disappeared. While no one had any proof, everyone who was connected with her felt that Pernell had spirited her away once more. He was contacted, but claimed to know nothing about Jeannie's latest disappearance.

On May 10, 1989, four days after Jeannie went missing, her room-mate received a mysterious phone call. The caller claimed that Jeannie was dead and that he knew where her body was buried. He said he was fearful that Pernell would kill him if he learned about this phone call. Finally, after talking to Jeannie's father, the caller gave his name as Joey St. Augustine and informed the grieving father that he had driven Pernell and the body to a construction site for a new church. He had remained in the car while Pernell had buried the body. St. Augustine agreed to lead Jeannie's father to the body of his daughter.

Accompanied by police, the group, led by St. Augustine, proceeded to the construction site. Try as they might, they were unable to locate the body. Meanwhile, Pernell learned that police were on his trail. Next day he walked out of his place of employment and never returned.

On January 1, 1990, deer hunters Michael Spain and Randy DuClau came across the skeletal remains of Jeannie Butkowski near Nibbs Creek in central Virginia. A short time later, Jeannie's Nissan, which had been missing since her disappearance, was recovered after having been parked for months in front of an apartment building in Richmond. The Nissan had made the rounds of several small-time hoodlums. Police traced it back to a man named Wayne Scott, who was located and questioned. He decided to tell all in exchange for immunity from prosecution.

Scott claimed that he, together with Charles Zimmer, Mike Savin and Pernell Jefferson, had abducted Jeannie. After the abduction he was let out of the vehicle and went home. Next morning, Pernell told him that he had shot the girl and wanted to get rid of the car. Scott obliged and so started a series of purchases that led to the Nissan being abandoned.

Pernell wanted to move the body from the construction site. Using another vehicle, Scott, Zimmer, Savin and Pernell moved Jeannie's body to where it was found by the hunters. Both Zimmer and Savin verified Scott's story.

Pernell was traced to a cousin's home in Stuart, Florida, where he was arrested and charged with the murder of Jeannie Butkowski. He was tried, found guilty and sentenced to life imprisonment. Pernell Jefferson is presently incarcerated in Craigsville, Virginia. He will be eligible for parole in 2011.

Ted Kaczynski
(UNITED STATES)

THE PACKAGE WAS FOUND in the parking lot of the University of Illinois in Chicago. As a matter of course it was returned to the apparent sender, Professor Buckley Crist at Northwestern University in Evanston, Illinois. When Professor Crist didn't recognize the parcel, he turned it over to the campus police.

Next day, police officer Terry Marker was opening the package, when it exploded. Fortunately, he was only slightly injured. The pipe bomb, which detonated that May 25, 1978, was crudely constructed of match heads and wood. It would mark the first bomb in a reign of terror that would last for 18 years. The ensuing investigation into the serial bombings and the hunt for the perpetrator, who would become known as the Unabomber, is estimated to have cost the United States government in excess of $60 million.

A year after the first bomb exploded, 35-year-old graduate student John G. Harris found a cigar box on campus at Northwestern. When he opened the box, it exploded. Harris suffered little more than cuts and bruises. Unknown to all, the Unabomber was just warming up.

In November 1979, he struck again. The passengers aboard American Airlines Flight 444, in flight from Chicago to Washington, were terror-stricken when the cabin filled with smoke. Although the bomb found in a mailbag didn't explode, it caught fire in the cargo area, forcing an emergency landing. Several passengers required treatment for smoke inhalation. The bomber had graduated from a crude mechanism to a more sophisticated one. The bomb was set to go off when pressure in the cabin reached a certain level.

Seven months later, Percy Wood, president of United Airlines, opened a mail package at his home in Lake Forest, Illinois. It exploded, injuring Wood in the hand and face. The bomb had been disguised as a book.

The FBI connected the four bombing attacks as the work of one man. Because the first two were directed toward universities and the last two toward the aviation industry, the name Unabomber was assigned to the now-infamous criminal.

In 1981 and 1982, the Unabomber struck again. A bomb was found by a maintenance worker at the University of Utah in Salt Lake City. The alert worker called police, and a bomb squad successfully defused the device. A year later, a package addressed to Professor Patrick Fischer of Vanderbilt University in Nashville, Tennessee, was opened by his secretary, Janet Smith. The bomb exploded, inflicting lacerations to Smith's hands and arms. In July of the same year, Professor Diogenes Angelakos of Berkeley suffered severe burns to his right hand when he moved a parcel he had found in the fourth-floor faculty lounge.

As suddenly as the unexplainable attacks had begun, they ceased. For three years nothing more was heard of the Unabomber. As if to make up for lost time, he struck four times in 1985.

John Hauser, an engineering graduate student at UCLA, studying to become an astronaut, picked up a package atop a heap of notebooks on a shelf. The booby-trapped package ripped off several of Hauser's fingers. Hauser gave up his dreams of becoming an astronaut, but did go on to earn his Ph.D.

By now it was apparent the Unabomber was on a power trip. In particular, he harboured a grudge against the academic community. In an attempt to explain his motives, he wrote to the *San Francisco*

Examiner, revealing for the first time that he blamed advances in technology for the world's ills.

A month after Hauser's ordeal, a bomb arrived by mail at Boeing's Fabrication Division in Auburn, Washington. It was immediately defused. On November 15, James McConnell, a psychology professor at the University of Michigan, received a book in the mail. It exploded, injuring both McConnell and his research assistant, Nicklaus Suino. McConnell was rendered partially deaf, while Suino received burns to his arms and legs.

On December 11, 1985, the Unabomber killed for the first time. Thirty-five-year-old Hugh Scrutton picked up a paper bag outside his Sacramento, California, computer store. The ensuing blast killed him instantly. Two years passed before another bomb was placed outside a computer store. Owner Gary Wright moved a few pieces of wood in his parking lot. The wood was booby-trapped. Wright was only slightly injured, but this incident resulted in the famous composite drawing of the mustachioed man in the hood, which was widely distributed around the world. A woman looking down on the parking lot from an upstairs window had observed a man carrying pieces of wood about an hour before the bomb went off.

While law enforcement agencies across the country waited for the Unabomber to strike again, he inexplicably stopped planting bombs for several years. Then, in 1993, he placed two bombs during the same week. One, at the University of California at San Francisco, seriously injured Professor Charles Epstein. Two days later a package exploded at the office of computer scientist David Gelernter. The blast left Gelernter without vision in one eye, without hearing in one ear, and blew away a portion of his right hand. The Unabomber wrote to the seriously injured scientist, lecturing him on the ruination of the world by the use of computers. The United States government offered a one-million-dollar reward for the bomber's apprehension.

Undaunted, the Unabomber continued his attacks. On December 10, 1994, a bomb was mailed to the home of advertising executive Thomas Mosser in North Caldwell, New Jersey. When Mosser opened the package, it exploded, killing him instantly. The Unabomber had taken a second life.

Five months later, the same fate befell Gilbert Murray, a forestry executive in Sacramento. The bomb was so powerful it literally blew Murray apart. After the Murray murder, the Unabomber wrote the *New York Times*. He belittled the FBI's futile attempts at identifying and capturing him. He followed his letter to the *Times* with one to the *San Francisco Chronicle*.

It was this letter that threw the entire U.S. into a state of alert. The Unabomber declared that he would blow up an airplane after takeoff out of Los Angeles within the following six days. Air mail in California was terminated. Security was tightened. The Unabomber relieved the tension by sending letters to the *New York Times* and the *Washington Post*, stating that his threat was a hoax. The cunning bomber had a new proposition. If the newspapers would publish his manifesto, he would stop his bombing attacks. The newspapers had three months in which to make a decision.

In September, the Unabomber's 35,000-word manifesto was published in a special section in the *Washington Post*. In deciding to publish the rambling but learned tirade against technology, authorities believed that someone somewhere might recognize a word or phrase which they could attribute to a friend or acquaintance. They were right.

Ted Kaczynski, the alleged Unabomber, lived as a hermit in a shack near Lincoln, Montana. To say that Ted was different is to understate the case. He was born in Chicago in 1942. By the time he reached the age of six, his parents were so amazed at his reasoning ability and grasp of complicated problems that they had him tested. Their son had an IQ of 170. When he was seven, his little brother David was born. Ted was delighted. The two boys became close friends. In grammar school, Ted was so advanced that he skipped an entire year. In high school, the same thing happened. After completing his senior year, universities across the country offered him full scholarships. He accepted one from Harvard.

Ted majored in mathematics, graduating in three years. In 1964, he received his master's degree from the University of Michigan, and in 1967, his Ph.D. Ted's thesis won a prestigious award as the best written in Michigan that year. Dr. Kaczynski accepted a teaching position at UCLA. For five years he taught advanced math, keeping to himself and making no friends.

In June 1969, Ted abruptly left his position at the university and made his way to Montana. About five miles outside Lincoln, he purchased an acre and a half of land and pitched a tent. Eventually he replaced the tent with a crude shack. He had no running water, no indoor plumbing and no income. He got around on an old wreck of a bicycle. Occasionally, Ted's mother or his brother, David, would send him money. Infrequently he accepted a handyman's job in town, but always quit within a few weeks.

Gradually the trappings of the brilliant mathematician fell away, to be replaced by what the good folks of Montana felt was another eccentric hermit in their midst. No one asked questions. No one cared. The bearded recluse in the old shack wasn't harming anyone.

Meanwhile, Ted's brother had graduated from Columbia University, married and settled into a social worker's position in Albany, New York. Although Ted didn't bother to attend his brother's wedding, the two men remained close.

In January 1995, Ted's mother decided to move to the Albany area to be closer to David and his wife, Linda. David was helping his mother move when he came across a box of letters written by Ted to their mother. Like most people in the United States, David had read the Unabomber's manifesto. As he went through his brother's letters, he was disconcerted at the repetition of phrases in the letters that were exactly the same as those in the manifesto. A feeling of dread came over him. Could his brother be the Unabomber?

David did a little checking. He discovered that after he or his mother sent money to Ted, a bomb would be mailed from outside Montana. Was it possible that Ted had travelled and mailed bombs from distant points in the country in order to avoid detection?

David related his suspicions to his mother. She was certain he must be wrong. Her brilliant son a terrorist and serial killer? It was unthinkable. But she did agree to cooperate. Through a lawyer, David contacted the FBI.

The little shack in Montana was surrounded by FBI agents. Ted was taken into custody without incident. Inside the cabin, agents found sketches of explosive devices, pipes similar to ones used by the Unabomber, chemicals, a partially completed pipe bomb and an array of tools. Most important of all, they came up with the original typewritten draft of the Unabomber's manifesto.

On May 4, 1998, Ted Kaczynski was sentenced to life imprisonment.

Alex Kelly

(UNITED STATES)

DARIEN, CONNECTICUT, is located only 35 miles northeast of Manhattan and is reputed to be the most affluent community in the entire United States. The close-knit suburb oozes big bucks, with its exclusive country clubs, yachts and manicured tennis courts. This is the place to be, close enough to the Big Apple yet surrounded by all that nature and money have to offer.

Alex Kelly was born and raised in Darien. His father, Joe, a self-made millionaire who accumulated his money in the plumbing game, thought the world of his teenage son. So did his mother, Melanie. They had good reason to feel they had an extraordinary offspring. Alex, 18, was a straight-A student at Darien High School. He was co-captain of the school's wrestling team and had just completed an undefeated season. In addition, the five-foot-nine-inch, 155-pound Alex was a star on the football team.

Oh, sure, there had been a few dark moments in the boy's past. When he was 16, Alex had hung out with the wrong crowd. The preppy "in" students were heavy drinkers and drug users. To finance their drug habit, Alex and his friends burglarized houses. When he was caught by authorities, Alex spent four months in a drug rehabilitation program. Upon being discharged from the program, he became an outstanding achiever. Past indiscretions were forgotten. Boys will be boys. That wild Kelly boy had turned his life around. Everyone in town was proud of him—right up until February 14, 1986.

That was the day Alex was charged with raping two teenage girls in two similar and brutal attacks, which took place four days apart, on February 10 and February 14. The two girls identified Alex as their attacker without ever having shared their experiences with each other. The first victim, a native of Darien, was attacked just five days after her 16th birthday. The second victim, a 17-year-old girl from nearby Stamford, claimed to have been attacked in Darien at 1:00 a.m. on Valentine's Day.

Later that same morning, Alex was questioned. Five days later, he was arrested and charged with two counts of first-degree sexual assault and one each of first-degree kidnapping and threatening. He was also charged with rape. Alex pleaded not guilty to all the charges. After spending 17 days in jail, he was freed on $200,000 bail put up by his parents.

It was a year before Alex's trial was scheduled to take place. In the meantime, high school officials decreed it would be best if their most notorious student did not return to the classroom. Because he was in his senior year and had outstanding marks, it was arranged for Alex to graduate in advance of his class. He received permission to leave the state. An expert skier, Alex rented an apartment in Aspen, Colorado, and waited out the time until his trial date.

On the day before Alex was to appear in court, his parents met with him in Colorado. On February 15, 1987, Alex Kelly, allegedly with $10,000 given to him by his parents and a valid passport, disappeared. He would remain at large for eight years.

Back home, all hell broke loose when Alex didn't show up in court. The FBI learned he had taken off for Europe. The TV program *America's Most Wanted* featured him on four different occasions.

We now know that Alex, a handsome, charming teenager, kept on the move. His passport, later turned over to the courts, bore the stamps of 15 countries, including Egypt, Holland, Italy, Turkey, Greece, Spain, Portugal and India. As the years passed, he often wintered in Chamoix, a well-known playground of the rich and famous. He also frequented the slopes around La Grave, a luxury resort.

In 1990, Alex made his home in Kladesholmen, a fishing village on an island off the west coast of Sweden. He met blond Elisabet Jansson while skiing. Soon they were living together and often vacationed in Switzerland. Alex worked in Elisabet's father's grocery store. He wrote to his family, "I would like to live like this forever."

In July 1994, the FBI raided the Kellys' home on Christie Hill Road in Darien. They gained access to the Kellys' safe-deposit box. Authorities found letters from Alex to his parents, as well as photos of his parents visiting him at various European resorts. Many pictures included his girlfriend, Elisabet. Later, Joe and Melanie Kelly would admit they had visited their son four times while he was a fugitive.

The most startling find in the raid was a letter addressed to Alex found in his mother's purse. Interpol was contacted in Sweden. Next day, with Alex's address in hand, police arrived on the lonely island that had been Alex's home for so many years. They were too late. It is alleged that his parents had used a pay phone to contact their son immediately after the raid on their home.

On the advice of the Kellys' lawyer, it was agreed that the time was ripe for Alex to return home and face the charges against him. Accompanied by a lawyer, he walked into a Zurich, Switzerland, police station and gave himself up.

Returned to the U.S., Alex was his usual charming self. It was as if time had stood still. His victims were now in their mid-twenties. Alex, 29, looked exactly as he had at the age of 18, when the crimes had been committed. His Swedish girlfriend, Elisabet, joined him in Darien. At Alex's bond hearing, a judge set bail at a million dollars. Once again, the Kellys raised the funds necessary to gain their son's freedom.

Alex had an eventful summer while awaiting trial. For whatever reason, Elisabet, who had been introduced as Alex's fiancée, abruptly returned to Sweden. Alex would not be without female company for long. He and Amy Molitor had been an item in high school. They now renewed their relationship. Alex and Amy were inseparable. They were seen together at all the watering holes in the area.

On July 19, Alex, Amy and some buddies were having a few cool ones at Jimmy's Seaside in Stamford. Alex sidled up to three women and became abusive. Someone called police and Alex was charged with disturbing the peace.

Two months later, he and Amy were driving home from a barbecue. Alex was speeding. When a police car approached, he accelerated and tried to outrun the officer. He flipped Amy's Nissan. Alex left her bleeding on the pavement and ran home. In hospital, Amy was treated for five broken ribs, as well as cuts and bruises to the head. Alex was questioned later that night. He denied any involvement in the wild chase. Two days later police laid myriad charges against him concerning the incident.

At Alex's rape trial, the jury could not come to an agreement and a mistrial was ordered. They would do it all over again. In the summer of 1997, Alex Kelly stood trial for a rape that had taken place 11 years earlier. Adrienne Ortolano, who only revealed her identity at the end of the second trial, told what it was like to be raped by Alex Kelly when she was a 16-year-old virgin. Now 27, this remarkable woman revealed how she had rejected a defence plea bargain in 1987 and again in 1996. She never wavered throughout extensive cross-examination during two trials, in which she was called a drunk, a drug user and a liar who had consented to sexual intercourse.

This is Adrienne Ortolano's story: She had attended a basketball game, after which she went to a party. Because she had an 11:30 p.m. curfew, she asked a friend to drive her home around 10:45. Her friend wasn't ready to leave. Alex overheard the conversation and volunteered a lift. Adrienne didn't hesitate. Everyone knew Alex had a steady girlfriend.

On the way, Alex pulled over beside the Wee Burn Country Club and tried to kiss her. When she resisted, he drove past her house and parked. He told her he wanted to make love and grabbed her by the throat. Alex said he'd kill her if she didn't cooperate. He took off her pants and ordered her to take off her top. At no time did he loosen his grip on her throat. The rape took place. Adrienne bled profusely.

After the rape was over, Alex said he would do it again and kill her if she told anyone. Then he drove her home. Adrienne told her brother and sister what had happened and they convinced her to tell her parents. Next day she was examined by a gynecologist, who said there were obvious signs of first-time intercourse. Adrienne Ortolano stated that her life was never the same from that night on.

Four days later, Alex allegedly raped and sodomized his second victim. He also warned the teenager he would kill her if she ever told anyone.

Alex Kelly, 30, was found guilty of rape. He was sentenced to 20 years' imprisonment, with the final four years suspended.

Theresa Knorr
(UNITED STATES)

THERESA CROSS KNORR was the mother from hell.

Our tale of torture and murder begins on July 6, 1964. That was the day 18-year-old Theresa shot her husband, Clifford, with a .30-30 rifle that just happened to be lying around their Sacramento, California, home. The couple's 11-month-old son, Howard, was the only witness to the killing. Theresa pleaded not guilty by reason of self-defence. She claimed that Clifford beat her unmercifully. During a squabble, she said she was able to wrest the weapon from his grasp and pull the trigger. A sympathetic jury took only an hour and a half to find her not guilty. A few months after her acquittal, Theresa gave birth to her second child, a girl she christened Sheila.

Never one to let grass grow under her feet, Theresa met and married a handsome Marine, Robert Knorr, the father of her third child, Susan. In the two years that followed, Theresa gave birth to William and Robert. By 1968 she had five children and was still only 22 years old.

Following the birth of their first child, Robert Knorr started to abuse Theresa and the children. Despite this, Theresa had a sixth baby on August 6, 1970, a little girl whom she named Terry. By the time Terry was born, Theresa had separated from her husband and eventually divorced him. A quickie marriage to Ronald Pulliam just as quickly ended in divorce.

In 1973, Theresa, still an attractive, slender woman, married for the fourth time. Chester Harris was a wealthy newspaper executive who moved Theresa and her six kids into a large home in the suburb of Orangevale.

For a few years everything went well with the Harris clan. Gradually, Theresa gained weight. The trim figure gave way to rolls of fat. The five-foot Theresa blossomed into a waddling 250-pound behemoth. With the pounds came an increasing propensity to abuse her children. She left son Howard to his own devices. At 14 years of age he had grown into a six-foot, 190-pounder.

Theresa forced William and Robert into making their three sisters' lives a living hell. They would hold the girls while their mother beat them with a whip. All of the children received beatings on a daily basis, day after day, year after year. They came to believe that beatings were a way of life.

Throughout their ordeal the youngsters attended school. No one bothered with Theresa's kids. Chester Harris left the house and filed for divorce. Theresa now called herself Knorr, as did the children. Susan and Sheila were the main objects of their mother's wrath. Theresa burned them with cigarettes, whipped them with switches and made them lie still for hours on end.

In 1983, Theresa shot her daughter Susan with a .22-calibre pistol. The bullet entered Susan's body under her left breast and lodged in her back without striking a vital organ. She stumbled back and fell into a bathtub. All the youngsters witnessed the shooting, but such was Theresa's hold on them that none ran from the house. Instead, they complied when their mother had them wash their sister's blood from the floor and walls.

Although critically wounded, Susan was still alive. Theresa put a pillow under her head, removed her clothing and threw a blanket over her. Days passed. Then weeks. Somehow, Susan survived. Uncharacteristically, Theresa fed her daughter, who, thoughout her ordeal, remained in the bathtub. Theresa even gave her antibiotics to alleviate infection.

Eventually Susan recovered and was able to extricate herself from her bathtub prison. Of all the children, only Howard, who by now had left the Knorr nest, did not witness the shooting. Unbelievably, Susan recovered without any formal medical assistance.

In the fall of 1983, Theresa sold her large home and moved into a cottage on Auburn Boulevard in North Sacramento. By downgrading, she pocketed a cool $50,000. Nothing changed for the Knorrs in their new home.

For no apparent reason, Susan became the main object of her mother's beatings. She was handcuffed to her bed each night and was given sleeping pills to keep her quiet. On one occasion Theresa threw scissors, which stuck in Susan's back. Theresa pulled the scissors out and applied a bandage. Another time she stood on Susan's neck and stepped away only when the girl turned blue.

For reasons known only to herself, Theresa decided that the bullet imbedded in Susan's back had to be removed. Susan was forced to lie on the kitchen floor. Theresa had a few medical instruments, some painkillers and a bottle of Old Crow. Susan downed most of the bottle and passed out. Her mother hacked at her back. It took two hours before she managed to remove the bullet. Susan was near death. All the Knorr offspring other than Howard witnessed the operation. William and Robert put diapers under their sister and left her lying there on the kitchen floor. A week later she was still there, more dead than alive.

On July 17, 1984, 10 days after the operation, Theresa, accompanied by William, Robert and Sheila, carried the still-alive Susan out of the house and drove her in the family's Ford LTD to a secluded area near Squaw Valley Creek. William doused Susan and some of her clothing with gasoline. He lit a match. Flames leapt from the burning pyre.

Later that night, truck driver Robert Eden saw the blaze and ran from his vehicle. Using his fire extinguisher, he put out the fire. He had come across the body of Susan Knorr. Although recognized as a homicide, the identity of the burnt corpse was a mystery to investigating officers.

Back at the Knorr residence, nothing changed. It was Sheila's turn. William and Robert would hold the girl while Theresa administered vicious beatings. Each night she was handcuffed to the kitchen table to prevent her from escaping.

When William told his mother that he was leaving to live with a woman, Theresa was fit to be tied, but there was little she could do. William left his mother's home. Her aggravation was taken out on Sheila, who she locked in a tiny closet and left to starve to death. Terry, the youngest of the family, was now 14 years old. She would hold her hands over her ears when she heard her sister screaming to be let out of the closet. As each day passed, Sheila's screams became weaker. On June 21, 1985, there was no sound coming from the closet. Theresa opened the door. Sheila lay dead in her own filth.

Theresa summoned William from his home to assist in disposing of the body. With Robert's help, they managed to place Sheila's body in a cardboard box. Out to the LTD the strange family went with their gruesome cargo. The box was deposited near Martes Creek Lake. A fisherman stumbled across the box containing the body of Sheila Knorr. Authorities were unable to identify it. No connection was made between the two women's bodies found about 15 miles from each other one year apart.

In short order, Terry, the youngest of the Knorr brood, became a prostitute. Robert moved out and Theresa sought greener pastures. She changed her name to Theresa Cross and moved to Salt Lake City and a new life. Meanwhile, Robert Knorr got into serious trouble. He killed a bartender during a holdup and was sentenced to 16 years' imprisonment.

Theresa got a job taking care of an elderly lady. The 86-year-old woman adored her, as did the entire family. Although still a big woman, Theresa managed to shed 60 pounds. She had orchestrated the deaths of her two daughters and had escaped detection for nine years. She had manipulated her sons and daughter so that their fear of her ensured their silence.

It was the youngest, Terry, who could not live with her guilty knowledge. She contacted authorities and told the horrendous details of her life. Theresa was traced to Salt Lake City, where she was arrested and charged with double murder, as were her sons, William and Robert.

Robert was not difficult to locate. He was in prison. He pleaded guilty to being an accessory to the murder of his sisters. His prison sentence runs concurrent to the time he was already serving.

William, who was the only one of Theresa's family to lead a normal life after leaving her home, was able to plea bargain a sentence of time already spent in prison awaiting trial and was placed on five years' probation.

Theresa pleaded guilty to the first-degree murder of her two daughters, Susan and Sheila. She was sentenced to 25 years to life for each murder, the sentences to run consecutively. She will be eligible for parole in 2027, when she will be 80 years old.

Pamela Knuckles

(UNITED STATES)

YOU WOULDN'T CALL NANCY KNUCKLES a good mother. Still, she didn't deserve the fate doled out to her by her not-so-loving children.

Nancy's own parents were highly devout Roman Catholics who raised their daughter in the strict tenets of the church. As a teenager, Nancy rebelled at the regimented life and left home. At the same time, she left the Catholic Church and became a Southern Baptist.

Soon after switching religions, Nancy met Robert Knuckles, a part-time singer of western ballads. When Bob wasn't singing in bars, he was downing those establishments' main stock-in-trade. Bob was a boozer through and though. The marriage lasted eight years and produced a son, Barton, and two daughters, Pamela and Deborah. Upon becoming a single mother, Nancy took up the responsibility of raising her children. At the same time, she managed to graduate as a registered nurse. Once more, she switched religions, this time giving the Seventh Day Adventists a try.

Nancy lived in a comfortable three-bedroom home on East Vermont Street in Villa Park, a suburb of Chicago. To make ends meet for herself and her children, Nancy worked as a nurse and held down a second job as a cook in a local restaurant. She really led four lives: nurse, cook, religious zealot and homemaker. She was terrific at the first three, but the methods she employed in bringing up her children left something to be desired.

Nancy was religious to the point of fanatacism. She forsook almost all worldly pleasures. There were no movies, TV or dancing in her life. Denial was her watchword. Trouble was, she expected her three offspring to follow her example. The children, who saw other teenagers enjoying themselves, rebelled at their mother's strict code of behaviour. Even the slightest indiscretion on the youngsters' parts resulted in a beating with a garden hose. These beatings were almost a daily occurrence and were followed by a prayer for forgiveness and a discussion about the offence committed. Pamela meekly consented to the continual punishment, but Bart argued with his mother and received further punishment, such as being locked in a dark closet for prolonged periods of time. On every occasion, Nancy explained that she was receiving commands from God and that she really loved them all dearly.

For some time, no one knew what was going on behind the pleasant facade on East Vermont Street. The children were beaten for making a noise, for failing to wash out a sink or for leaving a spot on a washed dish. Any little thing brought Nancy's wrath down on her children. This strict lifestyle and the continual beatings did not bring about the results Nancy desired. When 13-year-old Bart stole money from her purse and attempted to steal her car, Nancy sent him off to an institution for delinquent children in Nebraska. Her church helped out with the cost.

At home, Pamela defied her mother. She attended movies, watched television, dated, smoked and drank alcohol. In short, the very behaviour her mother had preached against was now Pamela's lifestyle. There was little Nancy could do. She worked at two jobs and didn't have much time to spend with her two girls. When she was at home, she reviewed the girls' foul deeds, had them confess, beat them and prayed with them.

At age 15, Pamela moved out of her mother's house to live with a boyfriend. The arrangement didn't work out. Pamela soon learned that her boyfriend was as possessive and cruel as her mother. She moved back home. Her move coincided with Bart's return home from Nebraska. For the first time in years, Nancy and her three children were once more living under the same roof. The Knuckles brood no longer listened to their mother. Nancy worked at her two jobs. The kids partied. They had a circle of rather wild friends who soon realized that here was an unsupervised house where you could smoke and drink all day long without being disturbed. Even when Nancy came home and hollered at everyone present to assist her in cleaning up, she was more or less ignored.

Nancy did seek some help. She spoke to friends at her church about her undisciplined teenage children. The church members told her they would pray for her. The prayers obviously didn't help.

One brisk day in November 1984, Nancy was preparing to leave her house to go to her job at the Health Oasis Restaurant. All three youngsters were at home, along with several of their friends. Pamela sneaked up behind her mother, placed a garrotte around her neck, pulled it tight and screamed, "Die bitch, die bitch!" Nancy fell to the floor. One of Pamela's friends, Dennis Morris, grabbed both ends of the ligature from Pamela and continued to pull it tighter. Bart walked into the room and felt his mother's pulse. Nancy was still breathing. He fetched a plastic garbage bag and placed it over her head. The next time he checked her pulse, she had ceased breathing.

Nancy didn't show up at either of her two jobs, which was unusual for her. Nothing much was done about her absence until police received an anonymous call a few days later informing them that Nancy's children had killed her and had placed her body in a trunk. The caller said the trunk had been dumped into nearby Salt Creek.

Investigators called at the Knuckles's home and found the three teenagers partying with several other youngsters. A few questions was all it took to have the details of the murder tumble from the participants' lips. The killing had been planned. The day before the murder, they had agreed that Nancy would no longer scream at them and tell them what to do. They would kill her and run the house themselves. Little thought was given to the fact that Nancy was the sole support of the entire family and hangers-on. Finally, it was decided: they would strangle Nancy. Pamela made the garrotte out of a strong piece of thin rope.

The day of her demise, Nancy was in a foul mood. She lectured her offspring about the difficulty she was having supporting them and their friends who had been hanging around the house for a full week. Bart gave the signal to strike. Pamela drew the garrotte around her mother's neck; Dennis pulled it tight and Bart finished the job with the plastic garbage bag. Everyone helped move the body down into the basement where it was placed into an old steamer trunk. Steve Wright and Dennis Morris loaded the trunk into David Duke's car. Together they dumped the trunk into Salt Creek.

The local fire department hauled the trunk from the creek. Sure enough, it contained the body of Nancy Knuckles. The strange case of the houseful of youngsters who turned on Nancy shocked the state of Illinois and the country. All were arrested and charged with various crimes. Pamela Knuckles and Dennis Morris pleaded guilty to murder. Both received 33-year prison sentences. Bart Knuckles was found guilty of murder and concealing a homicide. He was sentenced to a total of 37 years' imprisonment. David Duke was sentenced to four years' imprisonment for concealing a homicide. Steve Wright received two years on the same charge. Deborah Knuckles was charged with concealing a homicide and was sentenced to two years' probation.

On August 31, 1990, Pamela Knuckles was released from prison on a technicality and a new trial was ordered. She had been told by her lawyer at her original trial that she faced the death penalty. That was erroneous information, since she was 17 at the time of her mother's murder and the minimum age for the death penalty in Illinois at that time was 18.

While incarcerated, Pamela received her bachelor of arts degree. She is now free, awaiting a new trial.

Harold Loughans

(ENGLAND)

ROSE ADA ROBINSON was a capable 63-year-old who operated the John Barleycorn, a well-known pub in Portsmouth, England. Rose had been running the place for 40 years since her husband's death shortly after their marriage. Rather than take up another profession, resourceful Rose had continued to run the pub until it became one of those bustling establishments that always seemed to be full of chatty, thirsty patrons.

Each night Rose cleared the cash register of the day's take, which usually amounted to approximately £500. She would joke with her last customers of the night as she placed the cash in two large handbags. She would then retire to her quarters above the John Barleycorn, where she lived alone.

On the night of November 28, 1943, Rose's barman, a man named Welch, closed the establishment at around 10:30 p.m. and cleaned up before leaving the premises. As he left, he heard Rose bolt the front door behind him. Next morning, a woman who helped clean the upstairs flat found Rose's body on the floor of her bedroom. She had been strangled. The flat had been ransacked and the cash contents of her handbags were missing.

Police were summoned. They noted that a downstairs window had been broken and the catch had been forced. The back door to the John Barleycorn was unbolted and unlocked. It was apparent that the killer had gained entry through the window and had exited through the door. The intruder had left no fingerprints, but had lost a lone black button, which was found on the sill of the broken window.

An examination of the pub owner's body indicated that Rose had been manually strangled to death. There was a clear thumbprint on her throat and three minor bruises, no doubt made by the killer's fingers.

Detectives thought that they were investigating a rather routine murder committed during the course of a robbery, yet as events unfolded, Rose Robinson's murder would become unique in the annals of English crime and, arguably, the only such case ever to take place in the entire world.

A month passed without a solution to the identity of Rose's killer. Then, quite unexpectedly, the killer was found. Two police officers were tailing a suspicious-looking rounder along Waterloo Road in London. Their quarry walked into a restaurant, and there, attempted to sell a new pair of men's shoes. The officers, believing that the shoes were stolen, took the man into custody. He surprised them by stating, "I'm wanted for things far more serious than this. The Yard wants me. It's the trap door for me now. I'm glad you picked me up."

At the police station, Harold Loughans continued to talk, "I'm glad I'm in. I've been through hell for the past three weeks. I've been a bastard all my life and I'll finish as I've lived. I was sorry for it the moment I done it. I haven't slept since. It preyed on my mind. She must have had a weak heart, poor old girl."

Harold broke into crying jags from time to time, but had an uncontrollable urge to continue talking. He told officers, "It's a relief to get it off my mind. I had to stop her screaming. All the jobs I have been doing have been worrying me, and since I did the big job at Portsmouth, where I got the money when I strangled the old woman at the beer house, to get it off my mind I've been doing jobs every day."

An examination of Harold's jacket revealed that it had no front buttons. He told police that when he noticed he had lost a button after the killing, he pulled all the buttons off his jacket. Fibres gathered from a mat in Rose's bedroom matched fibres taken from Harold's clothing. Harold was charged with Rose's murder. He stood trial in March 1944 in Winchester.

At his trial, Harold denied that he had confessed to the murder. From the witness stand he stated that the entire story had been made up by the police. He displayed his right hand, which was deformed. Harold had only a thumb and four half fingers. He argued that he couldn't strangle anyone if he tried with all his might. In addition, the defence produced four witnesses who swore that Harold had been in an air raid shelter on the night of the murder. They all remembered him because of his deformed hand. The jury reported that they could not reach a verdict and the presiding judge reluctantly ordered a retrial.

Two weeks later, Harold's second trial was held at London's Old Bailey. This time, the defence produced famed pathologist Sir Bernard Spillsbury, who emphatically stated that it would have been impossible for Harold, due to his deformed hand, to have strangled Rose Robinson. The jury, deeply impressed, found Harold not guilty.

As Harold walked out of court, police were waiting for him with open arms. He was immediately arrested and charged with the various robberies he had confessed to when he told officers that he had killed Rose. During one of these robberies, he had very nearly killed another woman, whom he had struck over the head with a heavy flashlight.

Harold was still serving his prison sentences over 19 years later when he sued the Sunday newspaper, *The People,* for libel. The paper, in publishing the memoirs of J. C. Casswell, the lawyer who had twice prosecuted Harold, had mentioned that at both trials Casswell had said that Harold Loughans had been fortunate to be acquitted.

In 1963, Harold found himself once more in a courtroom. This time he was the plaintiff and as such had to prove his case against the newspaper. In essence, the old murder case was retried in a civil court. It was proven that Harold was the killer of Rose Robinson two decades earlier. The newspaper won the strange case. Harold, who could not be tried again for murder, was returned to prison.

A few months later, Harold, suffering from stomach cancer, was released from prison. One day he showed up at the office of *The People* newspaper. The old killer, now a frail, dying man, wanted to get something off his chest. He confessed to the murder of Rose Robinson and had his photo taken writing out his confession in longhand. In part it read: "They tell me I have cancer and haven't long to live. Before I die, I want to make a confession. I want to say I done that job. I did kill the woman in the public house in Portsmouth."

Harold Loughans died in 1965, at age 69.

Earl Lund & Fred Phillips

(CANADA)

PLAIN AND SIMPLE, they were two bad cats. That's what the good folks of Charlottetown, Prince Edward Island, thought of Fred Phillips and Earl Lund.

At age 17, Fred was convicted of breaking and entering. For that indiscretion he was sent to reform school. A few years later he was caught stealing a truck, an offence that landed him in the local jail. In 1939, he was apprehended breaking into houses. This time he landed in Dorchester Penitentiary.

Earl's record was just as impressive. As a teenager he was arrested for breaking and entering. Upon his release, Earl dabbled in the illegal liquor trade, a profession which saw him charged with no less than 35 offences. When he was captured after escaping from jail, the local law threw him in Dorchester Penitentiary, where he became good friends with fellow Islander Fred Phillips.

On the night of January 30, 1941, the two young men (Earl was 29, Fred 25) were celebrating Earl's release from Dorchester pen, where he had spent the last seven years on an armed robbery charge. It had snowed heavily on the island that January and five-foot snowbanks lined both sides of Charlottetown's King Street. Earl and Fred slipped into the Capitol Theatre with a bottle of bootleg hootch to comfort them. When they came out of the theatre at the conclusion of a double bill, they were feeling no pain. Fred brushed back his mop of red hair and suggested that conditions were getting mighty dry. Where could a fellow get a bottle of that lousy two percent beer or, at worst, a bottle of pop?

It was after 11:00 p.m. Not much was open. The two men strolled down deserted King Street until they found themselves in front of Trainor's Meat Market. The sign in front of the store was a misnomer. While Trainor sold meat, he also sold just about everything else. Peter Trainor, at 78 years of age, was an energetic, healthy man who never missed a day's work. He lived in a flat above the store.

Earl and Fred saw a light on in the store. They tried the door and were mildly surprised to find it was open that late at night. The two men stepped inside, closing the self-locking door behind them.

As luck would have it, a short time after the men were in the store, two local constables, Sterns Webster and Anthony Lund, were making their routine rounds of Charlottetown's streets. They were surprised to see that the lights were still on in Peter Trainor's store. As they were pondering this rather strange circumstance, they observed a man dashing around the corner. It was only a fleeting glance. Because the snow was so high, they only saw the top of the man's head. He was wearing a hat. The two officers knew that Trainor turned off his lights and closed his store promptly at 10:30 each night.

Constable Anthony Lund, who incidentally was a cousin of Earl Lund's, peered into the store. He recognized his ne'er-do-well cousin standing behind the cash register. The constable tapped his billy against the store window. When he received no response, he smashed in the plate-glass window and quickly entered the store.

All hell broke loose. One of the intruders turned out the lights. The two desperate men dashed around attempting to find a back door in the pitch dark. They bumped into stacks of boxes and bottles in what was Trainor's storage space. Earl was cornered trying to exit via a rear window.

A voice from the top of the stairs leading to Trainor's flat shouted, "Come on up and get me too." There stood Fred Phillips aiming Trainor's .22-calibre Smith & Wesson at the unarmed officers. Fred attempted to fire the weapon, but it didn't function. In desperation he threw the gun, along with a number of pop bottles, at Constable Webster.

Undeterred, Webster managed to get up the stairs and grapple with Fred until both men tumbled down the stairs. In short order, the two police officers got the best of the scuffle and turned on the lights.

Webster and Lund were shocked at the sight that greeted them. There was blood everywhere—on boxes, on the walls, as well as a distinct trail of blood on the floor leading to the rear of the store. There the police found the horribly hacked body of Peter Trainor. He had been stabbed 22 times. One of the thrusts had nearly decapitated the elderly storekeeper.

Next morning, the two men had sobered up and were made to realize the seriousness of their predicament. This was no big-city murder. This was the land of Anne of Green Gables. Murders were few and far between on Prince Edward Island.

In June 1941, the two accused stood trial for the murder of Peter Trainor. There seemed little doubt they had committed the crime. Still, no one had actually seen the murder take place. The defence attorney put forward the theory that the stranger the police had seen dashing around a corner was the real culprit. He claimed his clients had been half-drunk when they strolled into the store, not realizing they had stumbled onto a murder scene.

Through the testimony of doctors who took the witness stand, he was further able to prove that the knife produced by the prosecution was not the murder weapon. The doctors stated the knife on exhibit could not have inflicted the horrendous slash that had almost decapitated Trainor. The defence claimed the real murder weapon was never found because the real murderer had taken it away with him.

In addition, the defence produced a friend of Earl Lund's, one Benjamin Gauthier, who claimed to have seen the elusive stranger run from the store before Earl and Fred went through the door. Gauthier said he was across the street at the time and saw the whole thing. He also recognized the two police officers when they showed up. Unfortunately, Gauthier didn't recognize the man in the hat who he claimed had run from the store.

Under cross-examination, Gauthier admitted that although he heard the window breaking, he continued on up the street. Because he had a police record himself, he didn't want to get involved. Besides, he was known to take the odd nip of the devil rum himself and felt he had better keep his nose clean. Benjamin Gauthier wasn't the most reliable witness ever to grace a witness stand.

The two accused testified on their own behalf. Earl told of going to the movies, drinking a bottle of moonshine and seeing the light on in the store. He claimed that just before he and Fred went inside, they saw a stranger going around the corner up the street.

Once in the store, they hollered out for Trainor, but received no response. All of a sudden there was a knock on the window. Earl recognized his cousin, Anthony Lund, and told Fred that cops were outside. Fred turned out the lights. Quickly the two men decided to get out the back way. It was rough going in the dark. Boxes and bottles tumbled to the floor. The officers approached with flashlights. The two men scurried about until they were overpowered.

Fred Phillips told much the same story as his fellow accused. Under cross-examination he was asked, "If you were in the store not doing anything improper, why didn't you open the door and let the policemen in?" Fred replied, "They would have arrested us if there was anything wrong."

No one believed the two small-time career criminals. Everyone in the courtroom knew that Fred Phillips had stood on the stairs and had attempted to shoot the officers in cold blood. Would he take such desperate measures if he really believed he was caught in the store doing nothing wrong? On the other hand, being convicted of any offence meant long prison terms for both men.

As for the stranger seen near the store—if he was totally innocent of any involvement in the crime, he certainly heard of the murder and chose not to come forward. If he was the killer as the defence insinuated, he had good reason to maintain his silence. He has never been identified.

At the Phillips/Lund trial, the prosecution put forth the theory that the unknown stranger could have been an accomplice of the two accused. Quite possibly, following the code of honour among thieves, they never revealed his identity.

Fred Phillips and Earl Lund were found guilty of the murder of Peter Trainor. On August 20, 1941, they consumed a last meal of chicken sandwiches and tea. At 2:00 a.m., both men walked unaided to the gallows. They have the dubious distinction of being the last men executed in the province of Prince Edward Island.

Lynda Lyon & George Sibley
(UNITED STATES)

THE JULIA TUTWILER PRISON FOR WOMEN is tucked away off the beaten path, about 25 kilometres north of Montgomery. It is here that the state of Alabama houses its female prisoners. The institution is the only women's prison in the state.

It is 1997. Warden Earnest Harrelson, an ardent bow-and-arrow hunter, sits in his office surrounded by his mounted trophies, which seem to stare down at us through hollow sockets as we discuss the prison population.

According to Harrelson, there are approximately 700 inmates in the institution. A smile crossed his face when I told him five years ago that Ontario had just abolished the $5-a-week stipend received by all inmates. He was quick to point out that no such remuneration was available in Alabama. "It used to be 25 cents a week. We called it tobacco money, but that was cut out about a year ago."

At the time, there were four women on death row in Julia Tutwiler Prison. One of these women, Lynda Lyon, was the reason for my visit to the Deep South.

The ivory-painted floor-to-ceiling bars opened electronically as a prison official led me to a private cubicle. Apologetically, he instructed me to return to my car and leave my wallet locked and secure. Upon my return, he explained, as he pat-searched me, that my car keys would be returned to me when I left. My shoes were removed and tapped on the concrete floor. Contraband can be smuggled into the prison concealed in the heels of shoes. At last I was led to a stark-white office containing nothing but a table and two chairs. A guard told me that Lynda Lyon would be joining me shortly.

Lynda entered, accompanied by a guard. Could this attractive woman with the bleached-blond hair, large blue eyes and trim figure be the killer I travelled so far to see? I extended my hand. Lynda stepped away, explaining that her hands were handcuffed behind her back. After a guard unlocked them, we shook hands. The stern-faced guard took her position outside the office door.

In her spotless white jumpsuit produced by fellow inmates at 25 cents an hour, Lynda related her tale as she had so often since that day in October 1993, when she shot and killed a police officer. She was born in Orlando, Florida, graduated from high school and completed some college courses before she left school for a career as a hairstylist. At age 19, Lynda married a colleague in the hairstyling game, the first of her five husbands. The couple had one child. In the succeeding years, Lynda, who we can only assume was a free spirit, sailed the Gulf of Mexico for over a year with one husband; with another, she toured the country on a motorcycle.

It was an altercation with Karl Block, husband number four, that precipitated the series of misadventures that would ultimately land her on Alabama's death row. She was 35 when she married 71-year-old Karl. Lynda was quick to point out that, despite his age, Karl was an active, virile male. In short order, the pair had a son, Gordon.

In 1991, Lynda met George Sibley at a Libertarian meeting in Orlando. The pair became friends and eventually lovers. A year later, she and husband Karl agreed to disagree. They would divorce. Karl would leave their home to Lynda and young Gordon. Meanwhile, she and George became deeply involved in the Libertarian movement. Together they launched a magazine containing articles that railed against corruption in government. In the process, according to Lynda, they made many enemies.

For reasons of his own, Karl changed his mind about legally turning over the home to Lynda. She decided to have a tête-à-tête with him in an effort to change his mind. George accompanied her to Karl's residence. Lynda told me, with a degree of pride, that she didn't carry along her gun to the meeting. Instead, she took a knife.

During the meeting, an argument escalated into a scuffle. Karl was cut in the chest. To hear Lynda tell it, the wound was little more than a superficial scratch, although she admitted, "It did bleed." George and Lynda bandaged the wound and left.

At 2:30 a.m., the pair was arrested and charged with domestic violence. They spent five days in jail before being released on bond. According to Lynda, they were advised to plead no contest. While awaiting sentencing, they deluged officials with documents claiming corruption in high places and their denial to a fair trial. They were now in danger of being sent to prison for three years. They decided to flee the state. When they didn't show up for sentencing, Lynda and George officially became fugitives.

Lynda, George and nine-year-old Gordon made their way to Alabama. Near the small town of Opelika, they stopped at the Pepperell Shopping Center. Lynda walked to a pay phone in front of a Wal-Mart store, while Gordon and George remained in the car. Unbeknownst to the fugitives, a woman, Ramona Robertson, thought something was amiss in the Mustang hatchback. A young boy, alone with a man, plus pillows and bedding in the car, aroused her suspicions. She spotted Officer Roger Motley of the Opelika Police Department coming out of a nearby store and told him of her concern. Later, at Lynda's trial, this same woman swore that the young boy in the car was attempting to get her attention. She believed he was being held against his will. Lynda vehemently claims that this witness was lying.

Officer Motley drove his cruiser up and down the rows of cars until he located the maroon Mustang described by Robertson. He got out of his vehicle. George saw the officer approach and he too got out of his car. Officer Motley asked to see George's driver's licence. George, who didn't have a licence, tried to explain that he had documents in the glove compartment of the Mustang exempting him from carrying a licence. Motley responded by asking George to place his hands on the vehicle. When George didn't react to the command, Officer Motley, according to Lynda, appeared to reach for his weapon. Investigating officers claim George was the first to reach for his gun.

At any rate, George pulled out his own gun. Motley turned and dashed behind the police cruiser. Lynda heard shots, saw shoppers scampering for cover, and then took in the scene of the gunfight between the policeman and George. She ran up behind the officer, who didn't see her. Lynda drew her gun and fired several shots. One plowed directly into Motley's chest as he turned in surprise to face a second adversary. Officer Motley was able to crawl into his police car and radio the code for "Officer needs all possible assistance." He attempted to drive away, but smashed into several parked cars and came to a stop. Rushed to nearby East Alabama Medical Center, he was pronounced dead six minutes after the gunfight. Later, an autopsy revealed that Officer Motley had been shot four times.

What actually took place during the shootout? George claims that the police officer was about to shoot him. Lynda says she shot the officer in order to save her husband's life. Both profess to have shot in self-defence. Investigators into the killing believe Lynda shot Officer Motley in cold blood while hubby George was firing several shots at the same time.

The situation begs the following question: Do law-abiding citizens drive around with two rifles, two handguns and enough ammunition to supply a small army? Lynda explained that both she and George had taken weapons training. When they loaded their car in Orlando with a few valuables from their residence, it was only natural for them to take their guns. "Besides, I always carry a weapon," Lynda told me.

George had been shot in the arm. With Gordon in tears, the desperate pair took off. A few miles down a country road, they sighted a police roadblock. George braked to a stop.

The police, weapons drawn, approached the Mustang. Lynda shouted to the closest officer, "Stop. I have a child in the car." After a brief conference on his radio, the officer responded, "Okay, ma'am, we won't shoot. You can let the child go." Lynda opened the door and saw her son scamper to safety.

George and Lynda sat in their vehicle for four hours. Their situation was hopeless. As evening fell, they observed that regular police officers had pulled back, while a SWAT team took up a position close by. Inside the Mustang, the fugitives discussed their options, not the least of which was double suicide. George and Lynda made deals with police in exchange for a peaceful surrender. In the end, police gave the stalling couple five minutes to make up their minds. They put down their weapons and, with raised hands, surrendered.

George Sibley was tried first. The outcome was something of a foregone conclusion. He was found guilty of capital murder. The Alabama jury recommended the death sentence.

Lynda dismissed her court-appointed lawyers and acted as her own counsel. Again, the result was predictable. She was found guilty. At the sentencing portion of her trial, Lynda stated that she had brought forth all the pertinent issues at her trial and refused to beg for her life. She was sentenced to death.

Now Lynda sits in her death row cell refusing to exercise the many appeals available to her. She is determined to go directly to the Congress of the United States, charging the American Bar Association with fraud and treason. She believes that by handling her own affairs she stands a good chance of success. Not many agree with her. Her husband, George, is on death row in Holman Prison in Atmore, a small community in southern Alabama. George and Lynda have the dubious distinction of being the only married couple sentenced to death in the entire United States. In August 2000, the pair filed an appeal of their sentences weighing a whopping five pounds, most of it railing against judicial and political corruption.

The United States, in common with many countries where capital punishment is practised, is reluctant to execute its female killers. Since the resumption of executions in 1977, only nine women, beginning with Velma Barfield of North Carolina in 1984, have been put to death in America.

Far more reluctant to execute females is the state of Alabama. The last woman to be put to death in the yellowhammer state was Rhonda Bell Martin, who was convicted of killing the fourth of her five husbands. She also murdered three daughters, her mother and another husband. Martin was executed at Holman Prison on October 11, 1957, decades ago.

Lynda Lyon is well aware of the electric chair in Holman Prison that awaits both her and her husband. I asked her one final question: "Lynda, as we sit here, do you feel you will be put to death in the electric chair?"

Without hesitation, she replied, "No."

As I retrieved my belongings and left the Julia Tutwiler Prison, I couldn't help but feel she might be mistaken.

Louis Mercier

(UNITED STATES)

LOUIS MERCIER CUT QUITE A SWATH among the single and oh-so-eligible young ladies of Pittsfield, Massachusetts. The transplanted French Canadian could be seen most winter evenings gliding across the city's outdoor rinks, decked out in a white cardigan and jaunty toque complete with pompoms bouncing in the breeze.

Louis was a snappy dresser, glib talker, and besides, that man could skate as smooth as silk. No wonder. Louis originally hailed from northern Quebec, where donning the blades is one of the few, if not the only, means of passing a cold winter's eve. *Pardonnez-moi,* great lovers also come from that part of the country. But that's another story.

Unbeknownst to the young women who skated across the ice with Louis was his little secret. His wife's name was Eugenie. Louis had her stashed away in a rundown flat in the city's slums. None of his lady friends knew of Eugenie's existence. She hardly ever left her seedy flat due to the flock of children she and Louis had brought into the world in the preceding years. Louis, the cad, was generally unemployed. He barely supported himself and his family with handouts from the city's welfare funds.

During that winter of 1924 Louis skated with one particular young woman. She firmly believed that her beau was unattached. The couple became an item. Louis, who had ice water running through his veins, asked the winsome lass to marry him. His girl-friend, possibly charmed out of her skates by the French Canadian accent, agreed to marry our Louis.

Things were going along more smoothly than a finely executed triple salchow when Louis's girlfriend discovered that her betrothed was a married man. What's more, he had a flat brimming over with children. She was furious. Louis begged. He pleaded. He promised an immediate divorce. Finally, the distraught girl told her lover to come back to her when he could show her proof that he had divorced his wife. All that day Louis thought and thought. There had to be some way to facilitate a clean separation from his Eugenie. After all, he was from Quebec, where separation has always been considered a viable alternative.

Louis decided to eliminate his wife. To implement his plan, he visited a silver-plating plant in town where he had performed odd jobs in the past. He casually strolled through the plant with the manager. While making small talk, Louis displayed an uncharac-teristic interest in a large crock of striking solution. The manager explained that the contents of the crock were partially made up of sodium cyanide, a poison used in the process of cleaning silver. To the manager's surprise, Louis said he just happened to have a small bottle with him and would like some of that solution to apply to a rusty penny bank he had at home. The manager told Louis that he was mistaken. The striking solution was not the answer to his problem. When Louis insisted, the plant manager told him in no uncertain terms that he wouldn't give that particular lethal liquid to anyone.

A discouraged Louis took a few spins around the rink before returning to Eugenie and the kids. Two days later he paid another social call to the silver-plating plant. This time, he unobtrusively made his way to the room where the sodium cyanide was kept.

Devious Louis had brought along a bottle labelled Paregoric. He attached a piece of metal wire to the neck of the bottle and lowered it into the deadly solution. Upon extracting the bottle, he put a stopper in its neck and tucked it into his overcoat pocket. Louis chatted with a few employees and left the premises.

Returning to his apartment, Louis placed the bottle on a shelf where it was usually kept. He knew very well that his wife used paregoric to ease her monthly menstrual pains. It was the day before Eugenie's menstrual discomfort was due.

Next day, young boys who lived in the flat below the Merciers went upstairs to visit their playmates. When they entered the flat they were shocked to find the children huddled in a corner, crying. As the youngsters took in this scene, they heard excruciating screams emanating from the bedroom. They ran out to fetch a neighbour. This neighbour made her way to the Merciers' bedroom. There was Eugenie, frothing at the mouth, eyes staring and glassy. The stricken woman was breathing spasmodically until she stopped breathing altogether.

At that precise moment Louis walked into the room. The neighbour, who was no great fan of the skater's, bluntly declared, "Your wife is dead. How did this happen?" By way of explanation, Louis pointed to a bottle on the shelf in the kitchen. "She took that stuff," he said. Louis went on the explain that when his wife rose that morning she said to him, *"Louis, je me sens étourdie,"* which, as everyone knows, means, "Louis, I am dizzy."

According to Louis, his wife collapsed. He helped her into bed and asked her if she had taken anything. Eugenie, in great distress, could only mumble, *"Ma médecine."* Louis then explained to his neighbour that he had gone out to fetch a doctor, but unfortunately the doctor was out. The best he could do was leave a message for him to come to the Merciers' flat as soon as possible. Louis philosophically added, "I guess it's too late now."

Louis's neighbour wasn't swallowing the tale of woe. She went directly to the police with her suspicions. Detectives visited the flat and immediately solicited medical assistance. Dr. Colt confiscated the bottle marked Paregoric and sent it for analysis to the local General Electric Co. chemical laboratories. Within an hour they reported that the bottle contained sodium cyanide.

Authorities then did something that would never be tolerated today. In 1924, they got away with the subterfuge. Eugenie's funeral was attended by those few who knew her, as well as funeral officials and her husband. The coffin was lowered into the grave but, unbeknownst to Louis, it was not covered with earth. Instead, when the funeral party had dispersed, the body was raised and removed for an autopsy.

The autopsy indicated that Eugenie had been poisoned. The contents of her stomach revealed the presence of sodium cyanide. The bottle marked Paregoric contained traces of silver as well as the poison. Police traced the solution in the bottle to the silver-plating plant, where the manager told detectives of the great interest Louis Mercier had expressed in the poison.

Police picked Louis up at the local outdoor rink, where he was vigorously attempting to alleviate his sorrow by getting that salchow down cold. Taken into custody, Louis initially professed to be innocent. He then surprised all by confessing, but soon recanted his confession.

It mattered little. Louis stood trial for the murder of his wife. When the prosecution produced Louis's overcoat as evidence, his goose was cooked. An expert had analyzed the pocket of the coat and found that it contained traces of sodium cyanide. When Louis had placed the wet bottle in his pocket, some of the solution had adhered to the cloth.

Louis Mercier was found guilty of murder in the second degree and received a sentence of 20 years' imprisonment. It is reported that before being transferred to prison he made several inquiries regarding the institution's recreational facilities. In particular, he wanted to know if it had a skating rink.

Richard Minns

(UNITED STATES)

THIS TEXAS TRAGEDY had its roots on the ski slopes of Aspen, Colorado. That's where Barbara Piotrowski met Richard Minns.

Barbara was 24 years old. She had the body and looks of a movie star. Long, blond hair accentuated her finely chiselled features. She had won several beauty contests and had been a part-time model since the age of 16.

No dumb blonde, our Barbara achieved straight A's in school. The day she met Dick on the slopes, she was taking pre-med courses at night. From the time she was little more than a child she had wanted to be a medical doctor.

When they met in 1977, Dick was 48 years old. On that fateful January day, he told Barbara he owned a chain of health clubs in Texas and made his headquarters in Houston. No flies on Dick either. He was a health nut and it showed. Dick Minns had the body of a Greek god.

Barbara was impressed, if a little dubious, about her new friend's financial status. By the time their stay in Aspen was over, the pair agreed to exchange telephone numbers. Barbara returned to California and her studies at UCLA; Dick to Texas and his health clubs.

Within a few weeks, Dick was on the phone imploring Barbara to join him in Aspen that March. Initially, she resisted the invitation, but gradually gave in. At Aspen the pair were inseparable. They soon became lovers. Both were totally intrigued with each other.

Dick coaxed Barbara to move to Houston and live with him. She could continue her medical studies there. He claimed he couldn't live without her. For her part, Barbara had never met anyone quite like Dick Minns. He was the answer to every woman's dream. She moved to Houston.

What Dick neglected to tell Barbara was that he was married—well-married for the past 25 years—and the proud father of three children. His daughter was older than Barbara. Wife Mimi was an active partner in his health club business.

Dick had started out in the advertising game and had switched to the health-club business when that industry was in its infancy. He made it big, real big. While still in his twenties, Richard Minns was worth several million dollars. He called his luxurious health spas Presidents Club.

Later he would pioneer women's health clubs, which he christened First Lady. At the zenith of his business success, Dick owned 32 clubs throughout the United States and employed more than a thousand people. He and Mimi were millionaire celebrities in a city of millionaire celebrities.

Dick let Barbara know he had been married and introduced her to his children. He had the gall to tell her he was divorced. Somehow he managed to spend two or three nights a week with Barbara. Friends were amazed at the open affair he carried on. For some time, neither Mimi nor Barbara knew of the other's existence.

Little by little, Dick stick-handled around the truth. He told Barbara he wasn't exactly divorced; he was legally separated. She accepted that.

That summer Mimi found out about Barbara. Within weeks, she informed Dick she would be seeking a divorce. For financial reasons, he implored her to stay married to him. They could come to some sort of arrangement short of divorce. Mimi eventually obtained her divorce and walked away with over $5 million as her cut of the business.

Meanwhile, Barbara was ensconced in a townhouse in fashionable Ethan's Glen. For some months all went well. Naturally enough, now that her man was free to marry, Barbara longed to become Mrs. Minns.

Dick expressed undying love, but constantly delayed the marriage. He felt quite content to live with Barbara. Sometimes the couple had heated arguments. According to Barbara, Dick struck her on a couple of occasions. Finally, she couldn't take it any more. She moved out, taking the contents of the townhouse with her. That was a big mistake.

When Dick came home to the empty townhouse, he was livid. He immediately had Barbara charged with the theft of their furniture. It had been three years since the blond beauty had moved to Texas to be with her handsome millionaire lover. Now he was charging her with theft.

If ever the bloom was off the rose, it was with this pair of lovers. Barbara attempted to build a life of her own. She taught aerobics classes to support herself and continued her studies at the University of Houston. She instituted "common law" proceedings against Dick, claiming some portion of his assets, while he continued to press the theft charges against her. Always in the back of her mind was the thought that Dick would punish her for leaving him.

On October 20, 1980, Barbara pulled into the parking lot of a doughnut shop. She made her purchase and returned to her red Firebird. A man leaned into the vehicle's open window, brandishing a revolver. She turned away, attempting to duck. The man shot four times. All four slugs tore into Barbara's back.

By sheer chance, two officers were driving by in their patrol car. One actually witnessed the shooting. They saw the gunman jump into a Cadillac driven by a second man. The officers gave chase and at the same time radioed for an ambulance. After a short chase, the

Caddy crashed into a pole. The two men ran away on foot. Hit men Patrick Steen and Nathaniel Ivery were apprehended while hiding in a nearby field.

Meanwhile, Barbara was undergoing emergency surgery, which saved her life. Two of the bullets had severed her spinal cord. She had no feeling from the waist down and was told she would never walk again.

Steen and Ivery told detectives they had been hired by a Bob Anderson to kill Barbara Piotrowski. They had no idea why she was to be assassinated. Anderson had provided them with the Cadillac. They were to receive $4,000 each, while Anderson, who had been hired by someone else, was to keep $2,000 for himself.

Bob Anderson was traced. Through him, it was learned that a private detective, Dudley Bell, had hired Anderson to arrange the assassination. Bell had also been hired to do an in-depth investigation of Barbara by none other than Dick Minns. He obviously was gathering material in defence of Barbara's claim to a portion of his assets.

When the smoke cleared, Patrick Steen and Nathaniel Ivery were charged with attempted murder. Both men plea bargained. In return for testifying against the man who had hired them, each received sentences of 35 years' imprisonment.

It took well over six years to legally nail Bob Anderson. In 1987 he was convicted of solicitation of capital murder and sentenced to 38 years in prison. Dudley Bell was convicted of the same charge and received the same sentence as Anderson.

The Minns-Piotrowski affair is still before the courts. Barbara learned that the Houston Police Department was aware, through an informer, that she was an assassination target long before the shooting took place. She sued the police department for $50 million. The case is still to be resolved. She has also sued Dick Minns in a civil action and has been awarded $32 million, but as of this writing has not collected one cent.

Dick Minns has never been criminally charged with the shooting. He has continually failed to appear in court, but is represented by high-priced lawyers. It is believed that he has divested himself of all his U.S. holdings and now lives abroad.

As for Barbara Piotrowski, she no longer exists. To wipe out her past life, Barbara has changed her name to Janni Smith. She managed to develop herself into an outstanding wheelchair athlete, winning several marathons throughout the United States.

In 1982, she became deeply involved in research conducted by Dr. Jerrold Petrovsky, who was experimenting with electrodes attached to the legs controlled by a computer. Unbelievably, using Petrovsky's method, in 1983 Barbara actually walked. In 1985, this courageous woman completed the Honolulu marathon. Since that time Janni Smith has received several honours for her work with the physically handicapped.

On November 30, 1991, the girl who was shot in the back four times, the girl who was told she would never walk again, married her doctor. She is now Mrs. Janni Petrovsky.

Raymond Morris

(ENGLAND)

CANNOCK CHASE IS AN 80-SQUARE-MILE AREA located about 20 miles north of Birmingham, England. This beautiful spot, dotted with woods, is a favourite location for family picnics. It was this area that gave rise to the most extensive child murder investigation in the history of English crime.

On Wednesday, September 8, 1965, seven-year-old Margaret Reynolds of Birmingham went missing after leaving her home to go back to school following lunch. Margaret's sister accompanied her partway to school, but the girls separated, as they attended different schools. No one saw Margaret after that Wednesday at noon. Police conducted an extensive door-to-door investigation, but didn't uncover a single person who had seen Margaret after she and her sister parted company.

Almost four months later, five-year-old Diane Tift of nearby Bloxwich left her grandmother's house to play outdoors. Her mother was in a Laundromat near the house. At 3:00 p.m., Diane's older sister, Susan, told her mother that little Diane had just strolled by the Laundromat window. Then she simply disappeared. When the child couldn't be found, her distraught mother reported her missing. An extensive house-to-house search was carried out.

In all, the occupants of 6,000 homes were interrogated without success.

The distance between the locations where the two girls had gone missing was eight miles. Although the police were in no way certain the two cases were connected, there was grave concern that a serial child murderer was stalking, abducting and killing little girls.

Months passed before a man walking along a ditch in Cannock Chase saw what he thought was a bundle of discarded clothing. He approached the clothing and was horrified at the sight of the decomposed body of a little girl. Police were summoned. One officer, searching along the ditch, saw what he thought was a rock. Upon examining his find, he realized it was a human skull. Margaret Reynolds and Diane Tift had been found at last.

Forensic experts were able to ascertain that Diane, who had been sexually assaulted, had probably been asphyxiated with the hood of her coat. Because of advanced decomposition, it was impossible to tell how Margaret Reynolds had met her death.

On August 19, 1967, it happened again. Seven-year-old Christine Darby lived with her mother and grandmother in nearby Walsall. At lunchtime she went outdoors to play with her friends in the bright sunshine along Camden Street. A light-coloured car pulled up beside the group of children. According to the youngsters, the man behind the wheel wound down the window, leaned over and said, "Could you show me the way to Carmer Green, please?" The youngsters responded in unison, "Up that way." The man, talking directly to Christine, said, "Could you get in and show me the way, please?" As he spoke he opened the passenger door. Christine jumped in the car.

And so a third child had been plucked off the streets in broad daylight. This time the abductor left clues. The pronunciation of the words Carmer Green indicated that he was a local man. Carmer Green was the local vernacular for Caldmore Green. The youngsters also described the man as being in his thirties, dark-haired, clean-shaven, fairly thin and wearing a white shirt without a tie.

Scores of officers fanned out over the neighbourhood. A mounted officer came up with the first physical clue, a pair of panties stuck on a tree branch. Christine's grandmother identified the panties as belonging to the little girl. Within 24 hours a total of 750 police and members of the military were involved in the search. Shoulder-to-shoulder they marched through Cannock Chase. Christine Darby's body was found covered with ferns at the foot of a tree. She had been viciously raped. Death was attributed to asphyxiation by suffocation.

Scotland Yard was called in to assist local police. To illustrate the vastness of Cannock Chase and the massive search undertaken by authorities, over 500 pieces of women's underwear were found in the search for clues into Christine's death.

Eventually detectives located a witness who lived close to where the bodies had been found. Victor Whitehouse had seen a car back into the woods around the time Christine was believed to have been murdered. Victor saw the driver face-on and was able to tell police the man was about 40 years of age with a ruddy complexion and dark hair. Victor thought the car in question was a light grey Austin. He swore he would recognize the man if he ever saw him again.

Another witness, Jeanne Rawlings, had been picnicking with her husband. She too had seen the man and gave police the same general description as that given by Victor Whitehouse. She described the car as a light grey Austin. Neither witness had noted the licence number.

The two witnesses, using an Identikit, came up with their version of what the suspect looked like. The picture was distributed throughout the British Isles without success. Months turned into years and still the Cannock Chase murderer evaded capture.

In January 1968, Scotland Yard decided to mount an all-out blitz to bring in their man. Two hundred police officers would conduct house-to-house investigations of the entire area. Each occupant would have to account for their time on the three dates the children had been murdered.

The task was a monumental one, often involving several return visits to the same house. As one can imagine, some occupants were on vacation, some in hospitals. Others had moved to different countries. For months police trudged from house to house. Several crimes were solved as a result of their inquiries. By spring, 54,000 homes had been visited. The hunt continued.

In November 1968, the mountain of reports on homes visited and the reports on grey Austins finally paid off. One man had owned a Vauxhall Cresta years earlier when that make of vehicle was observed at the scene of a rape and attempted murder of a little girl. This same man owned a grey Austin at the time of Christine Darby's murder. He also bore a resemblance to the Identikit picture. On those occasions when he had been questioned by police, the man's wife had given him an alibi for the time of the three murders.

The suspect had been in trouble back in 1966. In October of that year he had picked up two little girls and had taken them to his home. According to the children, ages 10 and 11, they were made to undress and were photographed. For this they were paid two shillings. The girls told their parents, who reported the incident to police. The man was questioned. He denied everything. Although photographic equipment was found, no photos were recovered. As investigators only had the word of the two children, the matter was dropped.

After years of frustration, police had a prime suspect. Raymond Leslie Morris was taken into custody. His wife of four years was again questioned. She now admitted that when she had previously told police her husband was at home at the time of the murders, she had merely confirmed what her husband had said. She had lied. After all, it was ridiculous to think that her kind, gentle husband was some kind of monster. To get the police off their backs, she had agreed with anything he said.

Both Victor Whitehouse and Jeanne Rawlings identified Morris as the man they had seen near the location of the Christine Darby murder.

When Morris was taken into custody, his wristwatch was found strapped around his ankle. The reason for this oddity became apparent when Morris's flat was meticulously searched. Detectives found photographs of naked little girls, some posed with Morris. The photos featuring parts of his body, but not his face, had obviously been taken by a camera fitted with a time switch. One of the photos clearly showed Morris's wristwatch, the one he had attempted to hide by strapping it around his ankle.

Raymond Leslie Morris was tried and found guilty of the murder of Christine Darby. He was sentenced to life imprisonment. Since his confinement he has been classified as a dangerous psychopath who would be a danger to children if he was ever released.

Edward Mueller

(UNITED STATES)

THE HONOURABLE PROFESSION of counterfeiting is generally carried on by well-organized gangs producing high-denomination bills. Much care is given to the paper and ink used in the process. A master engraver with larceny in his heart is a prerequisite.

Once manufactured, the "queer," as it is sometimes called, is often distributed through wholesalers for as little as 25 cents on the dollar. The wholesaler in turn may sell the bogus money to legmen for as little as 40 cents on the dollar.

Keeping all the above in mind, it is refreshing to report that the greatest counterfeiter the United States has ever known was not a master criminal but a little old man who lived with his dog in a flat on the top floor of a tenement building near Broadway and 96th Street in New York City.

Edward Mueller got into the counterfeiting profession through necessity. He was superintendent of several apartment buildings until 1937, when his wife died. At age 63, he found it increasingly difficult to look after the buildings in his care. Now that his children were grown up, Edward figured it was time to make a career change. He became a junk dealer. To complete the transition, he and his mongrel terrier moved into a smaller flat of their own.

Lugging a pushcart, Edward commenced to purchase junk, a venture which provided a precarious living at best. After a year of pushing that darn cart over the streets of New York, Edward took stock. It was time for another career change. He would become a counterfeiter.

Edward Mueller wasn't a man who made hasty decisions. He took his time. One day, while visiting his daughter in the suburbs, he noticed she had a studio camera. Gentle Edward took a picture of a dollar bill. He then produced zinc plates, which he touched up by hand. The finished product looked great to the rookie counterfeiter.

Later, the Secret Service, who profess to be experts in such matters, claimed the bill was the most amateurish counterfeiting job they had ever seen. One glaring error is worthy of note. In touching up the bogus plates, Edward had somehow transposed one of the letters in the word Washington. He'd spelled the president's name "Wahsington." Not one person accepting the bills ever noticed the mistake. Then again, neither did Edward.

In the fall of 1938, Edward went into production. He turned out his very first dollar bill on his rickety hand-driven printing press. Gingerly, he hung up the bill to dry on a clothesline in his flat. Nervous as a turkey at Christmas time, he took the bill down to a store and bought 10 cents worth of candy. Edward learned a valuable lesson that day. Nobody really examines a one-dollar bill.

It didn't take long before the phony bills came to the attention of the Secret Service. Right off, the feds were mystified. Whoever was making the phony ones was producing precious few bills. The Secret Service didn't know our boy. Edward was different from all other counterfeiters who had come before him. He simply wasn't greedy. He turned out only enough bills to provide for himself and his dog. The one exception was his purchase of candy for the neighbourhood children on Sundays.

For years, Edward cranked out his phony one-dollar bills in his tiny flat, and for years the Secret Service was baffled at the minuscule supply of bad bills that turned up. Edward's output never exceeded $50 a month. What's more, the bills were of such poor quality, the paper could be obtained at any stationery store. "Washington" was spelled wrong. To add insult to injury, one of Washington's eyes was an ink blot. At the end of five years, a grand total of $2,840 was successfully put into circulation. Folks, that's well less than two dollars a day. Secret Service agents held meetings. What sort of strange individual was manufacturing such a limited supply of counterfeit money?

For 10 long years, Edward successfully produced and distributed his phony ones. In the end, he was discovered only by accident. One day, while he was out, a fire broke out on the top floor of his apartment building. His flat was badly damaged and his faithful pet terrier was suffocated by smoke. Firemen, as is their custom, threw much of the contents of Edward's flat out a window into a vacant lot below. Saddened by his loss, Edward went to live with his daughter in the suburbs while his apartment was being repaired.

Nine boys, ranging in age from 10 to 15, used the lot as a playground. One of the lads found what he thought was play money. Ironically, for 10 years no adult had thought Edward's money to be anything but genuine. A 10-year-old spotted it as phony in two minutes. He took some of the bills home. Another boy carried home some money, as well as an old printing press. His father saw the boys playing with the money. He examined a bill and was suspicious enough to call police. One look at the misspelled "Washington" and the Secret Service knew they were getting close to their old nemesis.

The boys led police to the vacant lot, where they quickly learned that the half-burned junk in the lot had come from a fire-damaged flat in the building. And who was the tenant of the burned-out flat? None other than that kind, gentle old man, Edward Mueller.

Edward was questioned, and immediately confessed that he had produced those phony dollar bills. He explained that no one was harmed by his counterfeiting. He had made sure he never stuck any one person with more than one dollar, and never printed more than he needed to support himself and his late lamented dog. Oh, yes, he sometimes treated the neighbourhood kids to candy.

Everyone liked Edward, who seemed to bask in the notoriety he had achieved. Released on bail, he enjoyed dropping in to the Secret Service offices to pass the time of day with the agents. Wearing a perpetual smile and standing an imposing five foot three inches tall, he was an unlikely criminal who had cost the government more time and trouble than any counterfeiter in the history of the country.

The 73-year-old Edward came to trial. He loved every minute of the proceedings. He was charged with three offences—possessing plates, passing counterfeit bills and manufacturing counterfeit bills. Edward was found guilty of all three charges. He was sentenced to one year and one day in prison. A trickle of laughter went through the courtroom when the presiding judge fined him one dollar.

After serving four months in jail, Edward was released and moved in to his daughter's home. He spent most of his time telling neighbours and friends how he had hoodwinked the Secret Service for 10 years.

In 1950, a movie, *Mister 880*, was made about Edward's exploits. It starred famed character actor Edmund Gwenn, who was nominated for an Academy Award for his performance. Edward Mueller attended the premiere and told his daughter he had never enjoyed anything more in his life.

Hendryk Neimasz

(ENGLAND)

CONSCIENTIOUS POLICE OFFICERS often store away insignificant tidbits of information in their memory bank for possible future use. More often than not, the information proves to be of no value, but there are rare incidents when unusual recall has led to solving a murder. One such incident took place in the village of Aldington, England.

Listen up.

Alice and Hubert Buxton had been living in Aldington for only two years, which to the villagers meant they were newcomers. Hubert was employed as a gardener at a large estate near the village. A bungalow came with the job, and it is here that Hubert and Alice lived. Alice, a native of Belgium, was employed as a waitress in a nearby hotel.

The couple were accepted by the villagers as respectable, hard-working members of the community. Everyone liked the good-natured 38-year-old Alice. Well, not quite everyone. The person who killed her didn't like her one little bit.

It happened Saturday, May 13, 1961. On that day, milkman David Pilcher delivered milk to the Buxtons' bungalow, as he did six times a week. This day would be different. Instead of being greeted by cheerful Alice, he observed his customer lying on the floor with part of her head caved in. Beside the body, which was clad only in a slip and sweater, lay the broken-off barrels of a shotgun.

David ran all the way to the village police station. In minutes, a bobby was at the scene. He confirmed that Alice was dead, then went into a small room off the kitchen. There, on the scullery floor, lay the body of Hubert Buxton. Beside the body was the stock of a shotgun. The constable immediately informed his superiors of the double murder.

Initially, police speculated that the couple had interrupted a robbery or that Alice was a rape victim. Autopsies performed on the bodies were most revealing. Alice had not been shot or raped. She had been bludgeoned to death, while Hubert had been shot.

Early in the investigation, detectives discovered that Alice was not legally married to Hubert. She had left her husband for Hubert years before. Naturally, her legal husband was the one person who, logically, might have wanted both Alice and Hubert out of the way. This tangent of the investigation came to nothing when it was learned that Alice's husband had emigrated to Canada and could not possibly have committed the crime.

Neighbours of the Buxtons were questioned. One of them told investigators that Alice had confided in her that Hubert was a very restrictive husband who allowed her little freedom. Alice left her home only to go to work or to take the occasional trip to Belgium, where most of her friends and family lived. Alice also revealed that her sex life with Hubert had ceased sometime in the past.

Although inquiries were still in the early stages, the double murder was turning into one of those cases that could very well go unsolved. There were no clues that might lead to the killer. That was before Constable Fred Brisley turned on his police radio to a channel reserved for information on the Buxton murders. One of the pieces that came over the radio reported that a receipt in the Buxtons' bungalow made out to someone called Neimasz had been found.

A light went on in Fred's memory bank. He was positive he had heard that unusual name before, but for the life of him he couldn't remember where. All day as he observed traffic he couldn't get the name out of his mind. That evening he made the connection. It had been approximately seven months earlier, and the incident wasn't without humour. Fred had seen a suspicious-looking car partially covered with a tarpaulin parked in a nearby quarry. As he approached the vehicle, he heard a squeaky noise from inside. Fred pulled off the tarp and came face-to-face with a man and woman, almost totally undressed, having intercourse.

The couple was understandably embarrassed. So was Fred. He stuttered, "W-what are you doing?" The man, fumbling at his clothing, replied, "We are having some tea." As he spoke, he produced a thermos. Fred, repressing a chuckle, replied, "Carry on the good work." As he turned away, he inquired as an afterthought, "And what's your name?" The man replied, "Neimasz."

Fred was one of those conscientious police officers who took the trouble to write down his every activity at the end of his shift. He looked in his notebook to find the incident. Sure enough, there it was in black and white. The date had been September 29, 1960, the time was 4:45 p.m., and the vehicle was a Hillman Husky, licence number YKR 866.

Fred had no idea how important the incident was to the current murder case when he related it to his superior, who passed it along to New Scotland Yard. Yard detectives wanted to know if Fred would recognize the woman in the car if he saw her again. Fred said he would. As a result, he was asked to view the body of Alice Buxton. Fred took one look. There was no doubt about it. Alice was the woman he had seen in the Hillman the previous September.

Hendryk Neimasz and his wife, Grypa, had been acquaintances of the Buxtons. Grypa and Alice had met accidentally and become good friends. One day, Alice asked Grypa to her home for tea, suggesting she bring her husband along. Hendryk, who hailed from Poland, spoke only broken English. Evidentally, he took a shine to Alice who, due to her rather restrictive lifestyle, was very susceptible to the temptation of an extramarital love affair. The pair met clandestinely, sometimes doing what comes so very naturally in the close confines of the Hillman. It was one such coupling that Constable Fred Brisley interrupted in September.

Once Scotland Yard got on the scent, they turned up a love letter from Hendryk to Alice which by accident had ended up in the Buxtons' bungalow. Hendryk had written to Alice while she was on one of her periodic visits to Belgium. Because Alice had already gone back to England, her family had forwarded the letter to her home in Aldington.

The Neimasz residence in Mersham, about three miles from Aldington, was searched. Portions of the trigger mechanism of the shotgun used to murder Hubert Buxton were found in the home.

Hendryk was taken into custody and questioned. He confessed to his relationship with Alice, but swore he hadn't killed anyone. His story was rather fantastic. He told police that Alice had begged him to kill his wife and her husband so that they could be together forever. Her suggestion had preyed on his mind. He became fearful that Alice would kill Grypa and Hubert herself.

Hendryk admitted he had explained his fears to a man he knew only as George, whom he met in a pub. To prevent Alice from killing his wife, he had paid George £60 to kill Alice. He never really felt the man would carry out the job, but now he figured George must have done it after all. He had no idea why Hubert had been killed. Maybe he had gotten in George's way.

Scotland Yard searched for George, but could locate no one in the area who had ever heard of him. When they found a pair of blood-stained trousers hidden in Hendryk's home, they stopped looking for George.

Detectives theorized that Hubert had intercepted the love letter from Hendryk to his wife. When Hubert accused her of having an affair, Alice swore she wouldn't see Hendryk again and told him so. Furious at this turn of events, Hendryk called on the Buxtons with a loaded double-barrelled shotgun. He shot Hubert as soon as he arrived. Alice was clubbed to death with the weapon.

When Hendryk kept hitting her limp form on the floor, the old shotgun disintegrated, leaving the barrel portions beside her body. Hendryk tossed the stock away. It came to rest near Hubert's body. Hurriedly, he must have pocketed the trigger mechanism and taken it home.

In July 1961, Hendryk Neimasz stood trial for the double murder. He stuck to his story of a mystery man named George. The English jury did not believe the tall tale. Hendryk Neimasz was found guilty of both murders and was sentenced to death. On September 8, 1961, he was hanged at Wandsworth Prison.

Joe Nischt

(UNITED STATES)

IT WAS ONE OF THOSE MYSTERIES that occur every so often to puzzle and embarrass those whose occupation it is to serve and protect.

Back in 1950 in Chicago, a respectable 58-year-old housewife, Rose Michaelis, disappeared under mysterious circumstances. Rose had always been a creature of habit. At the same time each evening she prepared dinner for her husband, Milton, except on nights when he was held up at his work as an estimator for a glass company.

One day Milt called Rose at 4:30 p.m. to tell her that he would be working overtime. He expected to be home at eight o'clock. Rose, in her meticulous way, told her husband of many years that she would adjust her routine. Dinner would be ready promptly at eight.

A few minutes after eight, Milt arrived home. The front door was locked with a burglar chain. He rang the doorbell. No one answered. Milt went around to the back door, but it too was locked. Now, that wasn't like Rose at all. She knew very well that she had the only key. Milt was apprehensive. Could Rose have had an accident or a heart attack?

Milt elicited the assistance of a neighbour. Together, they broke in the front door and entered the house. Nothing was disturbed. The table was set. Dinner was simmering on the stove. Everything was as it should be, with one exception. Rose was nowhere to be seen.

Milt called a few relatives who lived nearby. They arrived in minutes to help him look for Rose. The group circled the house. At the rear of the Michaelis home was an alley that most residents used as a shortcut. In the alley, the search party found the key to the back door of the house and a broken water jug that had belonged to Rose. She often used it to fetch water from a nearby filtration plant. In addition, they found the heel of one of Rose's shoes. Milt called police.

The area around the house was thoroughly searched. Police found bloodstains on a telephone pole in the alley near the Michaelis home. Detectives believed it was possible that Rose had been the victim of a hit-and-run driver, who had stopped, seen the body and decided to dispose of it elsewhere. It was a far-out theory, but this kind of thing *has* happened. Police canvassed repair garages for suspicious vehicles.

Meanwhile, other officers pursued the theory that Rose could have met with foul play in the alley and might have been dragged into a nearby basement apartment. Milt volunteered that he knew the janitor of the building rather well. His name was Joe Nischt. Milt sometimes played cards with the janitor, who often did odd jobs for Rose.

Joe Nischt was a tall, handsome 30-year-old who took his janitorial duties seriously. You could eat off the floor of Joe's apartment building, it was so squeaky-clean. He was questioned by police and expressed great sadness at Rose's disappearance. Detectives were in a quandary. Although husband Milt was mildly suspected, as was Joe, there was no evidence against either man.

Joe told detectives that he had picked up his paycheque from his employer at about four-thirty on the afternoon in question. On the way back to his apartment building, he had stopped for a few cool ones at a local watering hole. He had arrived back in his apartment by 7:00 p.m. and had stayed there all night, except for a short while at 9:00 p.m. when he had stoked the fire in the boiler room. As was his custom after stoking the fire for the night, he had locked the basement door opening on to the alley. He hadn't heard or seen anything suspicious.

Joe's apartment building, including the 36 lockers in the basement, was searched by police. No Rose. Desperate for a clue, police conducted an in-depth investigation into Milt's background. He came up clean as a whistle. Not so Joe. There were a few bumps.

Joe had once been arrested for slugging a waitress in a restaurant. The charges had been dropped. On another occasion, he had been charged with illegal entry. Once again, the charges were dismissed when it was learned that nothing had been stolen. On both occasions, which had taken place years earlier, Joe had been slightly inebriated.

Then it happened—the hot clue that should have led investigators directly to the killer. A garage owner informed police that a customer had left a vehicle in his garage with a broken radiator and a twisted bumper. Police scraped human hair off the radiator grill. The owner of the car was located. The hair found on the vehicle came from his head.

Frightened and annoyed, the owner proved that his accident had taken place several days before Rose's disappearance. When he had examined the damage on his hands and knees, he had hit his head on the grill. This unfortunate gentleman proved without a doubt that he'd had nothing to do with Rose Michaelis's disappearance.

Just when they thought the mystery would never be solved, police received an anonymous phone tip. The caller informed officers that Joe Nischt had not been in his apartment building from 7:00 p.m. on as he had stated. That was enough for them to take another crack at the janitor.

Surprise! Joe broke down. He sobbed, "I killed her. Yes, I killed her." Joe went on to tell all. "I got home about six o'clock. I saw her coming up the alley and suddenly a kind of a fit got me. I grabbed her and she yelled for me to let her go. Then I hit her with my fist and she fell against the telephone pole. I dragged her into the basement. I shoved her into the furnace and closed the doors and turned up the heat. Then I washed the basement floor."

Joe cleaned out the ashes the next day and they were routinely hauled away by a private company that had the contract for removing ashes from his building. Detectives were led to a dump where the ashes had been deposited.

It took three days to sift through 25 tons of ashes. Dr. Wilton Crogman, professor of anthropology at the University of Chicago, supervised the proceedings, but the entire operation was in vain. Nothing was found; not a bone, buckle, tooth or piece of clothing, not a trace of Rose.

The previously co-operative Joe picked this opportune time to recant his confession, leaving the police with no eyewitnesses, no confession and no body. Determined to get the goods on Joe, authorities brought in experts who testified that the heat within the apartment building's furnace was many degrees hotter than a standard crematorium. They even went so far as to procure a corpse from a local medical school. Like Sam McGee, the corpse was stuffed into the furnace and was totally destroyed by the raging fire.

Joe Nischt, still protesting his innocence, stood trial for Rose's murder, despite the fact that no trace of her body was ever found. In the midst of the proceedings, he demanded a conference with the assistant district attorney. In a voice loud and clear, he announced, "I can't stand it. My conscience won't permit it. I killed her and I want to stick to my original confession."

Joe changed his plea to guilty and was sentenced to life in Joliet Prison. And, yes, even more than 40 years ago, you could be convicted of murder without the presence of a body.

John Perry

(WALES)

JOHN PERRY WAS A ROUGH, TOUGH WELSHMAN who hailed from the North Wales village of Higher Kinnerton. The Philippines were a long way from Higher Kinnerton, and a good thing too, thought John as he sat belly up to the bar in Manila. You see, John, at a not-too-well-preserved 52 years of age, had just gone through a rather nasty divorce back home. He had travelled to the Philippines to get away from it all. Was it just his imagination that the beauty at the other end of the bar was flashing him a come-hither smile? The next night she was occupying the same bar stool and was still smiling. And the next night, too.

Nothing ventured, nothing gained. John sauntered over. Her name was Arminda. For three weeks, John spent every day and every night with the attractive 20-year-old. He was smitten and had every reason to believe that Arminda was fond of him as well.

When the time drew near for him to fly home, Arminda was obviously saddened. She confessed that she was in love with John and didn't want him to leave. That's when he came up with his perfect solution. They would marry and settle down back in Wales. Arminda thought it was a wonderful idea.

The year of John's fateful marriage was 1984. For a while the marriage went along smoothly, but gradually John became annoyed when local youths lingered around his young bride. In time he grew downright angry, especially when Arminda reciprocated their flirtations. John was reluctant to admit the truth, even to himself. Arminda had married him to escape the poverty of the Philippines for a better life in Wales. Now that she was firmly ensconced, with food, clothing and shelter, she sought the company of younger men. Occasionally Arminda would stay away for a couple of days at a time. Such behaviour rarely makes for a harmonious marriage. John usually referred to his wife as "that slut."

In February 1991, a neighbour of the Perrys walked into the local police station and reported Arminda missing. She hadn't seen her friend for two weeks, which was most unusual. They normally spoke to each other almost every day.

The village police called on John to verify that Arminda was indeed missing. They found it a bit unusual that he had not notified authorities himself. John greeted the police amicably enough. He hadn't reported his wife missing because he felt she had just taken off with a man, as she had in the past. This time she was staying away longer than usual.

John explained that he had made a terrible mistake marrying Arminda and bringing her to Wales. She had been a prostitute and couldn't, or didn't want to, break away from her old habits. As a result, John had instituted divorce proceedings, even though his erstwhile true love was holding him up for £15,000. John told the police he would be happy to have her out of his life at any cost. He would make out just fine living alone with his cat, Katie.

As a matter of routine, the police asked John if he'd give them permission to look around the house. They might find something of his wife's that would give them a clue as to her whereabouts. The officers left the living-room area and opened a door leading to the kitchen. There was a decided odour in the untidy kitchen, but then again John had been "batching" it for two weeks. A bloody knife was visible on the kitchen table. On the floor around the table were several bloodstains. In fact, the more the officers gazed at the messy kitchen, the more blood spots they discovered.

Suddenly Katie the cat scurried across the room, coming to an abrupt stop beside two large plastic bags containing a quantity of chopped meat. Katie made threatening moves, attempting to get at the contents of the two bags. One of the officers brushed Katie aside. The large cat retreated under the table.

On a counter near the sink, in plain view, was a bloodstained hacksaw and screwdriver. Beside the tools was a medical encyclopedia, open at a page featuring the human skeleton, titled, "The Skeletal System."

It was time to seriously question John Perry. He explained that the meat in the plastic bags had been in his freezer. He had taken it out a few days earlier, but had not eaten any of it. Now the meat was a bit ripe and he planned on throwing it out. The answer didn't sit well with the officers. They didn't have to speak to each other. Each knew what the other was thinking. They called for assistance.

Within minutes the house was teeming with detectives. John's garage was opened. Inside, officers found two large wine-fermenting bins. One officer looked inside and recoiled in horror. The bins contained what appeared to be meat. Some of the meat had been burned, other pieces cooked, and still other portions were raw. The bin also contained human organs.

The police officers turned to John Perry. John knew the jig was up. He stammered, "All r-right, I killed her, b-but I didn't mean it. I lost my temper. She was standing right here, taunting me about her boyfriends and I just lost my head. I put my hands around her throat and before I knew what had happened, she was dead. I didn't mean to do it."

John went on, "I was in a panic. I didn't know what to do. I thought that if I disposed of her body and said that she had gone away with a boyfriend, everything would be all right. Nobody would suspect anything."

John's house was meticulously searched. Detectives found the utensils he had used to cook portions of his wife's body. Body parts were also found in the trunk of his car. In studying the body, pathologists found that certain portions were missing. It is believed that John fed pieces of his wife to his cat.

Doctors reconstructed most of Arminda's head. Although they were unable to establish the cause of death, they were able to ascertain that she had not been strangled. Bone fragments indicated that Arminda had received a vicious blow to the back of her head. John had also lied about killing his wife in the living room. The physical evidence proved she had been killed in the bathtub.

During the investigation into this repugnant murder, detectives located a friend of John's who was a butcher. This man told police that John had recently inquired as to how he went about cutting up a carcass. He asked about the tools required. Many tools the butcher had mentioned to John were found in John's house. In addition, at the factory where John worked, he had told fellow workers he was furious at having to pay £15,000 to Arminda as a divorce settlement. He speculated to them that there must be another way out of his predicament.

In November 1991, John stood trial for the murder of his wife. The prosecution produced all the damaging evidence related here. The best John's defence attorney could muster was his client's original statement that the murder had not been premeditated, but had been a spur-of-the-moment act.

The English jury wasn't swayed. John Perry was found guilty and sentenced to life imprisonment, a sentence he is still serving.

Robert Poulin

(CANADA)

WHEN STUART AND MARY POULIN had their third daughter, their 12-year-old son, Robert, moved into a basement bedroom. For the next six years Robert lived in a private, secretive world behind closed doors.

Outwardly, everything was normal. Robert's father, in his fifties, was a former armed forces pilot who taught elementary school in Ottawa. His mother, a nurse, was active in community affairs. Their two-and-a-half-storey Tudor-style home on Warrington Drive was spacious, their family close-knit. Unknown to his parents or his friends, Robert was spending more and more time in a fantasy world, a world he could enter at will when he closed his bedroom door.

Robert Poulin's parents respected privacy. The bedroom was Robert's place. They knocked on the door for permission to enter.

In his early teenage years, Robert had a newspaper route. For some time he worked in a pizza parlour. He attended church every Sunday. For relaxation he played complicated war games over the phone with friends or by himself. Robert attended St. Pius X Catholic High School. In the 12 months preceding October 27, 1975, Robert's parents never once saw the interior of their son's room.

When Robert was in Grade 10, he became acquainted with Kimberley Rabot. At his parents' request he invited Kim to his home. The two students played Risk, a beginner's war game.

To the outside world, Robert Poulin's actions were normal, but his secret life was taking hold. It would soon erupt into one of the most horrendous crimes ever committed in Canada's capital city.

Sex occupied more and more of Robert's thoughts. By the time he was 17, he had covered his walls with *Playboy* centrefolds. Normal for a 17-year-old? Maybe. But Robert went further than pictures. He purchased women's underclothing and acquired books on bondage. He bought weapons—a snub-nosed .38-calibre revolver and an ivory-handled knife. He kept a scrapbook of nude men and women.

Robert wrote about bondage, rape, murder and suicide in his diary. From his writings we learn that Robert grew to fear his own obsessions. In an attempt to alleviate his urge to rape a girl, he purchased a life-sized vinyl inflatable doll for $29.95 from a mail-order house in California. The ad appeared in magazines circulated throughout the U.S. and Canada.

Robert was extremely disappointed in his life-sized doll. His fixation with aberrant sexual behaviour increased. On Monday, October 27, it would explode into violence.

Robert left his home at 8:00 a.m. but returned 15 minutes later. He entered his basement room through the garage. His mother heard him but paid little attention. At around ten o'clock, Mrs. Poulin went down to the basement and inquired through a curtained-off partition if she could speak to her son. "Yeah, but don't come in," Robert replied.

Mother and son talked through the curtain. Behind that curtain Robert had already raped and killed Kim Rabot. She had been hand-cuffed to Robert's bed. Robert Poulin was now acting out his fantasies. He was no longer the normal boy outsiders knew.

Shortly after 11:00 a.m., Robert came up to the kitchen, chatted for a moment with his mother, had a peanut butter sandwich and watched TV. At 11:30 a.m., Mrs. Poulin left her home and returned at 1:30 p.m. The back door was open. Robert was gone. Black smoke was pouring out of a second-storey window. Mrs. Poulin called for help. Firemen found Kim Rabot's body handcuffed to Robert's bed. She had been raped and stabbed to death.

Robert had purchased a Winchester shotgun, model 2200, for $109 four days before, and sawed 15 inches off the barrel. He set his house on fire before heading for St. Pius X High School on his 10-speed bicycle.

Father Robert Bedard was just beginning to conduct his Grade 13 theology class. It was a little after 2:00 p.m. Late students straggled in. By 2:20 p.m. Father Bedard was well into the lesson. The door to the class opened one more time. Robert Poulin stood in the doorway with a shotgun. He smiled. Then he fired.

Seventy-eight students ran for cover. Some threw chairs through windows and climbed out. Four times the pump-action sawed-off shotgun roared. Mark Hough, 18, was critically wounded in the neck and head. He would die from his wounds. Barclay Holbrook, 17, was wounded in the chest. Terry Vanden Handenberg, 18, was hit by pellets in the right shoulder and back of the neck. Mark Potvin, 18, Benggawan Kurniadi, 18, Renzo Catana, 18, and Mark Holleran, 18, received minor wounds. All but Mark would recover.

Robert stepped back from the doorway. One last shot was fired. Then nothing but moans and cries and blood. Outside classroom 71, Robert Poulin had blown away half of his head.

Back at the Poulin residence, police discovered that a plastic bag had been placed over Kim Rabot's head. She had been stabbed 14 times. The knife used to take her life was found taped to Robert's chest.

What strange urges at work in Robert Poulin's mind that day would cause him to take three lives, including his own? Robert left a diary. He wrote that he planned to have intercourse with a girl, burn down his family's home and then kill himself. He was depressed and at the breaking point.

Robert had suffered from acute loneliness and had even advertised for a friend. He'd placed an ad in the *Ottawa Journal* from

October 3 to October 10, 1975. It read: "Male, 18, looking for companionship. P.O. Box 4021, Station E." The box had been rented by Robert to receive his supply of pornographic material. He never responded to the three homosexuals who answered his ad.

Robert's main disappointment in life had been his failure to be accepted for officer's training in the militia. Deeply resentful, he joined the Cameron Highlanders as a private for the summer before his October nightmare. As his fantasy world became more dominant, Robert could no longer control his urge to act out the fantasies contained in his pornographic literature.

In truth, a once-normal boy had lost contact with reality.

Daniel Rakowitz

(UNITED STATES)

DANIEL RAKOWITZ WAS BORN IN TEXAS in 1960. From the time he was little more than a toddler, he was convinced that he was Jesus Christ. The strange boy, who constantly hallucinated, was often seen talking to the Three Wise Men. On other occasions he attempted to perform miracles on school chums. Daniel's actions placed him in and out of several institutions by the time he was 14 years old. While confined to these institutions, he was introduced to drugs to control his behaviour. He would forever after be associated with drugs in one way or another.

Between periods of confinement to hospital, Daniel was well enough to attend school, where he was picked on mercilessly by fellow students. He shunned contact sports and had a fetish about washing his hands. When other students harassed him, he tried to look the other way. On the few occasions when he fought back, he was told he was crazy and was punished.

When Daniel's mother suffered a heart attack and died in front of him, the teenager was devastated. His only true friend was gone. Daniel was left in the care of his demanding father, Tony, a police officer, who never understood his son's illness. Daniel underwent shock treatments, which seemed to control his behaviour for a short while, but it wasn't long before he reverted to his old ways and began experimenting with drugs. When Tony found marijuana in Daniel's room, the split between father and son was complete.

A short time later, Daniel turned 18 and enlisted in the U.S. Army. He was happy there, and earned a marksmanship certificate and took a course in law enforcement. It was his intention to pursue a career in law enforcement after completing his army stint. However, things didn't work out that way.

After his discharge, Daniel applied for the position of deputy sheriff in his father's Texas community. When he was turned down, he blamed his father for blackballing his application.

A short time after this setback, while suffering from depression, Daniel met a girl. The romance was torrid and brief. The pair married, but the realities of Daniel's illness surfaced soon after the euphoric period of wedding and honeymoon. It wasn't long before his teenage bride filed for divorce. Daniel packed his meagre belongings and headed for New York and a new beginning.

Daniel obtained a room in a flophouse off the Bowery. He found he could raise a few dollars by begging. Instead of squandering his income, he purchased marijuana and made a substantial profit by selling the pot to students and young executives.

After working the streets for a few years, he moved his drug-dealing operation to Tompkins Square Park. In time he became known as one of the characters around the park. When the mood struck him, he would lecture to anyone about the world according to Daniel Rakowitz. No one took him seriously—just another one of the homeless crazies who lived in the park. Daniel begged, dealt drugs and killed small animals for the fun of it. The police knew him well. They too considered him to be just another of the Big Apple's lost souls.

Then life changed for Daniel. He took a room in an apartment occupied by a young couple who had been living together for some time. He had little difficulty raising the $200 a month the couple required as his share of the rent. He was elated. At last, a decent, clean place to live. Unfortunately, a short time after Daniel obtained a real roof over his head, the young couple decided to split up. Suddenly he was left with no legal claim to the apartment and no way of making the $500 monthly rent.

As if by magic, Daniel, 28, met Monika Beerle. It wasn't that difficult to make Monika's acquaintance. She strutted her stuff at Billy's Topless, a bar on West 24th Street. Monika, 26, was not your average stripper. She hailed from St. Gallen, Switzerland, and had earned a teaching certificate in choreography in her native land. An adventurous type, Monika had decided to emigrate to New York in search of fame and fortune. Billy's Topless was the first step in her anticipated climb to fame.

Coincidentally, that summer of 1989, Monika was in the process of having to move out of her old digs when she met Daniel. She quickly agreed to move in with him and share the expenses of the apartment. To Monika's way of thinking, she now had a room of her own. In Daniel's mixed-up mind, he had acquired a beautiful lover.

He told his friends in the park it would be only a matter of time before his Monika was sleeping with him. His friends told him to be wary. Monika was manipulative. She only wanted a private room. When the time was right, she would shove him out in the cold.

Trouble soon came knocking at the door of the apartment at 700 East Ninth Street. Monika brought home a male companion. Soon her habit of entertaining men in her room became the rule rather than the exception. The beginning of the end commenced when the young couple who had moved out had to have their lease transferred. Daniel, with no job and no verifiable income, was not eligible to assume the lease. Monika was another story. She had a steady income. The lease was transferred into her name.

Daniel's friends had been right. Monika wasted little time letting him know she wanted him out of the apartment within two weeks. Daniel pleaded. He begged. But Monika stood firm. She wanted him out of the apartment, which he felt had been his only days earlier.

Daniel turned ugly. He threatened Monika. She told friends that he had told her he was going to kill her and cut her up in little pieces. She laughed at him like the students in his school had laughed at him. She laughed at him like the police had laughed at him. Daniel told his few friends that he planned to kill Monika. They laughed too.

When Monika failed to show up at her usual haunts for a few days, one of her female friends decided to drop over to the apartment. Under the pretense of removing a few of her belongings, she procured the key to the apartment from the superintendent, who knew her well. The young woman walked into the kitchen. There, on the stove, in a large soup pot, was Monika's boiled head. Her initial impulse was to flee, but she forced herself to swing the bathroom door open. The tub was half-full of blood. Readily discernible was a human rib cage. The woman fled as fast as her feet could be made to move.

Strangely, the young woman who had discovered Monika's head didn't go to the police. She would later claim she didn't want to become involved. Meanwhile, Daniel told his fellow beggars in the park he had killed Monika and cut her up. They laughed. Daniel was hallucinating again.

Later, it was learned that Daniel had lived in the apartment for several days after killing Monika. He had disposed of her organs and skin down the toilet. He'd boiled her bones until they were free of flesh, then thoroughly cleaned the apartment. Daniel would relate that he had scrubbed until his hands hurt. Finally he was left with scores of bones and a skull. These he packed in a bucket and lugged down to the Port Authority Bus Terminal, where he checked the bucket into a baggage storage locker.

When the superintendent of Daniel's building couldn't locate either of the occupants of the apartment, he went to the police. They checked out the apartment, but so thorough was the cleaning job, they could find no evidence of foul play. Still, they were suspicious enough to question Monika's friends. One of the women questioned was the woman who had seen Monika's head on the stove. She broke down and told police what she had discovered.

Police picked Daniel up in Tompkins Square Park. He confessed to stabbing Monika to death and disposing of her body. He led police to the Port Authority Bus Terminal, where they recovered a bucket of bones and a skull from his locker.

Little old New York has been witness to some weird crimes, but finding a bucket of human bones at the bus depot made the good citizens of that community sit up and take notice.

As for Daniel, he had been rejected all his life. Monika was simply the last in a long line of people who had cast him aside. It was her misfortune to cross paths with a madman. Daniel Rakowitz was found to be not guilty by reason of insanity and was confined to a mental institution.

Robert Rossignol

(UNITED STATES)

STOCKHOLM IS A TINY TOWN in northern Maine, located only a few miles from the Canadian border. Not that much exciting happens in Stockholm. The 350 inhabitants are a close-knit group. They look after each other. No need for locks and keys in their town.

Winters are severe in Stockholm. That's why neighbours often looked in on 90-year-old Elvie Johnson. Moreover, everyone in town liked Elvie Johnson.

In 1988, Elvie wasn't as spry as she once was. She walked with one crutch and wore a hearing aid. Elvie appreciated her neighbours' concern, but at times that same concern was annoying. She often told them that although her body was wearing out, her mind was as sharp as ever.

On Monday, March 14, a neighbour delivered Elvie's mail to her as usual. He opened the unlocked door and was greeted by the bloody sight of Elvie's body on the floor. He ran from the house and called police. The Maine State Police would be at the scene soon, but not before a group of friends had gathered at the crime scene. The town itself had no regular police force. By the time the state police arrived, an acquaintance had moved the body and placed a blanket over it.

Detectives removed the blanket and were shocked at the vicious-
ness of the attack. A kitchen knife protruded from the victim's
stomach. Elvie's dress and sweater had been pulled up over her chest.
A rag had been stuffed into her mouth. There also appeared to be
stab wounds about her throat. On the floor lay Elvie's crutch.

Initially, investigators thought robbery had been the motive for
the murder. The contents of Elvie's purse were scattered on the
kitchen table, but the purse itself was missing. Police reconsidered
when they found $1,100 cash on the kitchen counter. If robbery was
the motive, the perpetrator must have been blind.

When officials were bagging the body, the broken handle of a
paring knife fell to the floor. It was this knife that had inflicted the
stab wounds to Elvie's throat. During the autopsy, a broken knife
blade was uncovered embedded in the victim's throat. The blade
matched the paring knife handle found at the scene. In addition,
Elvie had endured two stab wounds to the right temple and the
horrible knife wound to her stomach. She had also been raped.

Lab technicians took over the crime scene. They were furious that
the scene had been contaminated; well-meaning neighbours had
paraded through the house before officials had arrived. The entire
house was dusted for fingerprints, although technicians realized they
would uncover scores of prints of neighbours who had been on the
premises before the authorities had arrived.

While fingerprints were being lifted and categorized, detectives
went door to door taking residents' fingerprints. They realized that
they would receive many matches which would not necessarily point
to the killer. In fact, several matches were made concerning individuals who could prove they were elsewhere during the hours the
medical examiner estimated as the time of Elvie's death.

Who had committed such a terrible crime? Surely not one of the
locals. A madman, perhaps a deranged serial killer, had passed through
town and picked Elvie's house by chance. As the days passed and detectives recorded where every male citizen in town had been at the time
of the murder, it became obvious that the killer had to be a stranger.

Police tried one last test. They used the substance orthotolidine to see if they could pick up the killer's fingerprints on the body through a transparent film of blood. The chemical compound was sprayed over the body. Several areas of undetected blood became visible. On the inside of the victim's knees were two previously unseen blood spots. The technicians were able to lift one clear fingerprint and a palm print.

For two days detectives pored over the prints they had garnered from their house-to-house inquiries. Rumours of the investigation's progress spread through the tiny community. The culprit wasn't a transient after all. The police were looking for one of their own.

On March 18, four days after the murder, detectives matched the prints found on the body with those of Robert Rossignol, a 19-year-old neighbour of the victim. As soon as the match was made, Robert was arrested at the local high school.

Robert had been interviewed during the original survey of the community. At that time he stated that he hadn't seen Elvie for three weeks prior to her murder. He told his interrogators that on the night of the murder he had visited a friend and had left the friend's house at 8:15 p.m. and had gone directly home. A member of his own family told police that he hadn't arrived home until 9:15 p.m.

It took only 10 minutes of questioning before Robert broke down and related the details of how he murdered and raped Elvie Johnson. He said he had gone to Elvie's house to make a phone call. Elvie was standing there with the aid of her crutch. She had apparently been watching TV and wanted to get back to it. When she turned to continue watching her program, Robert attacked. Clutching the frail elderly woman, he grabbed a paring knife from the kitchen and proceeded to stab Elvie in the throat. When the blade broke off, he picked up a larger knife from the kitchen and stabbed Elvie in the stomach. He then undressed her and proceeded to rape her. While undressing his victim, he must have left his fingerprints on the inside of her knees.

The confession was a gory and vicious recital. Robert went on to tell police that he had disposed of Elvie's purse in a field as he ran from the crime scene. Detectives retrieved the purse in the exact location Robert had indicated. As for motive, Robert could only say that he had freaked out. He offered no further explanation.

A year later, in March 1989, Robert stood trial for murder. He recanted his confession, claiming that he had only said what he thought police wanted to hear. He took the witness stand in his own defence and admitted stopping at Elvie's to use the phone. He claimed that Elvie was already dead when he entered the house. He touched her legs to see if she was alive. When he was sure she was dead, he fled, fearing that he would be blamed for her murder.

Robert sat down, sure that he had covered all his incriminating tracks. Obviously he forgot that he had told detectives where he had thrown the victim's purse. The Maine jury found him guilty of murder. Robert Rossignol was sentenced to 75 years in prison. He has never explained why he, a 19-year-old high school student from the peaceful community of Stockholm, Maine, murdered and raped his 90-year-old neighbour.

As you read this, Robert Rossignol is in prison serving his sentence.

John Rowlands

(WALES)

IN COUNTRIES WHERE CAPITAL PUNISHMENT IS PRACTISED, there are well-documented cases of innocent men being executed. This is the story of one of them.

In 1927, Dai Lewis was a well-known boxer in Cardiff, Wales. He was also a bit of a horse-racing buff and augmented his boxing income at Monmouth Track. Dai sold bookmakers' supplies at the track. His stock-in-trade was tables, chairs, buckets, chalk and the like—anything that bookmakers required to carry on their profession on race days.

The business was competitive. Portions of the track were, by gentlemen's agreement, allotted to certain suppliers. Dai had the reputation of often selling in a competitor's territory.

On September 28, Dai openly sold supplies to a bookmaker operating in territory known to belong to Ed and John Rowlands, rough, tough brothers who, together with a gang of rounders, hung out at the Colonial Club on Custom House Street. The Rowlands brothers didn't take kindly to Lewis trespassing on their territory. They let it be known among the fringe element that Lewis was in deep trouble. Word drifted back to Dai that the Rowlands brothers and their buddies wanted revenge.

Nothing untoward happened that day. On September 29, Dai attended to his business at the track as usual. At the conclusion of the last race, he made his way to the Blue Anchor pub. It was a little disconcerting when Ed and John Rowlands and three friends, Daniel Driscoll, John Hughes and William Price, strolled into the pub. As the evening wore on, it became evident that the men were biding their time. When the pub was about to close, some of them went outside and lingered, waiting for Dai.

Eventually, Dai walked out onto poorly lit St. Mary's Street. John Rowlands and William Price advanced toward Dai. Others slipped behind the unwary boxer. There was a rush of men from front and back. Dai swung wildly at his attackers as he went down. A knife flashed. In seconds, the men ran into the darkness. Dai Lewis lay in the street with his throat slit. Several prostitutes tore away their dresses and shawls and applied them to the gaping wound. Dai was still breathing. He was rushed to the Royal Infirmary, where doctors worked frantically to save his life.

While Dai was fighting for his life, a nurse at the reception area of the hospital received a series of phone calls inquiring about the boxer's condition. When the caller refused to leave his name, the nurse informed police. The urgent inquiries were suspicious enough for the authorities to place a tracer on the phone. Sure enough, a fourth call was received. It had been placed from the Colonial Club, the hangout of the Rowlands brothers and their gang.

This information, coupled with an anonymous tip that the brothers had threatened Dai the day before the attack, precipitated a police raid on the club. John and Ed Rowlands, Daniel Driscoll, John Hughes and William Price were arrested and charged with attempted murder. Meanwhile, at the infirmary, the boxer was sinking fast. Doctors informed police that he wouldn't last the night. Authorities decided to conduct a police lineup at the dying man's bedside. Dai was told what was required of him. He nodded that he understood.

Mustering all his strength, Dai was able to talk. He said, "I do not know how I have been injured. I do not remember how it happened.

There was no quarrel or fight. I did not see anyone use a knife." He looked at Ed Rowlands and said, "You had nothing to do with it. We've been the best of friends." To Daniel Driscoll he uttered, "You had nothing to do with it either. We were talking and laughing together, my dear old pal." Dai couldn't continue. Talking had sapped his strength. The lineup was discontinued. Later that day, Dai Lewis died. So popular was the local pugilist that 25,000 citizens of Cardiff lined the streets in tribute to him as the funeral cortege made its way through the city.

A few days after the funeral, John Rowlands confessed that he had slashed Dai's throat. He claimed Dai had advanced toward him with a knife. He had been able to wrest the knife from his adversary. In so doing, he had accidentally slashed Dai's throat. He swore he had been acting in self-defence.

Ed Rowlands and Driscoll claimed they had come out of the Blue Anchor and had been attracted to the crowd. As soon as they realized what had happened, they ran away. They said they had no prior knowledge of the attack and had not taken part in it in any way. Neither man deviated from this story and no witness was ever brought forward to contradict their account. As the accused's trial date approached, no evidence was uncovered involving John Hughes. The charges against him were dropped and he was released from custody.

On November 29, the four accused stood trial at the Glamorgan Assizes. Thousands attempted to attend the proceedings. Streets for blocks around the courthouse teemed with citizens eager to hear of any current news concerning the case.

As the trial proceeded, it was clear that there were conflicting eyewitness reports as to what had actually happened in the few seconds it took to slash Dai Lewis's throat. John Rowlands stuck to his story of acting in self-defence. A police officer testified it had been so dark at the scene, all he had seen was a short man inflicting the fatal blow. The Welsh jury deliberated only one hour before bringing in a guilty verdict concerning John and Edward Rowlands and Driscoll. Price was found not guilty and released from custody. The remaining three men were sentenced to be hanged.

That winter the men were to appeal, but the strain had been too much for John Rowlands. On the day the appeal was to be heard, he went totally mad. He was later certified insane and was committed to Broadmoor Asylum. The appeal concerning Ed Rowlands and Daniel Driscoll was denied.

As the days passed, bringing their date with death closer, there was a groundswell movement to save the two men. Many thought they were innocent, particularly Driscoll. There was no concrete evidence against him. The possible innocence of the two men was discussed in the House of Commons, but despite the public outcry, the justice system was apparently not to be denied.

A sensational development occurred when a member of the jury, representing eight of his fellow jurors, called on a member of Parliament and presented him with a letter. It read: "We the under-signed, hereby state that we are of the opinion that the sentence of death should not be carried out. There has been so much brought into the case as to cause us great anxiety since we made our decision. Sentence of death should be waived as an act of mercy."

The missive was presented to the Home Secretary, but did nothing. He responded, "No regard can be paid to expressions of opinion by individual members of the jury by which a prisoner has been convicted."

A huge crowd gathered outside the prison gates. Driscoll walked briskly to the scaffold and quipped, "Which noose is mine?" Rowlands, almost unconscious, had to be assisted to the scaffold.

Most students of the Dai Lewis murder case feel that two inno-cent men were hanged. As for John Rowlands, the probable murderer, he died mad as a hatter while confined at Broadmoor.

Freda Rumbold

(ENGLAND)

IT IS IN DECIDEDLY BAD TASTE to kill your husband and leave the poor soul hanging around for three days. Some might call it downright rude. Yet that's exactly what Freda Rumbold did. Gentle Freda swore up and down that the entire incident was an unfortunate accident.

Frank and Freda Rumbold were married in 1933. They had one daughter, Sheila, who, mercifully, does not enter our tale of woe. By 1956, Frank owned a small but prosperous lumber business. The Rumbolds' marriage was not a happy one.

Freda simply didn't like her husband any more. For one thing, Frank's sexual demands had graduated from kinky to downright disgusting. For another, Frank habitually beat Freda black and blue for no apparent reason, which got Freda to thinking that, at age 44, there had to be something better in her future than Frank Rumbold.

Freda had a plan. She left her home in Bristol, England, on a warm but overcast July morning and travelled to nearby Yeovil, where she purchased a single-shot handgun. Later, she asked friends to buy ammunition for the weapon in Taunton. She told them she wanted the ammunition for another friend who was going deer hunting in Scotland.

On Tuesday, August 21, Frank and Freda entertained at their home. No one noticed anything unusual. Next evening, they were seen having a jolly old time at the village inn. They left the inn at about 10:30 p.m. and went directly home.

Frank undressed, put on his pyjamas and retired for the night or, to be more precise, for all eternity. Freda held the gun about three feet from her sleeping husband's head and pulled the trigger. The bullet entered Frank's head, killing him instantly.

Not satisfied that the job had been completed, Freda calmly reloaded the weapon and fired a second shot, which just missed Frank's head, passing through a wall and lodging in a wardrobe in an adjoining room.

That night, Freda slept in another room. Next morning, she was a busy girl. She secreted her gun between two mattresses in an unused bedroom. She then traipsed down to Frank's business and informed employees that he had gone away. From that day forward they were to take their instructions from her.

Later that same morning, Freda wrote her mother, informing her that Frank had left, but had generously given her all his worldly goods, including business, house and bank account. She even included a typewritten authorization, apparently signed by Frank.

All day Thursday and Friday Freda carried on as if nothing had happened. By Saturday morning there was a peculiar odour emanating from the bedroom. Poor Frank lay where he had been killed the previous Wednesday. Freda placed a crude sign on the handle of the bedroom door. It read: Please do not enter. She also stuffed a towel saturated with disinfectant under the door.

The pressure became too much for Freda.

That Saturday, she visited her sister, Mrs. Voisey Barge. Freda told Voisey that Frank had found her gun and had threatened to shoot her. There had been a struggle and the gun had gone off. Frank was dead. She was terrified and hadn't told a living soul that Frank was still in bed and hadn't moved a muscle since Wednesday night.

Police were notified and hurried to the Rumbold residence, where they found Frank, still in his pyjamas, with a bullet hole in his head.

Freda was taken into custody. Her trial for the murder of her husband took place in Bristol in November 1956. She professed that the shooting had been an unfortunate accident.

Frank had been in bed. She had been downstairs cleaning up when she heard a shot. She had raced upstairs and found Frank with a gun in his hand. She grabbed at the gun and it went off.

Freda was afraid to turn herself in as it was a matter of record that she and Frank didn't get along. She had called police on two previous occasions when Frank had beaten her.

Freda admitted to purchasing the gun and ammunition, but swore it was for self-protection in case Frank tried to kill her. She also confessed she had hidden the murder weapon between the two mattresses. There were no fingerprints on the gun, which obviously had been wiped clean. Freda told investigators she had wiped the weapon clean, not to get rid of the fingerprints, but because it was her nature to clean things.

Freda swore she had not intended to kill or harm her husband. She said she had held the butt end of the gun during the scuffle, while Frank had held the muzzle. But let's allow Freda to tell the story in her own words: "The gun went off and he said, 'Oh.' He turned slightly in bed and I ran out of the room because I was frightened. I spent some time outside and then went back in his room again. I could tell my husband was dead, so I covered him up with the bedclothes. I put his arms up on his body. Then I pulled the curtains and closed the door."

The prosecution pointed out, with the aid of experts, that the trajectories of the two bullets fired that night were almost identical. In addition, they stated that Freda's story simply didn't make sense. Why would Frank be shooting a gun while lying alone in bed?

All was not cut and dried. In summing up, the judge stated that Freda had been abused by her husband over a lengthy period of time. Would this have caused any reasonable person to crack under the pressure and fire the fatal shot? If so, Freda would be guilty of manslaughter. If Frank's death had been an accident, as the defence proclaimed, Freda should be acquitted. If the killing was premeditated, Freda was guilty of murder.

The English jury deliberated for only three hours. Freda had purchased the gun, arranged for the purchase of ammunition, wiped the weapon clean of fingerprints and covered up the killing by writing to her mother. It was all too much. Freda Rumbold was found guilty of murder and sentenced to death, a sentence which was later commuted to life imprisonment.

Terry Ruza

(UNITED STATES)

THE HANDYMAN WHO TOOK CARE of the public-storage sheds at Andros Place in San Diego thought he'd better have a look. The odour emanating from Unit 59 was far too strong. He unlocked the unit and noted the usual array of household effects in the small storage space, but his attention was drawn to a 50-gallon reinforced cardboard barrel. A blanket had been thrown over the top of the barrel. The handyman removed the blanket and peeked in. His gaze fell squarely on a pair of feet. Whoever was in that barrel was standing on their head.

It was May 18, 1988, and the heat inside Unit 59 had contributed greatly to the decomposition of the body. Police had the barrel and its contents sent intact to the city morgue for examination. While waiting for the results of this examination and an autopsy report, detectives determined from a rental contract that the renter of the storage unit had given a false name and address to the manager.

Next morning, the autopsy revealed that the body in the barrel was that of a woman. She had been clad in a colourful tank top and purple shorts. Three .22-calibre bullets from a handgun had pierced her skull.

A check of missing women revealed that on May 12, six days before the body turned up in the barrel, two relatives of 33-year-old

Leona Lara had reported her missing. After the report was filed, one of the relatives called police with an interesting tale. The relative said that a nogoodnik, Terry Ruza, was furious at her for reporting Leona as missing. She went on to state that Terry had been Leona's steady boyfriend, but the two had not been getting along. More startling still was the information that Ruza had once been in prison for killing his wife.

Detectives checked out the unusual story. It was true that Ruza had served a three-year prison term, for the murder of his wife, Pam. He had beaten her to death with a hammer, but was convicted, not of murder, but of voluntary manslaughter. Events were developing with unusual speed. Detectives visited Leona's residence. Not one item of clothing, jewellery or any other personal effects was missing. Police were certain that the dead woman was Leona, as people seldom disappear voluntarily without taking something of value with them.

While detectives were searching Leona's residence and interviewing neighbours, who should drive up but Terry Ruza with a cute young thing whom he introduced as his girlfriend. Police decided to question him then and there, although at this time there was no proof positive that the body in the barrel was Leona Lara. Ruza was extremely co-operative. He explained that he had last seen Leona the day before her disappearance. He had lived with her for three years but had recently decided to break off the relationship. According to Ruza, Leona had once been a pleasant companion and lover, but in the past several months, she had taken to the booze with a vengeance. She had, in fact, turned into a disgusting lush. Ruza said he had tried to help her, but had given up and had let her know that he couldn't tolerate her behaviour any longer. At the time of her disappearance, they had been in the process of breaking up.

Terry Ruza was an impressive cut of a man. He was tall, handsome and charming. It was somewhat difficult to keep in mind that he had once beaten a woman to death with a hammer.

San Diego detectives obtained and studied Ruza's record. His wife had been killed when the pair were in the midst of separating. After beating Pam to death, he wrapped her body in a blanket and drove to their cottage, where he buried her in a grave only inches deep. A few days later, when Pam was reported missing, detectives found bloodstains in the bedroom of the Ruzas' apartment. When they arrived at the cottage, they were attracted to a swarm of flies, which led to the discovery of Pam's body. A sympathetic jury must have been impressed with Ruza's appearance to find him guilty of only voluntary manslaughter.

After the body in the barrel was identified as that of Leona Lara, detectives felt that lightning had struck twice. They went about gathering circumstantial evidence against their suspect. Although Ruza had used a phony name and address when he had contracted to rent the storage unit, it had been necessary for him to initial several paragraphs indicating that he had read the contract. From habit, he had initialled each paragraph "TGR." Ruza's middle name was Guy.

The barrel in which Leona had been found was identical to ones used at the restaurant where Ruza worked. Other items in the storage unit belonged to Ruza as well. That was enough. Ruza was taken into custody. During the arrest procedure, the key to Unit 59 was found with the suspect's personal possessions. To add to the array of circumstantial evidence, employees of the storage company picked our boy out of a lineup as the man who had rented Unit 59. A graphologist told police that Ruza's handwriting matched the writing on the rental contract.

In December 1988, Terry Ruza stood trial for the murder of Leona Lara. He changed his tune, no longer claiming that he had no knowledge of the crime. Ruza now made a confession of sorts. He stated that Leona had pulled a gun on him when she learned of his relationship with his new girlfriend. The gun had gone off accidentally as the pair struggled, killing Leona. He realized that, because of his previous conviction, no one would believe this death had been accidental. He decided to put Leona's body in the storage unit that he had rented three months previously to store odd bits of furniture.

The prosecution made short work of Ruza's claim of self-defence. Leona had been shot three times in the head, which makes self-defence a difficult theory to swallow.

The California jury agreed. Terry Ruza was found guilty of murder in the second degree. He was sentenced to 22 years' to life imprisonment, a sentence he is currently serving.

David Schoenecker

(UNITED STATES)

THERE WAS NOTHING to distinguish David Lee Schoenecker from thousands of other residents of Anaheim, California. Dave had been an outstanding high school athlete back in Milwaukee, Wisconsin, excelling in baseball and football. In his senior year he was voted class president.

During the decade that followed his graduation from high school, Dave obtained a degree in chemical engineering and married his university sweetheart. The marriage was blessed with two daughters, but the union, which had shown such promise, fizzled and died.

Dave landed on his feet. After obtaining a divorce, he met and married Gail, an attractive elementary school teacher. Dave and Gail purchased a home and lived in Milwaukee for some years. When job opportunities opened up in Anaheim, the Schoeneckers moved there.

Gail accepted a position as a Grade 6 teacher at Adelaide Price School in Anaheim. She soon gained a reputation as a caring, dedicated educator, deeply involved in community affairs. By 1988, she was a valued member of the Yorba Linda United Methodist Church choir.

Dave also did well in California, although he lost his job and had recently become somewhat moody. Still, the Schoeneckers, comfortably ensconced in their pleasant home on affluent Amanda Circle, were leading a good life.

No one knew that, during the winter of 1988, Dave had begun to remember incidents long buried in his past. He vividly recalled any slight that had ever been directed his way over the years. He was convinced that the perpetrators of these slights had to be punished. He told Gail how he felt and was disappointed when she brushed aside what she believed were totally silly thoughts. When Dave insisted on discussing the matter, Gail grew angry and refused to listen to such rubbish. That was a mistake.

On May 6, 1989, Gail didn't show up for classes at her school. Her colleagues were concerned. This had never happened before. If Gail was as much as a few minutes late she would call the school and ask a friend to cover for her. On the second day of her absence, teachers phoned her home, but there was no answer. Messages left on her answering machine received no response. On the fifth day of Gail's absence, the teachers called police. Coincidentally, relatives contacted police on that same day. All wanted to know what had happened to Gail Mae Schoenecker.

On May 11, detectives were dispatched to the Schoenecker home. They easily gained entrance to the locked house through the garage door and found Gail's body in the master bedroom. She had been shot once in the head with a .357 magnum. Soon the house was swarming with investigating officers who quickly ascertained that Gail, clad only in a negligee, had not been interfered with sexually. Nothing had been taken from the house, nor was there evidence of forced entry. When found, Gail was lying in bed. Her reading glasses were on a night table beside an open book.

It was most logical for detectives to want to speak to Dave. That wasn't as easy as it should have been. Dave was nowhere to be found. His absence was explained in a most unusual way when police found a chilling poem:

I'll come in the night
I'll come in the day
I've chosen for each
Their own special way
I made my list
I'm checking it twice
I'm going to find out
Who's naughty, not nice
All on the list will
Go to their grave
All with the help
Of friendly old Dave.

In addition to the poem, Dave left a list of 54 individuals whom he said he intended to kill. All were from Milwaukee or the Milwaukee area. Dave's former wife and two adult daughters were on the list. So was his brother whom he hadn't contacted in 16 years. Several high school classmates who hardly remembered Dave were on his list, as were old girlfriends. All were contacted and told the startling news that they were on a suspected killer's hit list. Most had no memory of ever doing anything to bring down the wrath of Dave Schoenecker.

The day after the unusual poem and list were found, a newspaper, the *Orange County Register,* in Santa Ana, received a letter from Dave written on stationery from a Travelodge Motel in Missoula, Montana. In it, Dave confessed to the murder of his wife, explaining he had no hatred in his heart for Gail. It was just that she didn't understand and would have interfered with his master plan to take the lives of 54 people. Dave explained he had been having clear visions of long-past incidents where relatives, friends and neighbours had done him wrong. Now it was up to him to make matters right.

The newspaper turned the letter over to police. Realizing the urgency of their investigation, police in Missoula quickly learned that Dave had purchased a quantity of camping equipment at a local sporting goods store. Witnesses had seen him travelling in his 1989 Pontiac Bonneville. The vehicle was found abandoned by a search helicopter near the Idaho border. Dave had had a flat tire and had gone off the road into a ditch.

Although it was May, there was more than a metre of snow on the ground. Even during the spring months, temperatures often dipped below zero at night. Dave was on the run, carrying supplies on his back, estimated to weigh about 45 kilograms. His tracks leading from his abandoned car were discernible in the snow.

In true western style, a posse consisting of 11 men on horseback was quickly formed to pursue the fugitive through the waist-high snowdrifts. During the hunt, swirling snow sometimes obliterated Dave's tracks. A helicopter pilot spotted the fugitive from the air.

With his location pinpointed and encumbered with his heavy load, Dave gradually lost ground to the posse, who were also having trouble making their way through the snowdrifts on horseback. It was decided that two law enforcement officers would be picked up by the helicopter and dropped off in a thicket near Dave's location. The scheme worked. With two rifles pointed at his heart, Dave surrendered without a struggle. He was flown by helicopter to nearby Superior, Montana, and eventually to Anaheim to stand trial.

Dave's lawyers pleaded that their client had "an obsessive-compulsive disorder that causes gross impairment in judgement and violent mood swings" and that, in effect, he was insane. To counter this argument, prosecution attorneys pointed out that if Dave were judged to be insane he would be confined to a hospital environment. Should he later be judged to be sane, he could be released in six months. In addition, it was the prosecution's contention, and indeed, outlined in Dave's confession, that he had planned his wife's murder for months and had lain in wait for her to be in the most vulnerable situation possible so that he could kill her instantly.

After deliberating for more than four days, the California jury found Dave guilty of murdering his wife. On October 4, 1991,

David Lee Schoenecker was sentenced to life imprisonment with no possibility of parole. As you read this, he resides in California's state prison at Chino.

Pam Smart

(UNITED STATES)

GREG SMART WAS LOOKING FORWARD to the summer of 1990. It was his season to howl, and why not? He had just been named regional sales rookie of the year with insurance company Metropolitan Life. Besides, he and his 22-year-old wife, Pam, were planning to celebrate their first wedding anniversary in Florida. The future looked bright. But, as we all know, looks can be deceiving. On May 1, someone shot Greg in the back of the head and killed him instantly.

The Smarts lived in a townhouse at 4E Misty Morning Drive, in Derry, New Hampshire. Pam was a teacher at Winnacunnet Regional High School in nearby Hampton. She was pretty and well liked by both colleagues and students.

The day of the murder started out as a routine one for the Smarts. Pam drove the 30 miles to her teaching job. That evening Greg attended an insurance meeting. He returned to his home and to his death. It was Pam, arriving home later, who discovered her husband's body. She ran to a neighbour's, and soon police were swarming over the crime scene.

Investigating officers learned that a few items had been removed from the house. Drawers had been opened and their contents strewn about on the floor. It appeared as if Greg had been unfortunate enough to walk in on a robbery in progress. The perpetrator or perpetrators left absolutely nothing in the way of clues at the scene.

As the days turned into weeks, it seemed the tragic murder of 24-year-old Greg Smart might remain unsolved. All that changed abruptly a month later, when a local man, Vance Lattime, walked into the Derry police station with a .38-calibre Charter Arms revolver. He told officers he believed the gun had been used by his 17-year-old son, J. R., in the Greg Smart murder.

This startling information had been imparted to Mr. Lattime by a friend of his son, 17-year-old Ralph Welch. Ralph had told him that J. R. and another buddy, Pete Randall, 16, had revealed that they had killed the insurance salesman. Police immediately performed ballistic tests on the weapon, which proved beyond a doubt it had been used to take the life of Greg Smart.

When Welch was questioned, he told investigators he had heard rumours that J. R. and Pete, along with another boy, Billy Flynn, 16, had committed the murder. Welch said he couldn't believe his friends had actually taken a human life. He asked them outright if the rumour was true. The three boys admitted to the killing, but threw in the tidbit that their teacher, Pam Smart, the dead man's wife, was the one who had orchestrated the murder. It was this information that catapulted the Smart case into the international spotlight.

According to Welch, Pam Smart had seduced Billy Flynn a year earlier when he was only 15. Once she had him in her clutches, she kept bringing up the subject of disposing of her husband.

The three boys were taken into custody. In time the story came out. Pam had chosen Billy Flynn to do her dirty work, not because he had any criminal traits, but because, of all her pupils, he appeared to be the most vulnerable. It wasn't difficult. Billy, at age 15, must have thought he had died and gone to heaven. Here was this good-looking teacher coming on strong. They had sexual intercourse in her Honda, in Billy's house when his parents were out and in her home when her husband wasn't around; just about anywhere when the opportunity presented itself.

Billy bragged to J. R. and Pete. He was making love to the teacher whenever he wanted. What's more, she seemed to want him every bit as much as he wanted her. Billy told his buddies he was in love. There was one thing that bugged him. His girlfriend kept bringing up the subject of killing her husband. At first, Billy changed the topic. As the months passed, Pam hinted she would stop seeing him if he didn't do something about getting rid of Greg. When Billy told Pam he didn't have a gun, she suggested he ask his two buddies, J. R. and Pete, to help him. She said she would pay them well for their assistance.

Billy talked the plan over with his two friends. Surprisingly, they immediately agreed to help Billy with the murder. J. R. solved the gun problem. He borrowed his father's .38-calibre Charter Arms revolver. Pam gave Billy some money to purchase hollow-point bullets. She had read somewhere that they were the deadliest kind.

On May 1, Greg Smart's fate was sealed. Pam gave the boys last-minute instructions. They were to make sure not to get blood on her white leather couch and not to kill Greg in front of the family dog. Pam didn't want her pet traumatized.

All was in readiness. J. R. waited outside, parked near a shopping plaza. Billy and Pete waited inside the Smarts' home. Greg pulled up into the driveway. He opened the front door with his key. Pete pushed the startled man against a wall. He forced him to drop to his knees. Holding a knife against Greg's throat, he demanded, "Give me that ring." Greg replied, "No." Startled at the unexpected reply, Pete asked, "Why not?" Greg answered, "It's my wedding ring. My wife would kill me."

Pete was caught off guard. He froze. Billy took over. He placed the revolver against the back of Greg's head. As if in a trance, he said, "God forgive me," and pulled the trigger. And that was how Greg Smart died, totally unaware of his wife's involvement in his death.

Authorities had a problem. The three boys were obviously telling the truth, but in court a jury could be made to believe they had concocted the story to shift blame from themselves to the respected wife of the deceased. The police needed more, and the three boys provided the information.

One other person knew of the plot to murder Greg Smart at least a month before the event. Cecelia Pierce, another of Pam's students, had been told of the plot by Pam herself. At the time, Cecelia believed it was all talk. No one was actually going to kill anyone. Cecelia realized she was in a precarious position. After all, she had knowledge of a murderous plot and had done nothing about it both before and after the fact. She wisely agreed to co-operate with police. Under instructions, she phoned Pam and made a date to meet with her. Cecelia wore a body pack to record their discussion.

The conversation that took place between teacher and pupil left no doubt as to Pam's involvement. During the talk, interspersed with expletives, Pam discussed details of the plot. As a result, she was taken into custody and charged with her husband's murder.

In exchange for their testimony, all three boys managed a plea bargain agreement with authorities. Billy Flynn and Pete Randall were sentenced to a minimum of 28 years' imprisonment. J. R. Lattime was sentenced to a term of 18 years in prison.

On March 22, 1991, Pam Smart was found guilty of being an accomplice to murder and of conspiracy to commit murder. She was sentenced to life imprisonment with no possibility of parole, and is presently confined in the New Hampshire State Prison for Women.

George Joseph Smith

(ENGLAND)

WHEN EDITH PEGLER ANSWERED an advertisement requiring a housekeeper, she had no idea that within 30 days she would become her employer's wife. Edith was hired by George Joseph Smith on July 1, 1908. On July 30 the pair became husband and wife.

At 33 years of age, Smith was tall, dark, but not all that handsome. Edith was pleasant to look at and healthy. All this is being revealed because Edith was to be an exception in her husband's future dealings with assorted members of the opposite sex.

George told his wife he was an antique dealer, a profession which allowed him to be absent from their Bristol, England, home for weeks and even months at a time. In 1910 Smith was on one of his antique-purchasing sorties in Clifton when he made the acquaintance of Beatrice Constance Annie Mundy, better known as Bessie.

Our boy, who could charm the birds out of the trees, charmed Bessie right out of her corset. On August 26, after a whirlwind courtship, they were married. Smith neglected to tell Bessie he already had a wife back in Bristol. Then again, he rarely told Bessie anything that smacked of the truth. During their courtship and marriage she knew him as Henry Williams.

Bessie had inherited £2,500 from her late father. By 1910 standards, that amount was a fortune. Smith looked for ways to divert his wife's loot into his own pockets. There was a problem. The money was being doled out to Bessie by trustees at the rate of £8 a month. At the time of their bigamous marriage, Bessie was owed £138. On the very afternoon of the wedding, Smith took legal steps to procure that sum. As soon as he had the cash in his jeans, he took off, leaving dear Bessie penniless.

Smith returned to Edith. Now flush with cash, which he explained had been derived from astute antique deals, he actually opened a small antique store on Bath Street in Bristol.

Seven weeks later, Smith was getting itchy feet once more. It was time for another trip. Would you believe it? Quite by coincidence, he bumped into Bessie in Weston-super-Mare. So slick was Smith and so gullible was Bessie that the cad had her eating out of his hand within hours of their chance meeting. He explained that he hadn't stolen her money, he had simply borrowed it.

The couple travelled for a few days, finally settling in a little house at 80 High Street in Hearne Bay. Smith knew very well it would be difficult to lay his hands on Bessie's £2,500. Of course, if they both made out wills naming each other as beneficiaries, there would be nothing standing in his way should dear Bessie depart this cruel world.

The wills were drawn up quickly. That same day, Smith purchased a bathtub. It had no taps or fittings and had to be filled by hand. It would have to do.

Three days later, Smith took his wife to the local medic, a Dr. French. He told the doctor that Bessie was suffering from fits. The doctor prescribed bromide of potassium, a general sedative. The following day Smith fetched Dr. French and brought him to his house. The good doctor couldn't find much wrong with his patient. He again prescribed a sedative. That same afternoon, Smith again had Dr. French visit. He described another fit to the doctor. All the while, Bessie nodded in agreement. A few hours later she wrote to her family that she was suffering from strange fits, possibly epileptic, but that her husband was being extremely attentive.

Next morning, at 8:00 a.m., a note was delivered to Dr. French. It read: "Can you come at once. I'm afraid my wife is dead." Dr. French rushed over to find Bessie dead in her bathtub. She was lying on her back, still clutching a piece of soap.

An inquest into the untimely death concluded that "The cause of her death was that while taking a bath she had an epileptic seizure, causing her to fall back into the water of the bath and be drowned, and so the jurors say that the said deceased died from misadventure."

"Brides in the Bath" Smith, as he would soon become known, had successfully disposed of his first victim. He returned to Bristol to spend a short time with the ever-patient Edith before once again casting his net for another victim. Smith made his way to Southsea, where he met Alice Burnham in, of all places, a chapel. It took only a week for the unsuspecting 25-year-old Alice to become engaged to Smith. A few months later, they were married at the Portsmouth Registry Office. Alice had £27 in the bank and was owed £100 by her father. No sooner were they hitched than Smith had his wife insured for £500. He then went about scheming how to lay his hands on her money. Through a lawyer, Smith collected the £100 from his father-in-law. Next step—a bathtub.

The Smiths took rooms at Regents Road in Blackpool. That same day they called on a Dr. Billing. Evidently Mrs. Smith had been suffering from severe headaches and had been losing her hearing. The doctor prescribed a sedative. A day later, Alice took a bath. Her husband found her on her back in the tub with her head submerged. Dr. Billing rushed to the scene, but there was little he could do.

As Smith himself so sensitively put it: "When they are dead, they are done with." An inquest was held and a verdict of death by drowning was returned. After the funeral, Smith went home to Edith in Bristol.

Alice Reavil, a domestic, was the next female to fall under the spell of Smith's many charms. She deserves special mention because she managed to live. Using the name Charles Oliver James, the heartless bigamist married Alice on September 17, 1914, one week after they met. He acquired her entire life savings of £75. On September 22, while out for a walk with his new bride, Smith excused himself to go to the washroom. He never came back.

When Alice returned to their rented rooms, she was aghast to find that Smith had absconded with her clothing and the few pieces of jewellery she owned. She was left with only the clothes on her back. As usual, Smith rejoined Edith.

Toward the end of 1914, Smith got that old urge once again. In Clifton, he met Margaret Elizabeth Lofty, a 38-year-old unmarried woman who was ripe for the picking. Using the name John Lloyd, he told Peggy he was a man of independent means. On December 4, he had the lovestruck Peggy take out a life insurance policy for £700, naming him beneficiary. On December 17, Peggy became Mrs. John Lloyd in, of all places, Bath.

The pair travelled to London, renting a furnished room at 14 Bismarck Road, Highgate. Their landlady, Miss Blanche, would later recall that Smith was extremely curious about the availability of a bath with their accommodations. That same day, Smith took his Peggy to see a Dr. Bates, with the now familiar complaints which seemed to have affected all of Smith's wives. Next day he had Peggy make out a will, leaving everything to him. That night, she took a bath and became the third of George Smith's wives to drown.

This time, the chance reading of a newspaper article by Charles Burnham, Alice Burnham's father, did Smith in. Mr. Burnham read about the particularly sad death of a Mrs. Margaret Elizabeth Lloyd, who had drowned in her bathtub after having visited a doctor. Her husband had found her with her head submerged in the bath. Mr. Burnham was amazed at the similarity between this latest accident and the circumstances that had resulted in his daughter Alice's death.

Charles Burnham told police and the jig was up. They learned of all three deaths at the hands of Smith. On June 22, 1915, George

Smith stood trial for the murders of Bessie Mundy, Alice Burnham and Margaret Lofty. One of the memorable events of the trial took place when a policewoman in a bathing suit was placed in a bathtub. To illustrate how Smith drowned his wives, a lawyer quickly lifted the woman's legs in the air. Her head immediately disappeared under the water.

"Brides in the Bath" Smith was executed on Friday, August 13, 1915, in Maidstone Prison.

George Stephenson

(ENGLAND)

JOSEPH CLEAVER WAS AN 82-YEAR-OLD RETIRED BUSINESSMAN who could look back on his career with a degree of satisfaction. Ten years earlier, in 1976, the aristocratic millionaire had retired from his prosperous publishing firm to take up the life of a country gentleman in the county of Hampshire, England. His wife, Hilda, at 82, was confined to a wheelchair, having suffered a stroke around the time of her husband's retirement.

The Cleavers were wealthy enough to maintain a household staff to tend to the housework and the extensive grounds. They also employed a nurse to take care of Mrs. Cleaver's needs. Their home, Burgate House, located on the river Avon, was a luxurious country mansion. Built in the war years, when lumber and metal were devoted to the war effort, the home was primarily constructed of cement. Inside, strict regimentation was maintained. Meals were served promptly at designated hours. Dinner was a formal affair, with the men in jackets and ties, the ladies in evening gowns.

On September 3, 1986, Mrs. Hillary Carpenter, a part-time housekeeper, walked up to Burgate House to the servants' entrance as she did each morning. Upon approaching the house, she detected the smell of smoke. She was appalled at the sight that greeted her.

The dining room table was formally set, but the meal which had been served the previous evening appeared to be half eaten. As she proceeded from room to room, Mrs. Carpenter noted a gun cabinet door was open and all the weapons were missing.

Totally apprehensive, Mrs. Carpenter went upstairs. One look was enough. In the master bedroom lay the bodies of Joseph Cleaver, his wife, Hilda, still strapped in her wheelchair, their son, Thomas, 50, and Hilda's 70-year-old nurse, Margaret Murphy. Thomas's wife, Wendy, 45, was found dead in a smaller bedroom. She had been taken there and repeatedly raped before being strangled.

All five victims had been horribly burned. Later investigation into the tragedy revealed they had been strangled and sprinkled with gasoline before being set on fire. Horrendous as it is to relate, the five victims had still been alive when they were set ablaze.

The obvious motive for the house invasion was robbery. Several items were missing from the home, including three shotguns, a rifle, ammunition, a TV set and a video recorder. The killers had spread fire starters throughout the bedroom, indicating they had arrived well prepared to burn the house and its occupants, thereby leaving no witnesses and little evidence. Burgate House simply wouldn't burn. In gathering up any cash the victims had on their person, the killers had missed £700. Unbeknownst to them, Thomas Cleaver had that amount secreted in his artificial leg.

Over the years Joseph Cleaver had employed hundreds of individuals. Detectives went about searching for a disgruntled employee. They didn't have far to look. George Stephenson, 35, a man known to hold a grudge, had been fired a month earlier. Stephenson and his wife had lived in a cottage on the grounds. He had been employed as a handyman, while Mrs. Stephenson worked in the house. The suspect had a checkered past, having served two prison terms for theft. In addition, he was a violent man when drunk.

On the day he was fired, he was drunk and was savagely beating his wife. Her screams brought assistance, but the damage was done. Cleaver dismissed the couple on the spot and had them evicted from the cottage. Stephenson was not having a good day. He lost his job and his house. Before the day was done, his wife left him.

Police across the country were alerted to be on the lookout for the suspect. Meanwhile, references which Stephenson had given to the Cleavers in order to obtain his employment were checked. One reference from a couple who lived in Bournemouth was followed up. The couple who had vouched for Stephenson told police the wanted man had visited them sometime before the murder. He noted they could use a good TV and video recorder and told them that he could procure these items for them at a cheap price.

On the day after the multiple murders, the couple had found the equipment on their doorstep and assumed Stephenson had made good on his promise. Later that day, he had phoned them to verify they had received the equipment. He said he would drop around in a few days to pick up some money from them. The unsuspecting couple had no idea the TV and video recorder had been stolen.

A car rental company employee contacted police. He had recognized Stephenson's wanted picture on TV. Two days before the murders, he had rented a red Rover to Stephenson. Two men had been with the wanted man when he rented the vehicle. One companion, George Daly, 25, had paid for the rental by cheque. Daly and his brother John, 21, were traced to Coventry. Both had criminal records for petty crimes.

Police learned Stephenson had holed up with George Daly and his common-law wife immediately after the murders. The brothers, under intense questioning, admitted their involvement in the crime. Stephenson, with his likeness being featured across England on television, had nowhere to hide. On September 4, 1986, he phoned police and made arrangements to give himself up. He claimed he had driven the brothers to Burgate House, but had stayed in the Rover until they had completed their grisly task.

From the Dalys' confession and corroborating evidence, detectives were able to piece together exactly what had happened inside Burgate House the night of the tragedy. Stephenson had sought revenge on Joseph Cleaver for firing him. He also was planning a large payroll robbery and needed weapons. He figured he could accomplish both the same night. If he could lay his hands on any cash in the house, so much the better. It was the cash that had tempted the Daly brothers. The not-too-clever trio rented the Rover and paid by cheque, which led directly to them. On the murder night, they equipped themselves with pickaxe handles, firelighters and two cans of gasoline. Stephenson knew exactly when the elderly couple would be seated for dinner. He had no idea that the Cleavers' son and daughter-in-law would be there that night.

One can only imagine the terror felt by this gentle family when they were confronted by three armed and desperate masked men. When told to pass over their valuables, all complied. Joseph assured the robbers they would co-operate with them in every way.

All five occupants were herded upstairs. Stephenson forced Wendy Cleaver into a small bedroom where the helpless woman was raped. Armed with a shotgun, he ordered the Daly brothers to rape Wendy so that the three of them would be equally guilty. John Daly admitted it was he who had strangled Wendy Cleaver.

The intruders searched the house for money. They not only missed the £700 in Thomas Cleaver's artificial leg, they also over-looked a wall safe located behind a picture. Their total cash take from the Cleaver home was £90. The four remaining captives were bound in the master bedroom and strangled into unconsciousness. Heartlessly, they were doused with gasoline and set ablaze. Firestarters were spread throughout the room. In moments, the room was a blazing inferno. The cement construction of the house prevented the fire from spreading beyond the bedroom.

On October 5, 1987, the three accused stood trial. After deliberating a full day, the English jury found George Stephenson guilty of rape, robbery and four counts of murder. He was found not guilty of murdering Wendy Cleaver. In all, he received six life sentences. George Daly was acquitted of all five murders, but was found guilty of manslaughter and sentenced to 22 years' imprisonment. John

Daly, who had confessed to all five murders, was found guilty of rape, robbery and five counts of murder. He was sentenced to seven terms of life imprisonment.

Five lives had been taken for a few guns, a TV set, a video recorder and £90.

William Suff

(UNITED STATES)

ADVOCATES OF THE DEATH PENALTY are quick to point out that executed men and women can never be released from prison to kill again. Had William Lester Suff been executed, as many as 19 individuals might very well be alive today.

William was born in California in 1950. The Suff family settled in Riverside, a city located a few miles southeast of Los Angeles. As a youth William didn't distinguish himself in any way. He played the trombone in the high school band and regularly attended church. When he entered his senior year, his father deserted the family, leaving his mother to raise William and his four younger siblings. The Suff family survived on welfare.

In 1968, at age 18, William fell in love with 15-year-old Teryl Rose, a girl he met at a football game. Soon after, he joined the air force and married his youthful sweetheart. The pair set up housekeeping at the Carswell Air Force Base in Fort Worth, Texas.

Things didn't go well for the newlyweds. William was extremely jealous, constantly accusing his wife of being promiscuous. The unfounded accusations wore down Teryl Rose, who was living away from home for the first time in her life. When William began hitting her, she twice left him, but each time he enticed her back.

On November 27, 1971, William Suff Jr. was born. When the child was only a few months old, Teryl Rose noticed bruises on the baby's arms and legs. She asked her husband about the bruises. William said the baby had incurred the injuries by swinging his arms and legs against his cradle. Teryl Rose accepted the explanation. Once, when she saw her husband slap the baby very hard, she berated him, but nothing seemed to stop William from abusing his little son.

In March 1972, the four-month-old was admitted to hospital with bruises on his back, abdomen and face. Hospital staff suspected abuse and had the child turned over to child welfare. Because there was no proof of wrongdoing, little William was soon returned to his parents.

On July 20, 1973, the Suffs had a further addition to their family. Dijanet was a healthy, active baby. Two months later, Teryl Rose noticed bruises on her daughter's body. Once again, she asked her husband about the telltale marks. He blamed it on William Jr., who he said hugged his little sister too hard. Teryl Rose accepted his explanation.

Two months later, Dijanet was rushed to hospital by ambulance. Apparently William had found the baby face down on the floor instead of in her crib. He phoned his wife at work. She hurried home and had an ambulance take the child to hospital. It was too late. Baby Dijanet died of a ruptured liver.

After examining the child, doctors were amazed to find that she had a broken arm, bruising to her face, bite marks on her forehead, 13 broken ribs and a cigarette burn on the bottom of her foot. There was little doubt this baby had been tortured and stomped to death.

It didn't take long for an investigation to reveal that the Suffs' home life was anything but ideal. Neighbours and acquaintances told of William's tirades toward his two children. Several had seen him abuse little Dijanet.

William and Teryl Rose were taken into custody and charged with their daughter's murder. Most felt it would have been impossible for Teryl Rose to have lived in the same house and not to have been aware of what was going on.

Both husband and wife claimed to be innocent. The jury didn't believe them. It took only 30 minutes to find both guilty of murder. Each received a sentence of 70 years' imprisonment. Two years later Teryl Rose's conviction was reversed by the Texas Court of Criminal Appeals. William's conviction was upheld.

Teryl Rose immediately filed for divorce. William Jr. was diagnosed as retarded due to the many beatings he had suffered at the hands of his father. He was adopted by a loving couple and has since grown up. He presently exhibits no signs of the problems he originally had as a result of his father's abuse.

William Suff went to prison and should have remained there, but such was not to be the case. Once behind bars, he displayed none of the vile characteristics that had been the cause of his incarceration. This reprehensible wife-and-child abuser played in the prison band and became something of a bookworm. He earned a bachelor's degree in sociology in 1980 from Steven F. Austin State University in Nacador.

As luck would have it, William's excellent behaviour in prison coincided with acute overcrowding of the Texas prison system. Those prisoners with exemplary records were being granted parole. The fact that William had earned a university degree since his incarceration didn't hurt his chances. After serving only nine years and nine months, he was paroled and moved back to Riverside County, California.

William's parole officer saw him every month for three years. He was then considered such a good risk that his parole status was relaxed to a visit once a year. William complied with this condition only once and then simply never contacted the parole board again. No one bothered him and he didn't bother anyone. William Suff, who had been sentenced to 70 years in prison, was as free as a bird and had effectively slipped through the cracks.

William quit or was fired from several jobs. He worked as a stock boy for a computer company and, for a short while, flipped burgers at a McDonald's franchise. He purchased a 1973 Toyota

Celica and discovered that he was able to pick up prostitutes with his new wheels.

In 1986, William obtained employment as a stock clerk at the Riverside County Warehouse. One of the agencies he filled orders for was the sheriff's office. He enjoyed passing the time of day with the sheriff's deputies when they dropped in to pick up office supplies. Things were looking up. William had a good job and even had a live-in girlfriend. Besides, he now had enough money to have a prostitute pretty well whenever he wanted. William loved what prostitutes did, but hated the girls for doing it.

In 1988, William Suff, who had tortured, stomped on and murdered his own child, decided that the world would be better off without prostitutes. He figured the best thing he could do would be to kill one—who knows, maybe more.

In January 1988, William cruised the streets of San Bernardino looking for a hooker. It didn't take long. The girls were out in full force displaying their wares. William pulled up, offered the first one he saw $20 for straight sex.

Lisa Lacik, a 21-year-old prostitute, a bit high on cocaine, jumped into William's vehicle. Three days later her body was found by hikers in the San Bernardino Mountains. She had been raped, strangled and stabbed to death. Her killer had cut off her right breast.

When William read about the body being found, he was ecstatic. It had been easy. He had murdered and no one was any the wiser.

A year later, William struck again. This time he picked up his victim off the streets of Lake Elsinore, where he was well known. It was a much riskier operation, but that only added to his enjoyment. Rhonda Jetmore suggested a vacant house where she usually took her tricks. William agreed. Once there, he attacked, but Rhonda was strong and sober. She fought him off and ran out of the house. That had been close, but it served as a lesson to William. Next time he would be more careful.

William purchased a grey 1989 Mitsubishi van. That June he murdered 28-year-old Kim Lyttle. Her murder was followed by those of Tina Leal, Darla Ferguson and Carol Miller. All these girls were tortured and mutilated. Between murders William had steady girl-friends who never knew that the gentle, polite man they were dating and, in some cases, living with, was a serial killer.

In November 1990, William murdered Cheryl Coker and tossed her body in a garbage enclosure in Riverside. A month later, he picked up Susan Sternfeld, who suffered the same fate as all the others. In January 1991, William raped, mutilated and murdered Kathleen Puckett.

He had now been operating for years in the towns and cities around Riverside. Police organized a task force to apprehend the serial killer, but the clues were vague. William took his victims' clothing with him when he left the crime scenes. He left no telltale fingerprints. The now out-of-control serial rapist and murderer loved to read about his exploits in the local newspapers.

Eventually, William became bolder. He decided to leave one of his victims where she would be found immediately. Cherie Payseur's body was deposited outside a bowling alley. Despite finding the body only hours after it was dumped, detectives failed to come up with any clues that would lead to the killer's identity.

The next victim to fall prey to the serial killer was Sherry Latham. Sherry managed to scratch William's face before succumbing to her attacker. William passed off his injuries with a laugh, claiming he had received the scratches when he broke up a fistfight.

In August, William picked up prostitute Kelly Hammond. She was murdered in the same manner as her predecessors, but not before another prostitute had seen the vehicle and the driver. This witness was able to describe the vehicle she had seen Kelly enter as being a grey van. She said the driver was a white man.

A month later, William raped and murdered Catherine McDonald. In October, Delliah Zamora met the same fate. Two days before Christmas, prostitute Eleanor Casares was murdered by the seemingly invincible serial killer.

William had long since perfected a method of disposing of his victims' clothing and jewellery. He washed the clothing immediately and, along with the jewellery, gave the items away. Apparently the recipients of the gifts never questioned their origin.

From tire tracks left at the Casares murder scene, authorities were able to identify the vehicle's tires. The murder van had been equipped with two new Uniroyals and a single Yokohama tire. The fourth tire couldn't be identified. They already knew they were looking for a grey van.

On January 9, 1992, police surveillance teams were, as usual, located at strategic points throughout the area. William was on the prowl. As he propositioned a prostitute, he was sighted by motor-cycle police officer Frank Orta. William spotted the officer at the same time, made a U-turn and sped away. Orta spun around and overtook the Mitsubishi. He had pulled over grey vans in the past, but none had been operated by the serial killer.

Orta thought this would be just another false alarm. To be on the safe side, he radioed in the incident, which brought two officers, Duane Beckman and Don Taulli, to the scene.

Orta checked the driver's licence on his computer. It had been suspended. William couldn't produce the vehicle's registration. Orta made the decision to impound the vehicle. He bent down and checked the van's tires. Two were Uniroyals and one was a Yokohama.

Eventually, trace evidence taken from the vehicle and William's person were found to match samples collected from several of his victims.

In March 1995, William stood trial, charged with 13 counts of first-degree murder and one count of attempted murder in the case of Rhonda Jetmore. Many believe that he was responsible for at least 19 murders.

The California jury deliberated for one week before finding William guilty on 12 first-degree murder charges and guilty of the attempted murder of Rhonda Jetmore. The lengthy deliberation was the result of one juror believing there was a reasonable doubt about one of the murders. There was never any doubt in anyone's mind that William was a monster whose main object in life was to rid the world of prostitutes.

At the sentencing portion of William Suff's trial, the jury retired for only 10 minutes before returning the death sentence. Today the Riverside Serial Killer resides on death row in San Quentin Prison.

Marty Tankleff

(UNITED STATES)

TAKE A SEAT with your fellow jurors and listen to this most disturbing evidence, much as the New York State jury did back in 1990. You decide whether the defendant was guilty of murder or not guilty. Ready? Here we go.

Seymour Tankleff had it made in the shade. In 1984, the 58-year-old Seymour sold his lucrative real estate and insurance business. Together with wife Arlene, he retired to affluent Belle Terre, Long Island. Their large waterfront ranch-style home usually had a couple of the family's vehicles parked in the spacious driveway. Years before, the childless Tankleffs had adopted a son, Marty, who had turned out to be their pride and joy. Marty, a fine cut of a lad, was attending high school.

On Tuesday September 6, 1988, Seymour had some friends over for their regular poker game. The men played cards until 3:00 a.m. There was nothing unusual about the game. None of the men behaved any differently than they had at previous games. Winners and losers alike bade Seymour good-night and drove away from their host's home.

At 6:00 a.m., the 911 operator received a desperate call from Belle Terre, which was unusual in itself. The community of 800 souls is

240

virtually crime free. This morning would change all that. The caller was 16-year-old Marty Tankleff. He blurted out that he had awakened at 5:30 a.m. to find his mother on the floor of her bedroom. He could see she had been bludgeoned and stabbed. Marty was sure she was dead. His father was in the den, fully dressed, but horribly beaten and stabbed as well. Marty felt his father was still breathing. He desperately wanted to know if there was any emergency procedure he could perform until assistance arrived. Following the 911 operator's instructions, Marty worked on his father until medics took over. Seymour was rushed by ambulance to Mather Memorial Hospital in nearby Port Jefferson. Unfortunately, Arlene Tankleff was beyond help.

The affluent, well-insulated community was aghast that one of their own had been murdered. Things like that just didn't happen in tranquil Belle Terre.

Marty told police he had arisen from bed, dressed, and was preparing to go to school when he ventured into his parents' bedroom. There lay his mother on the floor in her nightclothes. Seeing she was dead, he rushed through the house, looking for his father. He found Seymour in the den, badly wounded, unconscious but still breathing. He assumed his father had not yet gone to bed after the poker game had ended. Both of Marty's parents had been beaten with a blunt object and their throats had been cut.

Marty Tankleff was taken to police headquarters and questioned by Suffolk County detectives. By noon, he was charged with the murder of his mother and the attempted murder of his father.

The community and old friends of the Tankleffs believed there had been some terrible mistake. They had known Marty since he was an infant. He was a polite, obedient youngster who had never given his parents any cause for concern. The Tankleffs had been generous, loving parents, who had showered Marty with all the creature comforts any teenager could want. In fact, detectives investigating the case admitted that Marty's first-aid actions may have saved his father's life. The family rallied around Marty. They posted a $25,000 reward for information leading to the arrest and conviction of the killer.

While Marty awaited trial, other developments took place concerning the murders. Eight days after the murder, one of the men who had attended the poker game at the Tankleffs' disappeared. The missing man's car was found in Hauppauge, Long Island, with the engine running and the door open. There was grave suspicion that the man had attacked the Tankleffs and fled. Maybe he had killed himself. All doubts were put to rest when the gentleman was located alive and well in a motel in Redondo Beach, California. He had suffered from depression after the death of his wife. He now had a girlfriend and felt if he disappeared, his girlfriend and a child by his first wife would collect two million dollars in life insurance and be better off without him. He swore he had nothing to do with the Tankleff incident.

Another bombshell was dropped when the chief prosecutor in the case revealed that Marty had confessed to the attack on both his parents. On Friday October 7, 1988, Seymour Tankleff died of his injuries without regaining consciousness. Marty was released on bail of one million dollars, raised by his family.

On April 23, 1990, the double-murder trial of Marty Tankleff, 18, took place. The prosecution charged that Marty had confessed to the crime. The motive had been a disagreement about the family's new Lincoln. Marty wanted to drive it to school, but his father had insisted he make do with a 1978 Lincoln.

According to the prosecution, Marty confessed to detectives that he had hit his mother with a barbell and had cut her throat. He had then sneaked up on his father, who had said, "Marty, why are you doing this?" Marty told police, "I didn't reply. I knocked him silly."

The prosecution claimed that Marty had committed the murders in the nude to avoid getting blood on his clothing. He had worn gloves to prevent leaving fingerprints and had then showered with the barbell and the knife. After cleaning both thoroughly, he had placed the kitchen knife beside a watermelon on the kitchen counter, so it would appear as if it had been used for slicing the melon. He had then dressed and called 911. In addition, the prosecution brought forth several school chums who testified that Marty had often commented that he would have plenty of money and could do anything he wanted if only his parents were dead.

Regarding the confession, it was explained by the prosecution that one of the detectives had lied to Marty when he told him his father had regained consciousness and named him as the attacker. It was then Marty had confessed.

Marty's lawyer categorically denied his client had anything to do with the murder of his parents. Susan Ryan of the Suffolk County Criminalistics Laboratory testified she had extensively tested the barbell taken from Marty's room. There were several hairs and fibres adhering to the barbell, none of which matched either Marty's or his parents' clothing or hair. This effectively countered the prosecution's theory that Marty had thoroughly washed the barbell after the killings.

Marty took the witness stand in his own defence. He explained that a detective pretended to be talking to the hospital and had told him his father had named him as the killer. "I couldn't understand why my father should say that. He had never lied to me. I started to believe that I had done it. I thought I was having a bad nightmare and would soon awake. I finally said, Yes, (I had done the killings), because that's what they wanted to hear."

The defence also pointed out that if Marty was the diabolical killer, why had he single-handedly kept his father alive when it would have been so easy for him to have finished the job? All the evidence against the accused was circumstantial. There were no witnesses to the murders.

There you have it. On June 12, 1990, the jury convened to reach their verdict. It would take them eight days. What do you think? Was Marty guilty, as the prosecution claimed, or was he caught up in a web of circumstantial evidence and had nothing to do with his parents' murders?

The Suffolk jury returned a verdict of guilty concerning both murders. Marty Tankleff was sentenced to two terms of 50 years' to life imprisonment, to run concurrently.

John Tanner

(ENGLAND)

IT WAS LOVE AT FIRST SIGHT. Pretty Rachel McLean, a 19-year-old student at Oxford University in Merrie England made no bones about it. She had fallen madly in love with John Tanner, a student at Nottingham University in 1991, when our tale of dastardly deeds unfolds.

The two attractive students met at Rachel's nineteenth birthday party. They were immediately physically attracted to each other and were intimate from that very first meeting. Whenever they were together they engaged in intercourse, sometimes several times a night. The idyllic romance continued for eight months until Rachel disappeared.

It happened after Rachel had spent a pleasant weekend with her family in Blackpool. She returned to Oxford on Sunday morning and phoned her parents that afternoon, advising them that she had arrived safely at her Argyle Street digs. The three girlfriends with whom she shared the house were out of town for the weekend. Rachel had the run of the place for the rest of the day and for the best part of Monday.

Next day, Rachel didn't attend her regular lectures. Students sometimes party too hard and too long over the weekend and decide to sleep in on Monday morning, but one of Rachel's classmates remarked that it wasn't like Rachel to miss a Monday morning class. In fact, Rachel had never missed any classes, ever.

When Rachel's three housemates returned on Monday afternoon and found out that no one had seen her all day, they became alarmed. On Tuesday morning, the police were informed that Rachel McLean was missing.

Within a day, investigators realized the subject of their inquiries was a conscientious student and a loving daughter. They couldn't turn up any clue as to why or how she had dropped out of sight. They were informed of her involvement with John Tanner, who attended university in Nottingham, some 100 kilometres from Oxford.

Detectives visited John, who was devastated to find out his girl-friend was missing. He told detectives Rachel could not have disappeared on Sunday because he had been with her until Monday morning. John explained he had visited with Rachel on Sunday night. When he learned that her friends wouldn't be back until the next day, he decided to spend the night. John emphasized they had spent a very pleasant night, making love seven times. Next morning, the pair took a bus to the station, where he caught the 10:00 a.m. train to Nottingham. They parted on the station platform.

John told detectives that he and Rachel wrote to each other almost every day when they were apart. So deep was their love, he had composed a letter to her on the train. He remembered looking out the window and seeing Rachel talking to a man in the parking lot. As a matter of fact, he had mentioned the man in his letter to her.

Police felt the man Rachel had been speaking to was by far their best lead to her fate. They decided to re-create the scene John had witnessed. A policewoman of the same height and weight as the missing girl was outfitted with clothing similar to that worn by Rachel. John enacted the kiss he had given Rachel as he boarded the train. An officer, dressed in clothing described by John, took the part of the man in the parking lot. The press was invited to take photos of the re-enactment in the hope that someone had seen the lovers part and Rachel join the man in the parking lot.

While they waited for results from the newspaper pictures, detectives searched Rachel's room. Everything was neat and tidy. Evidently, Rachel was a meticulous housekeeper. The girl's room was spotless. Inside a closet, police found Rachel's diary. They pored over the contents. Initially, the diary revealed that Rachel was totally enthralled with John. However, more recently, her ardour had cooled. The relationship, as far as Rachel was concerned, had deteriorated to the extent that she had grown to dislike John intensely and had wrestled with how to tell him she wished to terminate their romance. Once, when she hinted she wanted to break up, John informed her that he was dying of cancer. Later, she found out he wasn't ill at all but was using the dreaded disease as a ploy to gain her sympathy.

Rachel's true attitude toward John and the poor response received from the re-enactment photographs convinced police they were on the wrong track. Instead of attempting to trace Rachel's last movements from the railway station, they now felt she had never left her home.

Detectives again descended on Rachel's Argyle Street lodgings. A search of the entire house failed to uncover any sign of the missing girl. It was now 18 days since Rachel had gone missing. If her body was in the flat, surely it would have given off a distinctive odour by now. Despite the lack of an odour, it was decided to take up the floorboards of Rachel's bedroom. Rachel McLean's body was found between the floor and the ceiling of the room below in a remarkable state of preservation. The outer wall of the house was made of air brick, which had allowed cold air to circulate around the body. The unusually cold weather, combined with this circumstance, had delayed decomposition.

An autopsy indicated that Rachel had been strangled from behind with a ligature. The bus company's computer records revealed John had travelled to the railway station alone.

Faced with the discovery of the body and the incriminating insinuations in Rachel's diary, John admitted his guilt and made a full confession. He told his interrogators he had arrived at Rachel's room at 8:00 p.m. on Sunday. Rachel had informed him in no uncertain terms that she wanted to break off their relationship once and for all. John saw red. He ripped off his necktie and strangled Rachel until she stopped moving. Then he placed the girl's body under the floorboards. John wore the necktie when he left the premises. After all, it had sentimental value. Rachel had given it to him as a present the previous Christmas.

In December 1991, John Tanner was found guilty of murdering Rachel McLean. He was sentenced to life imprisonment, a sentence he is now serving.

George Trepal

GEORGE TREPAL HAD A NATURAL FLAIR for anything scientific. He was particularly interested in computers and chemistry. George was bright, no question about it. He graduated from the University of Southern California with a bachelor of science degree, majoring in chemistry.

At a Mensa meeting (an organization which emphasizes high intellectual function, and whose members comprise the top 2 percent of the population), George met Diane Carr. Diane was no lightweight herself. She was a medical doctor and had earned three other degrees—a bachelor of science, master of science and a masters in clinical pathology.

The pair married and settled in the tiny central Florida town of Alturas. Their lifestyle was strange in that George spent most of his time in front of his computer. Diane, the breadwinner of the family, soon established a lucrative medical practice. Their home was in an isolated area surrounded by orange groves. The Trepals had only one neighbour, Peggy and Pye Carr (no relation to Diane). Forty-year-old Peggy brought three teenage children from previous unions to her marriage with Pye. Cissy, Allen and Duane got along well with Pye's two youngsters, Tammy and Travis. Cissy was the mother of two-year-old Kacy.

Peggy rose every morning at 6:00 a.m. to work at her waitressing job at Nicholas Family Restaurant in nearby Barlow. Everyone liked Peggy Carr. Pye was a miner who was well regarded by colleagues and friends.

The Carrs and the Trepals were as diametrically opposite as two families could be. George and Diane, who socialized mainly with other members of Mensa, considered the Carrs to be white trash. They rarely spoke more than a few words to them. Neither family had ever been in the other's home.

On October 23, 1988, Peggy had to drag herself to work. She simply didn't feel well. At the end of her shift at the restaurant, she returned home and, uncharacteristically, lay down on the sofa. Pye was concerned. Peggy grew pale. She had difficulty opening her eyes and complained of cold fingers.

Cissy thought her mother should be taken to hospital, but Pye disagreed. That night, near midnight, Pye had a change of heart. He and Cissy rushed Peggy to Barlow Memorial Hospital. Doctors couldn't come up with a diagnosis. Peggy failed to improve. She now complained of feeling as if she were on fire.

As suddenly as Peggy had fallen ill, she rallied and was sent home. To celebrate, the family had some fried chicken brought over to the house by Pye's sister, Carolyn Dixon. Since there was still suspicion that a flu bug had been the origin of Peggy's distress, it was suggested she take a lot of fluids. The chicken was washed down with Coca-Cola, which Carolyn found in a carton containing eight 16-oz bottles. Peggy drank the Coke, as did her son Duane and Pye's son, Travis.

Next morning, Peggy once again became ill. So did Duane and Travis. Strangely, they complained of the same symptoms Peggy had voiced earlier. Peggy was rushed to hospital by ambulance. Doctors there now felt that she had somehow come in contact with poison.

Initially, they suspected lead, mercury or arsenic, but when they noticed big clumps of Peggy's hair falling out, they came to the conclusion that she was being poisoned with thallium. Colourless, tasteless and odourless, thallium is deadly. It is outlawed for most uses, but continues to be used under tight restrictions in the photographic and medical fields. Peggy tested positive for the deadly poison, as did Duane and Travis in lesser amounts.

Peggy's condition didn't improve. She was unable to breathe without mechanical assistance or to open her eyes. All muscular control was leaving her body. Her daughter Cissy believed that Pye was poisoning Peggy. She remembered he had been reluctant to take her mother to hospital. Besides, Peggy and Pye had recently had a severe argument.

Police were called in to solve the attempted murder. Meanwhile, Duane and Travis were admitted to hospital. Slowly, they were transformed from active, husky teenagers to pale imitations of their former selves. Both told police their bodies felt as if they were on fire, but could shed no light on who might want to poison them.

Detectives learned that four months prior to the poisonings, the Carrs had received a threatening letter in the mail. It read, "You and all your so-called family have two weeks to move out of Florida forever or else you all die. This is no joke."

While everyone who knew the Carrs was being questioned, Peggy slipped into a coma. Pye came under serious suspicion until tests indicated that he too had ingested thallium, but to a far lesser degree than his wife and the two boys.

Police tested more than 450 items taken from the Carr home before they were successful in finding the source of the thallium. The poison was discovered in the remains of five Coca-Cola bottles which had already been consumed. Three full bottles also contained thallium. The tops of the bottles showed no evidence of tampering. The bottles had been opened, laced with thallium and the tops replaced expertly and with great care.

Was it possible that a madman somewhere in a Coca-Cola bottling plant was indiscriminately poisoning vats of the beverage? This horrific scenario was quickly put to rest when the eight contaminated bottles were found to be the only ones containing poison. All Coca-Cola from the originating plant was and had been free of any foreign substance. It was apparent that one individual had targeted only the Carr family.

At this point, despite the participation of the FBI, the investigation stalled. On March 3, 1989, Peggy Carr's life support system was disconnected and she died. In time, Duane and Travis would recover from the effects of the poison.

Because of his scientific background, neighbour George Trepal came under suspicion. Being the only neighbour, George could have had the opportunity to lace the Coke. But why would he do such a thing? Detectives thought they knew the answer, although they felt it was a bizarre motive for murder.

On a hot day shortly before the poisonings, Duane and Travis were washing their truck in the backyard. They turned on the truck's stereo, which blared across the orange groves. Peggy shouted to the boys to turn down the volume. They paid no attention, if they heard her at all.

Diane Carr stormed onto the property in a rage, demanding that they turn down the radio. Although Duane lowered the volume, Diane insisted on speaking to Peggy, who came out of the house. Diane threatened to call police. She waved her finger in Peggy's face. Peggy retaliated by telling the angry woman in no uncertain terms to leave her boys alone. In the end, Peggy ordered Diane off her property.

When questioned, Diane admitted to having had the heated argument with her neighbour. Both she and George said they hated the loud music played by the two boys. Taking a further look into George's past, detectives learned that he had once been charged with operating an illegal methamphetamine lab in North Carolina. For that indiscretion, George had spent some time in prison.

Police were sure they had their man. George was a chemist, who no doubt could lay his hands on thallium. He had the opportunity to lace the Coke and he had a motive, weird as that motive was. Officials felt it still wasn't enough. A female police officer was assigned to go undercover, ingratiating herself into George's life in order to somehow find a connecting link between him and the deadly poison. It took a full year, but in the end investigators had enough grounds to obtain a search warrant, enabling them to enter the Trepal home. Inside a work area, they found a bottle of thallium.

George Trepal was arrested and charged with Peggy Carr's murder, as well as six counts of attempted murder, seven counts of poisoning food with intent to kill and one count of tampering with a consumer product. He was found guilty of all 15 charges.

On March 6, 1991, George Trepal was sentenced to death. He is presently residing on death row. Ironically, each prisoner has a radio in his cell. To cut out the sound along the row, each is equipped with a private headset. We can only assume that George is happy with the low volume.

Dr. Paul Vicers

(ENGLAND)

YOU WOULD HAVE TO SAY THAT Dr. Paul Vicers, a man of honour, integrity, character and culture should have known better. The good doctor was a big wheel at Newcastle Royal Victoria Infirmary in not-so-sunny England, where he specialized in orthopedic surgery. But Paul roamed off the beaten path. Let me explain.

Vicers, 46, lived in apparent harmony with his conservative spouse, Margaret, in a lovely old home on a prestigious street simply called The Drive. The prim-and-proper couple met while both were attending Oxford University.

Funny how things change. During their college days, Margaret had been the outgoing, gregarious type, but as Paul climbed the professional ladder, Margaret took a back seat. Some women accept the role of second banana to illustrious husbands; others insist on pursuing their careers. Margaret chose the former route, but her decision took its toll. Shortly after their son, James, was born, she became depressed, a depression that was to stay with her the rest of her life.

In 1976, Paul attended a medical convention in Brussels. He enjoyed the break from his regular duties back home. Besides, it was a chance for him to socialize with important medical dignitaries.

There he was, in his rumpled suit, with his balding dome, when who should stroll into the Hotel Trafalgar but Pamela Collison. Pam, 32, hailed from London, where she was employed as a political researcher for the British minister of health. Although Pam's position was fairly high-profile, it wasn't her career that fuelled her engines. No, Pam was a lady on the prowl. She was looking for a male with money and prestige. Dr. Paul Vicers fit the bill absolutely.

There was one little scorpion in the broth. Make that two. Paul had a wife and adult son back home in Newcastle. Never mind, Pam would cross that bridge when she came to it. First and foremost, there was work to be done.

Pam arranged to be introduced to Paul. The conversation was pleasant and, above all, suggestive. This would be easy, Pam thought to herself. A risqué remark, a double entendre, and before you could say why not, the pair was having a quiet drink in the hotel lounge.

Paul was smitten. Here was a woman far more intelligent than Margaret, definitely more youthful, with a superior figure. There was a subtle insinuation that she would not be averse to experiencing sexual pleasures with the older medic.

Home was never like this. Margaret was so staid. Living with a woman who had been depressed for almost 25 years hadn't been easy. Paul and Pam exchanged telephone numbers. As she rose to take her leave, Pam was certain that the hook had been firmly placed. She and Paul would meet again. She was sure of it.

A short time later, Paul did call. Pam was flattered and pleased. He explained that he was attending another medical convention in London and would like to take her to dinner. They made a date to meet at the Moulin Rouge, the most expensive restaurant Pam could think of on the spur of the moment.

The dinner was a success, with just enough tension to elicit sexual urges that Paul had not experienced in years. Pam too was thrilled at the way things were going. She had made up her mind to play her cards just right. (Translation: She wasn't going to hop into bed with him that first night.) At the conclusion of dinner, Paul suggested she visit with him at his hotel. Pam pretended not to hear the invitation. The date ended with a polite, restrained kiss on the cheek.

Of course, Paul called Pam again. She wasn't nearly as conservative on their second date. (Translation: She did hop into bed.) Within a matter of weeks, Paul had rented a quaint bachelor apartment. For two or three days a week, Pam played house with the well-known surgeon.

Paul's nature was such that he didn't attempt to conceal his new-found love. As the months turned into years, his colleagues became quite accustomed to seeing Pam Collison on Dr. Paul Vicers's arm. He passed her off as a medical researcher, which didn't fool anyone for a moment.

Around the three-year mark of their romance, Pam suggested marriage more and more often. Paul thought of divorce, but the strain and scandal of it all was too much for him to face. There had to be another, simpler way to solve this most vexing problem. What to do? Margaret was depressed all the time. She continually complained of headaches. Sexual relations had ceased long before. The woman was no fun any more.

Paul came up with a rather illogical solution. He would stick with his mistress and kill his wife. It would be easy.

Margaret was forever requesting medication for her depression. Paul had just the ticket. He injected his wife with the drug CCNU. Within a few days, Margaret felt like a new woman.

When the effects of the drug wore off, Margaret begged for and was given another shot. She felt so much better. The couple's relationship became more amicable, but that wasn't in Paul's plans. He knew that in time the massive doses would take their toll.

In a few weeks, Margaret felt so weak she decided to stay in bed. Soon she was spending most of her time in bed. She had no way of knowing that she was suffering from aplastic anemia, a leukemia-like disease brought on by the injections given to her by her husband.

It took four weeks before Margaret was hospitalized. She continually received blood transfusions. In all, 30 pints were given to her in an attempt to save her life. Paul was beside himself with concern. His medical colleagues asked him if Margaret had been given any drugs recently. Paul assured them that she had not. It is interesting to note that no one asked Margaret this question. Then again, her husband was a well-known doctor. It was a mistake everyone except Margaret would live to regret.

Margaret's condition deteriorated. She died in July 1979. Paul was free as a bird to continue his relationship with Pam. The lovebirds billed and cooed in that bachelor apartment for another seven months until a suspicious Scotland Yard inspector decided to take a further look into Margaret's death. He dug up copies of prescriptions for vast amounts of CCNU made out to some of Pam's closest friends. He learned that none of the people named on the prescriptions had received the drug.

Both Paul and Pam were arrested and charged with the murder of Margaret Vicers. Pamela Collison was acquitted of all charges. There was no evidence to indicate that she had any guilty knowledge of Paul's diabolical plot to do away with his wife. Dr. Paul Vicers didn't fare nearly as well. He was found guilty of murder and sentenced to life imprisonment. In addition, he was stripped of all licences to practise medicine.

Maxine Walker

(UNITED STATES)

WHEN MAXINE WALKER'S HUSBAND UP AND DIED of a heart attack, the good hill folk of the Appalachian town of Sylacauga, Alabama, were mighty grieved. It wasn't right that a woman still in her prime would be left with two young'uns to bring up without a papa.

At the wake, Maxine put on a spread featuring big slices of pecan pie accompanied by sweet iced tea. As luck would have it, her husband had taken out a small insurance policy on his life, which would leave his widow with a few extra dollars to comfort her in her sorrow. Not to be overlooked was the snazzy white Ford pickup, which was an integral part of the late Mr. Walker's worldly goods.

Despite landing on her feet, it was a lonely existence for Maxine, living in the house with only her two children for company. Under normal circumstances, she would not have given a hound's tooth for the likes of W. C. Berry.

Let's face it, the 42-year-old W. C. didn't have a lot to recommend him. For starters, he had once spent a few years in prison for manslaughter, but that was of no concern to the locals. W. C. simply didn't do much but tool around the county in a beat-up old car, which more often than not wouldn't start. The best that could be said for him is that he could mow a mean lawn and straighten out a barn door if pressed. Most days he didn't tax his intellect with these pursuits, but preferred to spend his time hunting wild turkeys in the nearby woods.

One fine day in 1988, shortly after Maxine's husband went to his great reward, W. C. called on Maxine to pay his respects. Ordinarily she would have accepted his condolences through the screen door, but a girl gets lonesome. What the heck, thought the widow as she invited W. C. inside for a slab of that pecan pie, which evidently was her specialty.

In the following weeks, W. C. visited Maxine often. He did some mowing, repaired a broken window and, in general, did a whole lot of fixin' around the house. Well, folks, how can I put it? W. C. fixed more than the house. Before you could say Tuscaloosa, W. C. and Maxine were doing what comes naturally between the sheets. They were discreet. They waited until the children were asleep.

Eventually, W. C. moved right in with Maxine. Sure enough, tongues wagged, but the convenience was worth it. Everyone was happy. W. C. had an attractive partner in bed and, what's more, he had the use of the Ford pickup whenever he wanted. As for Maxine, we all know why she was so pleased.

This tranquil state of affairs could conceivably have gone on forever, if it hadn't been for a couple of things. There's only so much fixing that can be done around a house. In time, all the doors were oiled, the broken windows replaced and the lawn was as smooth as the top of a pool table. With nothing much to do, W. C. proceeded to do nothing.

Time rests heavily on idle hands.

To add spice to his life, W. C. wasn't above wandering by Mary McDaniel's house to do whatever he did with Mary. When Maxine heard of W. C.'s extracurricular activity she was madder than a hound dog with fleas. As if his philandering wasn't enough, that no good W. C. used the Ford pickup to call on Mary.

Maxine took inventory. At 44 years of age, she still had many a good year ahead of her. She looked in the mirror and admired herself. No sirree, she wasn't on the shelf just yet. She didn't need W. C. any longer, but there was a problem—how to get rid of the rascal.

Maxine's problem sort of solved itself, in a way. Due to an unpleasant gynecological condition, Maxine found it advisable to consult a physician in nearby Birmingham. Her worst fears were realized. She had contracted venereal disease from W. C. She ordered him out of her home. W. C. left, but didn't take the rejection well. He began stalking his former lover.

Maxine couldn't go anywhere without that annoying man trailing her. Sometimes he would park his nondescript car outside her home and just glare. On occasion, he would hurl threats at Maxine and the kids. The situation became so intolerable that Maxine had one of her nephews, 22-year-old Charlie Lawhorn, move in with her.

Charlie loved his Auntie Max. To prove the point, he gave W. C. a thorough thrashing, and for a while they didn't see hide nor hair of the rejected suitor, but it wasn't too long before W. C. resumed his old annoying ways.

Maxine couldn't stand it, so she sat Charlie down and came right to the point. Would her sister's boy help her get rid of W. C. on a permanent basis? She even offered to pay. Would $50 be enough to cover the inconvenience? Charlie thought the $50 was more than generous. In fact, for another $50, his brother Mark would be a willing participant.

And so the plan was hatched. Maxine called W. C. and arranged to pick him up. W. C. figured the gods had decided to smile upon him; obviously Maxine realized she couldn't live without him. Maxine drove Charlie and Mark into the woods near a well-known lovers' lane. She knew she would have no trouble enticing W. C. to the spot where they had made love in the good old days.

The scheme worked like a charm up to the moment that W. C. heard voices emanating from the woods. While he wasn't the brightest guy in the world, he immediately smelled a rat, opened the truck door and ran for his life. Maxine shouted at her nephews to hop on the back of the pickup. The chase was on. When she drew abreast of the unfortunate W. C., both Charlie, with his shotgun, and Mark, with his pistol, opened fire. In all, the brothers fired 16 times. Every shot found its target. W. C. was literally blown apart.

The day after the murder, April Fool's Day, 1988, was uneventful. But the following day, Wayne Martin, who was hunting wild turkeys in the woods, stumbled across what was left of W. C. The amateur murder scheme wasn't difficult to figure out. It was common knowledge among the mountain folk that W. C. had been Maxine's lover and that he had recently fallen out of favour. Likewise, everyone knew that nephew Charlie had moved in as Auntie Max's protector.

The local sheriff picked up Charlie and accused him of killing W. C. Poor Charlie didn't know what to say. But true to his Appalachian heritage, his first instinct was to protect his brother: "My brother didn't have nothin' to do with this. I did it for my Auntie Max."

Maxine was questioned and the entire story spilled from her lips. It wasn't much of a trial except for the fact that Maxine felt she was justified in sending W. C. to that great turkey shoot in the sky. The Alabama jury took only 50 minutes to disagree. They found her guilty of murder and sentenced her to death in the electric chair. Since then, Maxine has won an appeal on a technicality and was granted a new trial. This time around, she was found guilty but sentenced to life imprisonment. At a separate trial, Charlie was found guilty of murder, and sentenced to death. He currently resides on death row in Alabama. His brother Mark was found guilty of murder and sentenced to life imprisonment.

Fred & Rosemary West

(ENGLAND)

IS IT PREORDAINED that monstrous couples meet and go on killing sprees? What would Bonnie's life have been like without Clyde? Would Karla Homolka's life have been far different had she not met Paul Bernardo?

But they do meet and form their evil partnerships.

Fred West was employed as a bread deliveryman when he met Rose Letts at a bus stop in Cheltenham, England. Sweet-talking Fred had a crop of curly hair, a swarthy complexion and pale blue eyes. Rose thought he was very sexy. Besides, they had occupations in common. Rose worked in a bakery. When they met, Fred was 28, Rose, 16.

Fred had a shady past, having been in and out of prison for a variety of minor offences. Along the way, he met a lass from Scotland named Rena Costello, who was totally smitten with the charming Fred. On November 17, 1962, Fred and Rena became husband and wife. The couple settled into holy matrimony in the Scottish town of Coatbridge. The marriage wasn't a happy one. Fred insisted on having sex on command and was fascinated with bondage. To make ends meet, Rena tried her hand at prostitution, with Fred acting as her pimp. Sometimes he beat her up. No, you wouldn't say the Wests were your average family.

In March 1963, Rena gave birth to a baby girl, Charmaine. Fred wasn't the child's father. He hated the brown-eyed, dark-haired, beautiful little girl. In 1964, the Wests were blessed with another daughter, Anna Marie. This time Fred was the biological father of the new addition. He doted on Anna Marie. Sometime after her birth, the family moved to England.

Fred, who outwardly appeared so very average, had begun attacking young girls, which didn't sit well with Rena. Finally, she left him. Rena attempted to take her children, but Fred physically held on to the two girls until Rena, sobbing, left her offspring behind in England and returned to Scotland.

Anna McFall was hired on as the children's nanny. It wasn't long before the impressionable 16-year-old succumbed to Fred's charming, if coarse, ways. In the spring of 1967, Anna became pregnant with Fred's child. She suggested that he obtain a divorce from Rena and make her an honest woman. Fred wouldn't hear of it. Anna disappeared in July 1967. It would be 27 years before her fate would become the subject of headlines around the world.

At this juncture in the hectic life of Fred West, he met his Rose. Their lives would never be the same. By coincidence, they learned that they didn't live far from each other in the English hamlet of Bishop's Cleeve. Soon Rose was spending a lot of time at Fred's digs, looking after his two children. By now Charmaine was six years old. She was an intelligent, pretty child, but suffered from neglect and physical punishment meted out by her stepfather. Rose became the children's nanny. In addition to her nanny duties, she slept with Fred. It wasn't long before Fred had Rose selling her body to strangers. He liked to watch.

In June 1970, Fred, Rose and the two children moved into a flat at 25 Midland Road, Gloucester, a few miles from England's beautiful Cotswolds. That autumn, Rose gave birth to her first child, a girl, Heather. Rose ruled the children with an iron fist. Charmaine, now eight years old, had been physically abused since she was an infant. Fred and Rose were careful to strike her where bruises wouldn't be apparent to her teachers.

One day, while Fred was serving one of his brief prison stints, Rose told Anna Marie to go to school alone. Charmaine would remain behind. When Anna Marie returned home, she wanted to know what had happened to her sister. So did neighbours and the teachers at St. James school, where Charmaine attended. Rose told them all the same story. Rena, the child's mother, had taken Charmaine to Bristol to live with her. Everyone seemed to accept that explanation. No one checked out the story. When Fred returned home from prison, Rose confided that she had killed Charmaine. Fred took the news well. After all, he had never liked the child.

With the eldest offspring out of the way, Fred and Rose found that they could partake in deviant sexual practices more openly. Things were working out well, with one annoying exception. Rena kept inquiring about Charmaine. Tiring of her nosy ways, Fred agreed to pick up Rena and reunite her with her daughter. Rena was never seen alive again. Three human beings had disappeared. No inquiries were made, no reports filed—nothing. No one seemed to care. Life went merrily along at 25 Midland Road.

In January 1972, Fred and Rose were married in a registrar's office. No mention was made of his previous marriage. That June, Rose gave birth to May, her second child. With an expanding family, the Wests decided to move into a larger home. They chose 25 Cromwell Street, Gloucester. Fred, who was extremely deft with his hands, was employed as a carpenter. He planned on fixing the place up and taking in roomers. He also decided to renovate a private room for Rose to carry on her brisk prostitution business.

The family moved in and, true to his word, Fred went ahead with the renovations. He was constantly fixing or adding on sections to the rambling old dwelling. It wasn't long before the house on Cromwell St. was home to several roomers, many of whom were independent young girls living away from their parents.

The Wests were now a pair of loose cannons. They were practising every conceivable sexual act on each other and on some of their roomers. When their daughter, Anna Marie, was eight, her father raped her. Thereafter the terrified child performed for her father on a regular basis. At the time, Rose was pregnant with her first son, Stephen, who was born in 1973. Through the years Rose would have a second son, Barry, by Fred, and another four daughters fathered by various men.

In April 1973, Lynda Gough, a 20-year-old part-time babysitter, moved into the West residence. Shortly after, she became the sex partner of both Rose and Fred. But consensual sex was not enough for the evil duo. They tortured Lynda, performing unspeakable sex acts before their bound and gagged captive was dead. Fred methodically dismembered Lynda's body and buried her in a pit under his garage. Rose kept her victim's better clothing and tossed the rest into the pit with Lynda's body parts. Two weeks later, Lynda's mother showed up at 25 Cromwell. She was told that her daughter had left some time earlier. Jean Gough would learn of her daughter's fate 21 years later.

Carol Ann Cooper was only 15 years old when her boyfriend waved goodbye to her as she boarded a bus. It was Carol Ann's misfortune to cross the path of Fred and Rose, who were out cruising, looking for young girls to cart back to their house of horror. Their terrified captive was tied, gagged, raped and tortured before she was mercifully killed. By now the dismemberment was routine to Fred. He dug a three-foot-deep hole in the cellar and there deposited the mortal remains of Carol Ann Cooper.

The parade of young women continued to be lured into the couple's deadly trap. Lucy Partington, 21, Therese Siegenthaler, 21, Shirley Hubbard, 15, and Juanita Mott, 18, were all tortured, murdered and dissected. Fred buried the bodies in a semicircle in his cellar. There were cursory inquiries about the girls, but Rose and Fred were never suspected of wrongdoing.

Shirley Robinson was an 18-year-old prostitute when she met Rose West and began having sex with Rose and Fred. All were aghast when both Shirley and Rose found themselves pregnant at the same time. Although the identity of the father of the children was in some doubt, the three felt that Fred was the father of Shirley's child, while the father of Rose's was anyone's guess.

As the months passed, Rose was infuriated at the attention Fred showered on Shirley. The Wests had a chat. They decided it would be best for all concerned if Shirley were put to death. The pair strangled Shirley Robinson until she was dead. The dismemberment went well, as usual, but the burial proved to be a problem. The cellar was full of bodies. Shirley and her eight-month-old fetus were laid to rest in the backyard. Rose gave birth to her baby on December 9, 1977. They called the little girl Tara.

In the late summer of 1979, Alison Chambers, a teenage prostitute, was befriended by the Wests. She too ended up dissected and buried in the garden.

By 1986, Heather, the Wests' first child, was a pleasant, bright 15-year-old who, despite the abuse she had taken all her life, was a brilliant student. She actually believed that having sex with her father was normal behaviour. No one knows just why the murderous pair throttled Heather until she breathed no more. The young girl was dissected and buried in the garden. Unlike many of the other victims, Heather was missed by several people. The Wests told everyone that their daughter had gone away to work. Friends, teachers and other family members accepted the explanation.

The beginning of the end came when a teenager, who had been sexually abused but had managed to escape the fate of many who had preceded her, went to the police. This girl's name has never been made public. The surviving West children related a litany of abuse and violence. In particular, they told of the disappearance of their sister, Heather.

Rose and Fred were taken into custody. Fred, whose mental health deteriorated rapidly in prison, was the first of the pair to spill out their horrid secrets. The garden and cellar were excavated, uncovering the dismembered remains of the Wests' many victims. In addition, Fred revealed the location of Anna McFall's body, buried in a cornfield between Much Marcle and Kempley. In a rambling, almost incoherent recitation, Fred told detectives that Charmaine's body parts were buried in the yard near the back door of the flat at 25 Midland. Rena's body had been dissected and buried in a nearby park known as Letterbox Field.

Most students of the "House of Horror" murders believe that there were many more victims of the Wests who have never been found. Fred isn't telling. On New Year's Day, 1995, in Winson Green Prison, Birmingham, Fred tore his bedsheets into strips, made a rope and hanged himself. Rose pleaded not guilty to multiple murder. She was found guilty of 10 counts of murder and was sentenced to life imprisonment.

Pete Wheeler

(CANADA)

BEFORE THE TURN OF THE 20TH CENTURY, Bear River, Nova Scotia, then as now, was a tiny village surrounded by farms. When winter closed in on the area, not much happened around Bear River.

One must remember that, in those long-ago days, there were no cars, no airplanes, no television sets, but there was an abundance of peace and tranquility. On the night of January 27, 1896, all that was to abruptly change.

Annie Kempton was a 19-year-old beauty. She had long black hair, a voluptuous figure and pleasing personality. To add frosting to the cake, Annie's father was considered to be one of the wealthiest farmers in the county. At picnics and church socials, Annie was invariably the most popular girl in attendance.

On the night when our dastardly deed took place, Annie's father, Isaac Kempton, was away from home on a business trip. He was expected back late the following afternoon. Her mother was visiting a married daughter in Massachusetts. Two farmhands Isaac employed were off on a hunting trip and would not be back for several days. Annie was spending the night alone.

At around 11:00 p.m., Annie went upstairs, slipped into her nightgown and was about to retire for the night, when she heard a loud knock on the kitchen door. She put on her kimono, lifted her bedroom window and shouted down, "Who is there?"

The man, whom Annie knew well, identified himself in the dark and explained that he was sorry to call at such a late hour, but her father had told him he could borrow his rifle. Just an hour ago he had found out that he could go hunting in the morning and so had rushed over for the weapon.

Annie ran downstairs, lit a lamp in the kitchen and let the man in. The pair exchanged pleasantries. She couldn't help but detect the smell of liquor on the man's breath.

The visitor looked strangely at Annie. The intruder made his intentions abundantly clear. He told Annie, "For three long years, I've watched you and waited. I've seen the young fellows gather around at socials and parties begging for your attention. All the while I was promising myself that someday I would have you."

The man, now wild-eyed, went on, "I know I am much too old for you and have neither money nor looks. If I had attempted to court you, I knew everyone in the district would have laughed at me, including yourself."

Annie was frantic. She pleaded with the man to leave, but it was no use. In seconds the sex-crazed attacker was upon her, tearing her nightclothes from her body. Annie was raped repeatedly. From time to time, the intruder helped himself to Mr. Kempton's whisky.

After several hours, the rapist prepared to leave. Annie was understandably relieved, but not for long. In no uncertain terms, her tormentor told her he had to kill her to ensure her silence. Annie fought for her life, but her assailant struck her several times with a hardwood stick. He then bent down over the girl's fallen form and slashed her throat with a knife.

The sun rose over the snow-laden farm. All was silent. The Kemptons' neighbour, Mrs. Tilly Comeau, watched her hired man, Pete Wheeler, shovelling a path from her house down to the road. She shouted to Pete to go over and pick up milk from the Kemptons, as he did every morning. Pete nodded, picked up a pail and disappeared over a slight rise to the Kempton farm.

In moments Pete was running back, past the Comeau house and into Bear River. He burst into the general store shouting, "Annie Kempton's been murdered. Get the sheriff. Her throat is cut. There is blood all over the place. I saw it through the window."

The storekeeper and Pete notified the sheriff and then returned to the Kempton farmhouse. Along the way they gathered a raft of villagers. Bad news travels fast. Several walked into the Kempton house, saw the horrible sight of Annie Kempton, the blood and the hair-matted hardwood stick beside the body. There was blood everywhere.

Murder in peaceful Bear River! Impossible but true! An investigation was quickly undertaken. Pete Wheeler told how he had discovered the body. Reluctantly he added that he had met Ed Miller near the Kempton home just before seeing the body through the window. Ed, the village ne'er-do-well, had appeared to be drunk.

Ed was questioned. He admitted meeting Pete, but swore he hadn't killed anyone. The local police were stymied. Although a fresh snow had fallen on the night of the murder, all of the tracks, with the exception of Pete's tracks from the Comeau residence to the Kempton farm, made when he found the body, had been obliterated by the scores of curious villagers who had trampled around the farmyard.

Forty-eight hours after the murder, the local law called in well-known detective Nick Power of the Halifax Police Force. Power questioned everyone remotely connected to the crime.

During the course of his investigation he uncovered one Jack Kent, an old beau of Annie's. Jack was belligerent toward the detective for even suspecting that he had anything to do with the murder, but he did admit that he had threatened Annie when she had rebuffed him.

Jack had an airtight alibi for the time of the murder. He had been in his barn tending to a mare who was giving birth to a colt that night. His father, brother and a veterinarian had been with him.

After Jack's story was checked out with the veterinarian, he was absolved of any part in the murder.

Detective Power had another very real concern. Because everyone knew Annie would never unlock her door to a stranger, the villagers realized the killer was one of their own. The natives were getting restless. They wanted an arrest.

Now under a certain amount of pressure, Power reexamined the crime scene. Inside the house, he attempted to reconstruct Annie's murder. The place had been cleaned, but Power had no difficulty picturing the overturned furniture and the struggle between the terrified girl and her attacker. He imagined the killer bending over his fallen victim and slashing her throat. Finally, Power went outside and peered through the window, just as Pete Wheeler had peered seven days earlier.

A light went on in the detective's cranium. He knew very well who had taken the life of Annie Kempton. He re-entered the house and advised Isaac Kempton that he knew the identity of his daughter's killer. As the two men discussed the matter, Pete Wheeler paid a visit. He too was informed that Power had solved the murder.

Pete was thrilled. Was it Jack Kent? Maybe Ed Miller? "No," Power assured him. "It was you who killed Annie Kempton."

When he ran through the village, Pete had stated that Annie's throat had been slashed when he looked at her through a downstairs window. Detective Power had looked through that very same window and found that it was impossible to have seen Annie's throat by peering in that window. How could Pete Wheeler have known that her throat had been slashed unless he himself had done the slashing?

The colour drained from Pete's face. He couldn't answer. Detective Power arrested him on the spot. In an attempt to escape, Pete dashed out the door, but a warning shot from Power's revolver brought him up short.

Pete was lodged in the Kentville, Nova Scotia, jail. He was duly tried and convicted. While in jail awaiting execution, Pete confessed and wrote out all the details of his most despicable crime.

So hated was Pete Wheeler in the district that as his execution date drew near, there was grave fear that some citizens would take the law into their own hands. Rumour had it that 40 men were planning on making the short trip to Kentville.

Authorities decided to hang Pete several hours before the scheduled time. On September 7, 1896, when the Bear River crowd arrived, Peter Wheeler had already been executed.

Henry Williams

(CANADA)

THE DATE WAS AUGUST 19, 1974. It was to be the worst day of Julia Sheldon's young life.

The Canadian National Exhibition in Toronto had been great fun, thought 16-year-old Julia. She clutched the stuffed bear she had just won as she made her way to the GO transit station. Canada was everything she had imagined it would be when she was given the opportunity to travel from England with her parents to visit with friends in Mississauga.

Julia disembarked at the Clarkson GO station at around 3:00 p.m. and called a friend who had offered to pick her up. Unfortunately, he was outside and didn't receive the call. The city was in the midst of a transit strike. The young girl from England decided to hitch a ride. A presentable man in a presentable vehicle stopped. Julia glanced in the back of the car and saw a child's car seat. The driver was obviously a respectable family man. She accepted the lift.

Twenty-eight years have passed since that fateful day. Julia still has the stab-wound scars on her back, still has the vivid memories of her drive with a monster.

As they made their way through the suburban area, then far less populated than it is today, the man at the wheel suddenly changed direction and cut across a field to a wooded area. Julia grabbed the door handle, but it was no use. Henry Williams was on her in an instant, his hands firmly grasping the terrified girl's throat. The passenger door flew open and together they fell to the ground.

Julia can recall the details of her struggle as if it had occurred yesterday. The sexual attack, her hands being tied behind her back, her T-shirt being stuffed into her mouth. And then, most insidious of all, the thrusting of a knife into her back. Williams extracted the knife just as it broke his victim's skin and repeated his slow deliberate act a few inches from the first incision. It was as if he was probing for the helpless girl's heart. Once again, he withdrew the knife. Then he slowly and calculatingly pushed the knife into Julia's back. A rock came crashing down on her head. She went limp and held her breath, feigning death.

Julia felt that this was not a frenzied out-of-control madman, but a cold premeditated killer. The sexual attack had been secondary. His prime aim was to kill her. There she lay, helpless, blood pouring from her head, as well as from the stab wound in her back.

Williams and Julia had made small talk on their drive from the GO station. She knew a lot about her attacker, who even had his name and address on a sticker on his dashboard. She was certain he had no intention of letting her live. Survival was uppermost in her mind.

The cool rapist dragged Julia into heavier bush and commenced to bury her under rocks and branches. Her ruse had succeeded. Williams thought she was dead. Julia lay still in her makeshift grave. She could hear Williams scurrying about, cleaning up the scene. At long last, she heard his car start up and speed away. Only then did she dare commence the gut-wrenching task of digging herself out from under the rocks.

The courageous girl made her way across the field to the intersection of College Way and Winston Churchill Boulevard. By chance, an accident had taken place at the intersection. The teenager blurted out her story to ambulance attendants. Next day, police took Williams into custody. They recovered 26 one-pound notes he had taken from Julia.

Julia Sheldon spent three weeks in hospital. Among other injuries, she had suffered a concussion and a collapsed left lung. After travelling back to England, she returned to Canada to give evidence at Williams's trial. He was found guilty of attempted murder and sentenced to life imprisonment.

Twenty-five-year-old Henry Williams was married and the father of two young sons. Employed as a labourer in a brick factory, he could pass as your average pleasant young man. But Henry Williams was far from average. After his arrest he gave statements to police, confessing that he had killed two girls whose murders were unsolved at that time.

Constance Dickey was a native of Prescott, Ontario, who went missing on September 11, 1973, shortly after enrolling at the University of Toronto's Erindale Campus in Mississauga. Five days later her body was found in a wooded area on the campus. She had been strangled with a wire.

The second girl was Neda Novak of Mississauga, who disappeared on October 4, 1973. It wasn't until April 30, 1974, that her body was found close to a dam in nearby Streetsville under a pile of rubble. She had been strangled and stabbed to death.

In both these cases, Williams gave detailed accounts of meeting the girls, raping them and killing them. In each case he led police to the exact locations where the bodies had been found.

Eventually Williams was tried for both these murders. His lawyer attempted to have him declared insane, but despite his efforts Williams was found to be sane. He received life sentences for both murders to run concurrently with his life sentence for the attempted murder of Julia Sheldon.

Two girls had lost their lives to a cold methodical killer. The murderer himself languished in prison with three life sentences to be served. But time passes. In 1984, it was learned that Williams was receiving escorted day passes from Warkworth Penitentiary. It was Julia Sheldon who brought the matter to the attention of authorities. Strangely, Williams had been granted this privilege without being interviewed. The powers-that-be allowed the escorted day passes by studying his file only. After Julia made a presentation to the parole board in Kingston, the escorted day passes were rescinded. Twenty-eight years after being incarcerated, Henry Williams is still in prison.

Julia Sheldon, the survivor of Williams's reign of terror, became fascinated with police work as her case wound through the courts. She decided to make law enforcement her career. She joined the police and has been a member of the force for over 20 years.

As I interviewed the attractive police officer, she looked back at her ordeal and pointed out the positive aspects of what otherwise could only be termed a horror story. "I have used my personal experience to assist others. I advise them on how to help victims of crime."

In addition, Julia has lectured at the police college in Aylmer, Ontario. After all, who is better equipped than a woman who went through it all and survived? She explained to me that her attacker acted in a slow and deliberate manner. There was no madness in his actions. He was always in control of what he was doing and was "almost ritualistic" in his behaviour.

There is little doubt that by surviving her ordeal, Julia has saved lives. Had she been killed that day in 1974, other girls would surely have fallen victim to the same attacker. She is convinced now, as she was convinced then, that if set free, Williams would murder again.

As for Julia, today she is happily married to a former police officer and has a family of her own. Police work is her passion now as it was when she joined the police force over two decades ago.

Julia Sheldon is a survivor.